THE WORLD ECONOMY

THE WORLD ECONOMY

GLOBAL TRADE POLICY 2008

Edited by
David Greenaway
University of Nottingham

A John Wiley & Sons, Ltd., Publication

This edition first published 2009
Originally published as Volume 31, Issue 11 of *The World Economy*
Chapters © 2009 The Authors
Editorial organization © 2009 Blackwell Publishing Ltd

Blackwell Publishing was acquired by John Wiley & Sons in February 2007. Blackwell's publishing program has been merged with Wiley's global Scientific, Technical, and Medical business to form Wiley-Blackwell.

Registered Office
John Wiley & Sons Ltd, The Atrium, Southern Gate, Chichester, West Sussex, PO19 8SQ, United Kingdom

Editorial Offices
350 Main Street, Malden, MA 02148-5020, USA
9600 Garsington Road, Oxford, OX4 2DQ, UK
The Atrium, Southern Gate, Chichester, West Sussex, PO19 8SQ, UK

For details of our global editorial offices, for customer services, and for information about how to apply for permission to reuse the copyright material in this book please see our website at www.wiley.com/wiley-blackwell.

Library of Congress Cataloging-in-Publication Data
The world economy: global trade policy 2008 / edited by David Greenaway.
    p. cm.
  "Originally published as Volume 31, Issue 11 of The World Economy."
  Includes bibliographical references and index.
   ISBN 978-1-4051-8915-6 (pbk.: alk. paper) 1. Commercial policy. 2. International economic relations. I. Greenaway, David. II. World economy. Global trade policy.
  HF1411.W647 2009
  382'.3—dc22   2009001814

A catalogue record for this book is available from the British Library.

Set in 11/13 Times by Graphicraft Limited, Hong Kong

01 2009

Contents

Foreword   vii

List of Contributors   viii

TRADE POLICY REVIEWS

1   Demystify Protectionism: The WTO Trade Policy
Review of Japan ....FUKUNARI KIMURA   1

2   Indonesia – Trade Policy Review 2007 .... M. CHATIB BASRI
.... and HAL HILL   11

3   Missed Opportunities: The WTO Trade Policy Review
for the East African Community............................... OLIVER MORRISSEY
.... and CHRIS JONES   27

4   Liberalising Trends in Israel's Trade Policy: Trade Policy
Review of Israel .... ALFRED TOVIAS   51

5   United Arab Emirates Trade Policy Review .... WASSEEM MINA   61

INTERNATIONAL ORGANISATIONS: THE CHALLENGE OF ALIGNING

6   Conceptualising Globalisation: A Symposium for
the World Economy .... JOHN WHALLEY   73

7   International Organisations: The Challenge of Aligning Mission,
Means and Legitimacy .... ROBERT Z. LAWRENCE   75

8   Defining Globalisation .... JAN AART SCHOLTE   91

9   Globalisation and Values .... JOHN WHALLEY   123

Index 145

Foreword

Each year *The World Economy* publishes an issue dedicated to developments in global trade policy. That issue always includes a number of ingredients: evaluation of a range of WTO Trade Policy Reviews; a regional feature; and a 'special feature' devoted to a current issue. Because of the interest in this particular issue of the journal, it is always published also as a stand alone book.

Global Trade Policy 2008 includes Trade Policy Reviews of Malaysia, the United States and Trinidad and Tobago. This year's Special Focus is on the Doha Round, with contributions on not only what is at stake, but also possible outcomes. We also include an important agenda setting chapter on Trade Preferences, with a focus on how they can help Africa diversify its exports.

I am grateful to the contributors to this volume for preparing an excellent set of chapters and to Wiley-Blackwell for expeditious publication.

Contributors

M. Chatib Basri	University of Indonesia
Hal Hill	Australian National University
Fukumari Kimura	Keio University
Chris Jones	University of Nottingham
Robert Lawrence	Harvard University
Waseem Mina	United Arab Emirates University
Oliver Morrissey	University of Nottingham
Jan Aart Scholte	University of Warwick
Alfred Tovias	The Hebrew University Jerusalem
John Whalley	University of Western Ontario

1

Demystify Protectionism: The WTO Trade Policy Review of Japan

Fukunari Kimura

1. EFFECTIVE CHECKLIST IN THE TPR EXERCISE

𝕿HIS is the eighth Trade Policy Review (TPR) for Japan (WTO, 2007). The TPR initiative was not endorsed as a rigorous surveillance of countries' trade and other related policies in the Marrakesh Agreement, but the format of checking trade openness has become a key element in adding transparency to trade policy and generating helpful peer pressure for WTO member countries.

The TPR is particularly useful in the case of Japan. Japan has been viewed as an outlier among OECD member countries in various respects due to its historical, cultural and political background. The legal system and economic institutions have often been regarded as difficult to understand for people in other countries. A lack of visibility has caused frustration for outsiders and has provided good excuses for protectionists to preserve vested interests in Japan. However, well-organised scrutiny has gradually revealed that we can, in fact, apply the same logic and the same principles for Japan in almost all aspects of trade policy. Although Japan, of course, has its own institutional basis, most of the issues are well explained by standard economic logic. Changes in the approach to protectionism in Japan have gradually removed misunderstanding and unwarranted criticism by outsiders, while insiders have started to tackle well-specified problems for policy reform.

2. IMPROVEMENTS AND REMAINING ISSUES

As the TPR acknowledges, the Japanese economy has finally recovered from a long slump, and the upswing seems to be structural rather than cyclical, and accompanied by proper policy reform. Although some serious problems, such as a huge fiscal deficit and collapsing public pension system, remain, the Japanese economy is obviously normalised and back on a modest growth path.

1

FIGURE 1
Ratios of Exports and Imports (Goods and Services) to GDP in Japan

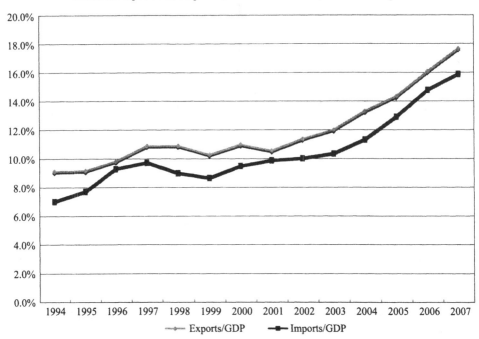

Source: The Cabinet Office, Government of Japan (http://www.esri.cao.go.jp/jp/sna/qe074-2/gaku-mcy0742.csv).

We can observe increases in trade–GDP ratios in the process of recovery; both exports and imports of goods and services have risen markedly (Figure 1). Although the TPR does not provide the reasons why, the enhanced openness is due to increased trade with East Asian countries in production and distribution networks. Growing economic turmoil in the world economy may disturb the growth performance of East Asia to some extent. However, the trend of Asian dynamism is likely to continue in the medium and long run.

As for trade in goods, not only customs clearance procedures identified by the TPR but also broader issues of trade facilitation have been granted policy priority, particularly in the context of international production and distribution networks extended in East Asia. Concepts of trade costs (Anderson and van Wincoop, 2004) and service link costs (Jones and Kierzkowski, 1990) are accepted as key even among policy makers and journalists, and the improvement of logistic infrastructure and services in terms of transport fees and time costs as well as their quality or reliability has been vigorously pursued.

As for the services sector, financial sector reform has finally borne fruit. Recently, non-performing loans have diminished rapidly, and the financial sector has gradually regained its competitiveness with enhanced openness. Reforms in telecommunications and professional services as well as the privatisation of public enterprises have been slow but are going forward. These are properly evaluated by the TPR.

Changes in the functioning of competition policy are a big surprise. The amendment of the Anti-monopoly Act (AMA) entered into force in January 2006. This included heavier penalties with possible criminal charges, a leniency programme to facilitate the disclosure of insider information, and possible compulsory criminal investigation.[1] Reinforcement of the institutional setting resulted in a significant outcome; Japanese competition policy suddenly started working strongly, most notably against hidden collusion (*dangoh* in Japanese) in bidding for public works. The lesson is that proper institutional design is crucial to successful policy reform.

However, some clouds remain. The most notable is heavy protection in agriculture and parts of the manufacturing sector such as leather and leather products. Policy distortion in agriculture is extremely complicated and presents a comprehensive 'cornucopia' of protection measures, which include tariff peaks, non-*ad valorem* tariffs (including not only simple specific tariffs but also differential tariffs, seasonal tariffs, and others), tariff rate quotas, state trading, suspicious sanitary and phytosanitary measures (SPS), and other non-tariff measures (NTMs). These measures are often employed in deliberately designed combinations; direct links of tariff revenues with subsidies for domestic producers are one example. Border measures with production targeting make the distortion even more serious. Special safeguards and emergency safeguards are frequently activated, the enforcements of which are almost automatic and barely publicised. The TPR correctly describes what is going on in agricultural protection in Japan in calm tones.

Other possible problems in Japan, though the TPR does not specify what to do about them, are in government procurement and inward foreign direct investment (FDI). According to the TPR, the share of government procurement of overseas goods and from foreign suppliers declined from 2002 to 2004. The smallness of inward FDI is a chronic problem, and continuous efforts to improve the investment climate in Japan are required.

3. MORE ON AGRICULTURAL PROTECTION

The agricultural sector is no longer a quantitatively important sector in Japan; its value added accounted for only 1.4 per cent of GDP in 2004. However, the TPR states that the total transfer to the sector amounts to 1.3 per cent of GDP in the same year. The TPR also presents a number of shocking figures. Net producer support estimates (PSE) for 2004 are 56 per cent (the OECD average is 30 per cent); consumer support estimates (CSE) for 2004 are 50 per cent (the OECD

---

[1] See http://www.jftc.go.jp/e-page/policyupdates/mainfeatureoftheamendedAMA.html for details.

TABLE 1
Japanese Imports of Agriculture-related Products, 2006 (1,000 yen, %)

Product Categories	Value	Share
Total	67,344,293,072	–
Agriculture-related products	8,085,915,262	100.0%
Agricultural products	5,004,147,619	61.9%
Animal husbandry	1,285,485,410	15.9%
Farm and plantation products	3,712,646,502	45.9%
Grain and grain products	643,562,183	8.0%
Fruits and fruit products	396,491,945	4.9%
Vegetables and vegetable products	403,857,826	5.0%
Sugar and related products	74,827,383	0.9%
Confectionery products	278,476,243	3.4%
Other processed foods and beverages	498,260,311	6.2%
Vegetable-based fats	397,165,023	4.9%
Tobacco	398,836,378	4.9%
Natural rubber	213,493,644	2.6%
Cotton	25,113,869	0.3%
Other agricultural products	382,561,697	4.7%
Forestry products	1,374,928,954	17.0%
Fishery products	1,706,838,689	21.1%

Source: The homepage of the Ministry of Agriculture, Forestry and Fishery, Government of Japan (http://www.maff.go.jp).

average is 20 per cent); the producer nominal assistance coefficient (NAC) is 2.3, indicating that gross farm receipts are 2.3 times as high as the level they would be at world prices without support; consumer NAC, the counterpart of producer NAC, is 2.0. The overall protection level for agriculture is obviously much higher in Japan than in other developed countries. It should also be noted that agricultural protection is still provided mainly by distortive border measures, rather than domestic support.[2]

To encourage Japan to reform its agricultural sector, we must conduct much more penetrative analyses than the general description provided by the TPR. Japan is one of the largest importers of agricultural products in the world, and its agricultural imports consist of a wide range of products (Table 1). The structure of the political economy differs across subsectors, and therefore not all parts of the agricultural sector are heavily protected. Even under the jurisdiction of the Ministry of Agriculture, Forestry and Fishery (MAFF), forestry and fishery products, for example, have low *ad valorem* tariffs (mostly single digits) because these products have not been included in the GATT/WTO agricultural negotiations. Vegetables and fruits also, in general, have low protection due to their diversified

[2] Japan does not have an export subsidy scheme except a small food aid programme for developing countries.

basis of political economy. Although complications such as SPS measures are sometimes a factor, these products are actively imported, and domestic producers are largely exposed to international competition.

Serious protection exists in products such as beef, dairy products, sugar, cereals (wheat, barley and rice), products/substitutes thereof (wheat flour, honey), tobacco and certain vegetable oils. In addition to tariffs, protection measures include state trading (certain dairy products, cereals, certain sugars and tobacco), price stabilising mechanism (beef), and special safeguards (certain dairy products, cereals and wheat flour). It should be noted that most of these highly protected products have geographically concentrated production bases. Kuno and Kimura (2008) calculated geographical concentration of production across 47 prefectures in Japan in 2006. The Hirfindahl–Hirschman Indices (HHI) present extremely high values for wheat and barley (HHI = 3,426), sugar beet (10,000), sugar cane (5,073), elephant foot (*konnyaku imo*) (8,701) and dairy cattle (2,028). These are classic cases of a common interest or pressure group model in the political economy literature (Baldwin, 1989). It is suggested that trade protection for these products depends heavily on specific politicians who try to maintain local protectionism. In other words, strong political determination at a high level is required in order to remove the protectionist measures, and this ought to be achievable.

In contrast, protection for rice is much more structural, symbolic and complicated. Production bases for rice do not show a clear geographical concentration. Raising rice is relatively easy with modern technology, and thus a large part of rice production is carried out by part-time, weekend farmers. They are getting old, and a considerable proportion of paddy land is not cultivated. Yet, heavy border protection and notorious subsidy for reducing production are maintained in order to push up the domestic price of rice. Unlike other agricultural products with local protectionism, rice reforms would require major structural adjustments with strong political will though actual costs of adjustment may not be huge.

The direction of agricultural reform taken by the Japanese MAFF looks fine in general. As the TPR notes, the revised Basic Plan for Food, Agriculture and Rural Areas announced in May 2005 presents its intention to shift away from price support to income support. At the same time, it emphasises more efficient land use and productivity enhancement together with fostering capable farmers for serious agricultural production. There are, however, two problems. First, the reform plan includes too much involvement of bureaucrats and agricultural cooperatives. It should rely more on market forces and price signals. Second, the link with international commercial policies is so tenuous that we cannot synchronise policy reform across policy modes. Agricultural reform is too slow to catch up with the proper timing of international commercial policies. The Council on Economic and Fiscal Policy (CEFP) chaired by the Prime Minister establishes the Working Group on Economic Partnership Agreements and Agriculture, in which the author personally participates, and tries to link agricultural reform with international commercial policies, though strong resistance still remains.[3]

As of March 2008, the political situation is even worse for agricultural reform. The leading Liberal Democratic Party (LDP) was beaten by the Democratic Party (DP) in the Upper House election in 2007 while maintaining a majority in the Lower House. The consequence is that both LDP and DP have become populists and claim an increase in subsidies for reducing rice production so as to raise the price of rice. This is even worse than the reform scenario proposed by the MAFF. We reformers will have to wait for the result of the next general election.

4. REGIONALISM

It is unfortunate that the WTO trade negotiations have gone too slowly for agricultural trade liberalisation, though the conclusion of the current agricultural negotiation would surely ignite substantial reform. Japan is already out of the main negotiating group for agriculture, which provides a good excuse for politicians and bureaucrats not to respond positively. Recently, however, some pressure for trade liberalisation has come from regionalism instead.

Japan's recent emphasis on free trade agreements (FTAs) is reviewed by the TPR. However, the characteristics of FTA networking by Japan and other East Asian countries are not fully discussed. The author would like to provide some supplementary comments on the implication of FTA networking.

Table 2 summarises recent developments in FTA/EPA negotiations by Japan. As of March 2008, Japan has concluded FTAs with two Latin American countries (Mexico and Chile) and six ASEAN forerunners (Singapore, Malaysia, Thailand, the Philippines, Indonesia and Brunei), and the negotiation with ASEAN as a whole has almost been concluded. The prime target of these FTAs is the improvement of the investment and business environment in order to further activate international production and distribution networks.[4] Therefore, FTAs are deliberately designed so as to include not only trade liberalisation but also various policy measures such as trade/FDI facilitation, institution building for investment and intellectual property protection, the establishment of private–government dialogues for trouble-shooting, and links with other policy modes such as economic policy cooperation and international financial policy. The movement of natural persons is also included in some of the FTAs. These policy

---

[3] As for the claim made by CEFP, see CEFP (2007). The home page of the CEFP discloses the detailed contents of straight talks in the working group meetings; such explicit discussion on agricultural protection could not have taken place 10 or 15 years ago.
[4] On the nature and characteristics of international production and distribution networks in East Asia, see Kimura (2006).

TABLE 2
FTA/EPA Negotiations by Japan (as of March 2008)

Counterpart	Negotiation Started	Agreement Signed	Entry into Force
Singapore	01/2001	01/2002	11/2002
Mexico	11/2002	09/2004	04/2005
Malaysia	01/2004	12/2005	07/2006
Chile	02/2006	03/2007	09/2007
Thailand	02/2004	04/2007	11/2007
Philippines	02/2004	09/2006	
Brunei	06/2006	06/2007	
Indonesia	07/2005	08/2007	
ASEAN	04/2005	(11/2007: major parts of negotiation completed)	
GCC	09/2006		
India	01/2007		
Vietnam	01/2007		
Australia	04/2007		
Switzerland	05/2007		
(Korea)	12/2003	(11/2004: negotiation suspended)	

Source: Ministry of Foreign Affairs (http://www.mofa.go.jp).

TABLE 3
The Ten-year Liberalisation Commitments by Japan in Japanese FTAs

Commodity (HS section)	Japan–Singapore	Japan–Mexico	Japan–Malaysia	MFN
Total	75.8%	85.4%	88.3%	40.6%
Agricultural products (sec. 1–4)	18.8%	41.7%	54.0%	18.8%
1 Live animals, animal products	19.9%	46.2%	38.5%	19.9%
2 Vegetable products	29.2%	50.0%	76.0%	29.2%
3 Animal or vegetable fats and oils, etc.	23.0%	36.8%	57.5%	23.0%
4 Prepared foodstuffs, beverages, tobacco	10.1%	33.1%	49.6%	10.1%
Manufactured goods (sec. 5–21)	92.4%	98.0%	98.3%	46.9%

Note:
The nine-digit HS tariff line basis.

Source: Kuno and Kimura (2008).

areas are not well covered by the WTO framework, and FTAs become an essential supplementary forum. The scope of the WTO is too narrow to meet policy demands in the globalisation era, which obviously causes a relative decline in policy weights on the multilateral channel vis-à-vis FTAs.

In concluding FTAs, interesting things happen to agricultural protection. Although it is not completely clean, trade liberalisation in the agricultural sector has steadily progressed. Table 3 tabulates the liberalisation coverage of the first three FTAs concluded by Japan. Figures present the percentage of tariff lines (HS nine-digit level) on which zero tariffs within 10 years are pledged. The liberalisation coverage in the agricultural sector is much lower than in the manufacturing sector. However, compared with the liberalisation coverage at the applied MFN level, coverage is substantially improved. Of course, trade liberalisation under the FTA scheme is discriminatory, and liberalised tariff lines are not necessarily important for bilateral trade. It is also true that highly protected sectors tend to retain protection in FTAs. But it is at least true that FTA negotiations generate strong liberalisation pressure even in agriculture in Japan, and the protection coverage is obviously narrowed through FTAs.[5]

The author is not claiming that the liberalisation coverage of Japanese FTAs is high enough. On the contrary, he would like to argue that a higher level of discipline is definitely needed for further trade liberalisation. FTAs recently concluded by Australia, the US and Korea reach very high levels of liberalisation coverage,[6] and Japanese FTAs must follow. In the course of extending its FTA strategy further in response to the Domino effects (Baldwin, 1995), Japan will surely face stronger pressure to enhance liberalisation coverage, particularly in agriculture. This is the liberalisation dynamism in FTA networking. The function of FTAs in accelerating trade liberalisation should not be understated.

5. CONSIDERATION FOR DEVELOPMENT

The recent emphasis on development issues in the WTO is by itself important and also necessary to maintain the commitment of developing countries to the WTO. The TPR praises Japan's effort in providing the generalised system of preference (GSP) scheme for developing countries. Japan has provided an extensive programme of GSP for developing and least developing countries (LDCs), which was further expanded in 2007.

However, there is some doubt on whether the GSP scheme is really helping developing countries in distress. Beneficiaries, as presented in the TPR, are strongly biased toward East Asian countries, notably China which occupies 58.9 per cent of total trade under the scheme in FY2004. In order to obtain a preferential status, traders must submit the certificate of origin and clear periodic quotas (in the case of GSP for LDCs, the quota system was recently abolished). In fact, quotas are not always binding even if imports exist from a designated country, which suggests the existence of fixed cost for obtaining preferential treatment. Small traders of a small country without any connection with Japanese trading companies may face difficulty in utilising the GSP scheme.

---

[5] More detailed tables are available in Kuno and Kimura (2008).
[6] For example, the 10-year liberalisation coverage in the Korea–US FTA is 99.7 per cent for Korea and 100 per cent for the US; the coverage in the Australia–US FTA is 100 per cent for Australia and 98.1 per cent for the US.

In addition, tariff reduction or removal for developing countries is of course important, but the East Asian experience suggests that the effort of reducing trade costs may be more important. The TPR discusses customs clearance procedures but does not fully deal with trade facilitation or trade costs in general. The East Asian model may provide some useful lessons on reducing trade costs for LDCs in other parts of the world.

6. CONCLUDING REMARKS

The TPR is a comprehensive review of trade-related policies in Japan. The well-developed format successfully discerns what has been improved and what sort of issues remain. The TPR initiative has now reached a level of maturity and is ready to seek more systematic interactions with other parts of the WTO activities as well as member countries' policy reforms.

Agricultural protection remains a serious problem in Japan. Because WTO agricultural negotiations have a wide scope in terms of policy measures, the conclusion of the negotiations will surely have a big impact. However, the Doha Development Agenda (DDA) negotiation is still going quite slowly. As a result, the current commitment to the WTO basis is almost at a standstill at the level of the Uruguay Round conclusion. In Japan, FTA negotiations have become more effective in promoting trade liberalisation.

Baldwin (2008) claims that the WTO must stop being an 'innocent bystander' and become an active player 'in making regionalism as multilateral-friendly as possible'. One of the key moves that the WTO could make is to establish proper discipline on regionalism. If this could be realised, the vigorous forces of regionalism might effectively accelerate trade liberalisation.

REFERENCES

Anderson, James E. and Eric van Wincoop (2004), 'Trade Costs', *Journal of Economic Literature*, **42**, 691–751.
Baldwin, Richard E. (1995), 'A Domino Theory of Regionalism', in Richard E. Baldwin, Pertti Haaparanta and Jaakko Kiander (eds.), *Expanding Membership of the European Union* (New York: Cambridge University Press).
Baldwin, Richard E. (2008), 'Multilateralising Regionalism: The WTO's Next Challenge', available at http://voxeu.org/index.php?q=node/959.
Baldwin, Robert E. (1989), 'The Political Economy of Trade Policy', *Journal of Economic Perspectives*, **3**, 4, 119–35.
Council on Economic and Fiscal Policy (CEFP) (Expert Committee on Reforms Addressing Globalization) (2007), 'Acceleration of Economic Partnership Agreements and Strengthening Agricultural Reform: The First Report of the Working Group on Economic Partnership Agreements and Agriculture' (provisional translation), available at http://www.keizai-shimon.go.jp/english/publication/reports_2007.html.

Jones, Ronald W. and Henryk Kierzkowski (1990), 'The Role of Services in Production and International Trade: A Theoretical Framework', in Ronald W. Jones and Anne O. Krueger (eds.), *The Political Economy of International Trade: Essays in Honor of Robert E. Baldwin* (Oxford: Basil Blackwell).

Kimura, Fukunari (2006), 'International Production and Distribution Networks in East Asia: Eighteen Facts, Mechanics, and Policy Implications', *Asian Economic Policy Review*, **1**, 2, 326–44.

Kuno, Arata and Fukunari Kimura (2008), 'Northeast Asia and FTAs: Issues and Perspectives', *ERINA Report*, **82**, July, 15–29 (Niigata, Japan: Economic Research Institute for Northeast Asia). Available at http://www.erina.or.jp/index.html.en.

World Trade Organization (WTO) (2007), *Trade Policy Review Japan 2007* (Geneva: World Trade Organization).

2

Indonesia – Trade Policy Review 2007

M. Chatib Basri and Hal Hill

1. INTRODUCTION

INDONESIA is the fourth most populous country in the world, and the largest economy in Southeast Asia. Its economic performance has been highly variable. It was dubbed the 'chronic economic dropout' by the major development economics textbook of the 1960s (Higgins, 1968), in recognition of the fact that income per capita at that time was lower than that of 50 years earlier. A quarter of a century later the World Bank classified it as one of the seven East Asian 'miracle economies', reflecting the rapid growth it had achieved since 1967. In 1997–98 it was deeply affected by the Asian economic crisis, and the resultant domestic political turmoil. In 1998 the economy contracted by over 13 per cent. The country suddenly lurched from an authoritarian, growth-oriented regime to a democratic state with under-developed institutions, and a greatly weakened national government wrestling with the fiscal, financial and social aftermath of the crisis.

The trade policy pendulum has also swung from closed to open. By the mid-1960s, the country had formally disengaged from the international economy, including most international organisations, and virtually all foreign property had been nationalised. From 1967, however, the new Soeharto regime decisively opened up the economy to international commerce. Serious protectionist pressures emerged in the 1970s but for most of this period, and especially since the mid-1980s, the economy has remained broadly open.

Against such an unusual backdrop, this chapter examines the authoritative 2007 World Trade Organization review of Indonesian trade policy (WTO, 2007). We summarise the report, update some of its analysis, highlight its key findings, and point to some trade policy issues that in our opinion warranted greater attention. The chapter is organised as follows. Section 2 provides a brief overview of macroeconomic outcomes and trade policy, extending the period of coverage of the WTO report to 2007. Section 3 examines Indonesian trade policy, both in

11

terms of the structure of formal trade policy making and the outcomes. Here too we update the WTO analysis. Section 4 provides a critique of the WTO report, briefly introducing several policy issues that were somewhat overlooked or perhaps regarded as too sensitive for inclusion in the report.

The main theme of the chapter, and implicitly that of the WTO report, is that Indonesia is a largely open economy, but that this openness on occasion remains precarious. There are both political economy, rent-seeking forces opposed to the current openness and, perhaps more importantly, much of the country's influential public opinion is sceptical of the merits of an open economy and deeper global commercial integration. Nor is there a deeply institutionalised support for openness in the country's bureaucracy and polity. Seen from this perspective, a key question is why the country has remained open, particularly since the devastating crisis of 1997–98.

2. THE INDONESIAN ECONOMY: RECENT DEVELOPMENTS

The Indonesian economy has now largely recovered from the 1997–98 economic crisis, although it is still growing more slowly than during the period 1968–96. Table 1 summarises recent macroeconomic developments, updating the statistics provided in the WTO report. Several features of the recent macroeconomic record need to be highlighted, as background to the analysis of trade policy.

First, growth has gradually accelerated, from the range 3.5–5 per cent in the early years of this decade, to 5–6.5 per cent since 2004. Initially this growth was consumption-led, as typically occurs after a crisis. Investment has gradually picked up, but it still remains well below that of the pre-crisis period. Net exports grew very strongly in the aftermath of the crisis, but for most of this decade they have not been a major contributor to economic growth. The indifferent export performance is a key feature of recent economic performance, and it has important implications for trade policy, to be discussed below.

Second, there is a serious labour market disequilibrium. In spite of the economic recovery, Indonesia's unemployment rate has remained stubbornly high, in the range 9–11 per cent since 2002. This 'jobless growth' (Manning, 2008) has been the result of both the slower overall growth rate, and a less labour-intensive growth path. The latter has arisen principally because of much more interventionist labour market policies, related to minimum wages, severance pay and other conditions. This too has implications for trade policy, since the country's general openness has not delivered on employment growth, as was the case in earlier periods, and therefore the constituency for liberal economic policies is weaker.

Third, macroeconomic management has been reasonably effective. Indonesia has continued a tradition whereby inflation is held in check, but is consistently above its major trading partners and neighbours, typically by around 3–6 percentage

TABLE 1
Indonesian Macroeconomic Indicators

	2000	2001	2002	2003	2004	2005	2006	2007
National accounts				*Percentage change*				
Real GDP (2000 prices)	4.9	3.6	4.4	4.7	5	5.7	5.5	6.3
Consumption	2	3.9	4.7	4.6	4.9	4.3	3.9	4.9
Private consumption	5.4	3.5	3.8	3.9	5	4	3.2	5
Government consumption	25	7.6	13	10	4	6.6	9.6	3.9
Gross fixed capital formation	16.7	6.5	4.7	0.6	14.7	10.8	2.9	9.2
Exports of goods and non-factor services	26.5	0.6	-1.2	5.9	13.5	16.4	9.2	8
Imports of goods and non-factor services	25.9	4.2	-4.2	1.6	26.7	17.1	7.6	8.9
Unemployment rate (%)	6.1	8.1	9.1	9.6	9.9	11.2	10.3	9.1
Prices and interest rates				*Per cent*				
Inflation (CPI, percentage change)	9.3	12.6	10	5.2	6.4	17.1	6.6	6.6
Time deposit, in rupiah	11.17	14.52	14.52	9.63	6.2	8.3	10.88	7.6
Time deposit, in US$			3.65	2.24	1.95	2.62	3.85	
Money credit (end period)				*Percentage change*				
Money supply (M1)	30.1	9.6	8	16.6	13.4	11.1	28.1	27.6
Money supply (M2)	15.6	13	4.7	8.1	8.1	16.4	14.9	18.9
Credit to private sector			25.1	22.1	30.4	19.7	14	
Exchange rate								
Rupiah to US$ (annual average)	9,595	10,400	8,940.00	8,465.00	9,290.00	9,830.00	9,020.00	9,158
Government fiscal policy				*Per cent of GDP, unless otherwise indicated*				
Total revenue (excluding grants)	14.8	18.3	16	16.7	17.6	17.7	19.1	18.2*
Tax revenue	8.3	11.3	11.3	11.9	12.2	12.5	12.3	12.9*
Total expenditure	15.9	20.7	17.3	18.5	18.6	18.3	20.1	19.3*
Overall balance (excluding grants)	-1.2%	-2.5%	-2.6%	-1.5%	-1.5%	-0.5%	-1.3%	1.1%*
Primary balance	2.4%	2.8%	2.8%	2.4%	1.4%	1.6%	1.3%	1.1%*
Public debt	82.8%	71.5%	59.7%	54.4%	51.0%	42.8%	33.0%	30.8%

TABLE 1 Continued

	2000	2001	2002	2003	2004	2005	2006	2007
Saving and investment								
Gross national savings	31.8%	30.0%	25.1%	23.7%	24.9%	27.5%	28.7%	28.7%
Gross domestic investment	19.9%	19.7%	19.4%	19.2%	22.4%	23.6%	24.1%	24.9%
Savings–investment gap	12.0%	10.3%	5.7%	4.6%	2.5%	3.9%	4.6%	3.9%
External sector								
Current account balance	4.8	4.3	3.9	3.4	0.6	0.1	2.6	2.4
Net merchandise trade	15.1	14.1	11.8	10.3	7.8	6.1	8.2	7.6
Value of exports	39.5	35.7	29.6	27	27.6	30.3	28.2	27.3
Value of imports	24.4	21.6	17.8	16.7	19.7	24.2	20	19.7
Services balance	−5.9%	−6.2%	−5.1%	0.0%	−4.2%	−3.2%	−2.7%	−2.7%
Capital/financial account balance	−4.8	−4.7	−0.6	−0.4	0.7	0.1	0.7	0.8
Direct investment	−2.7	−1.9	0.1	−0.3	−0.6	1.8	1.1	0.6
Terms of trade (2000 = 100)			92.4	94.8	93.3	92.1	93.7	
Merchandise exports (percentage change)			3.1	8.4	10.4	22.9	18.1	
Merchandise imports (percentage change)			2.8	10.9	28	37.2	5.1	
Service exports (percentage change)			21.1	−20.6	127.6	7.3	..	
Service imports (percentage change)			7.3	2.1	19.9	13.8	..	
Foreign exchange reserves (US$ million)	29,394	28,016	32,037.00	36,296.00	36,320.00	34,724.00	42,586.30	56,920
In months of imports			6.8	6.1	5	4.1	5	
Debt service ratio (end-period)			24.7	25.5	27.1	22.1	25.8	

* Taken from 2007 budget.

points.[1] With a floating exchange rate regime, loosely tied to the US dollar, the result has been a persistent tendency for the real effective exchange rate to appreciate, as discussed below. A major factor contributing to these macro-economic outcomes has been very prudent fiscal policy, with deficits in the range of 1–2 per cent of GDP in recent years. As a result, public debt as a percentage of GDP has fallen sharply, from 83 per cent in 2000 to 31 per cent in 2007. This is a remarkable achievement for a country so severely affected by a deep crisis just a decade ago.

Fourth, the country's balance of payments position remains comfortable. As often occurs after a crisis, Indonesia has been running a current account surplus. On the current account, there is an export response to the exchange rate depreciation, while imports slow as a result of this expenditure switching effect and also the slower economic growth. On the capital account, foreigners are more reluctant to lend to the country. Combined with renewed capital inflows since 2004, these have resulted in a large increase in foreign exchange reserves, which have almost doubled over the period 2000–07. The external debt–service ratio is also comfortable. Perhaps this build-up in reserves is excessive, but it reflects in part the strong aversion of policy makers to a repeat of the 1997–98 economic crisis.

Fifth, as the WTO report notes, alongside these mostly sound macroeconomic outcomes is a microeconomic policy environment that is much less conducive to growth. For example, the 2008 World Bank *Doing Business Survey* ranks Indonesia 123rd out of 175 countries in terms of ease of doing business; it also reports that it takes at least 80 days to register a business. Infrastructure investment is inadequate, particularly in power generation and roads. Most comparative business surveys report high levels of corruption. Moreover, unlike the Soeharto era, this corruption is unpredictable, in the sense that the link between bribery and desired outcomes is uncertain. Inevitably these outcomes reflect the major transitional challenges associated with building the institutions of economic governance on the road to democracy. The government, whose key economic policy makers are people of great technical proficiency and integrity, is of course aware of these challenges. As the WTO report notes, major investment reform packages were enacted, in 2006 (Presidential Instruction (PD) 3/2006) and 2007 (PD 6/2007), as well as a new Investment Law in 2007 (Law 25/2007). These initiatives are comprehensive, covering customs and excise, taxation, labour, infrastructure, financial sector development, foreign investment, small to medium-sized enterprises, and much else. They have also been accompanied by detailed time lines for implementation. It is too early to evaluate their impact, and in some

---

[1] The major spike in inflation in 2005 was the result of the government significantly reducing the subsidy on petroleum products. Inflation in 2008 is likely to be higher for the same reason, in addition to higher food prices and rising global inflation.

sensitive areas such as labour market policy the government has backtracked. But in principle the measures are highly desirable.

Since the completion of the WTO report, the major global macroeconomic developments have been the sharp rise in global fuel and food prices, and serious financial stresses originating from the US 'sub-prime' market. Of these, the greatest domestic impact to date has been the increased fuel prices. Indonesia is generally close to being self-sufficient in food, typically importing 2–4 per cent of consumption needs (although there are, of course, major distributional consequences of the increased food prices). Moreover, thus far the domestic financial sector has been little affected by international financial stresses, a reflection of the fact that it is less connected to global financial markets and the country is running a current account surplus.

The problem in the case of fuel prices is that, owing to political sensitivities, the government has been reluctant to allow domestic prices to follow international trends.[2] As a result, Indonesia has among the lowest petroleum prices in the world, at about 60 cents per litre. However, this has been achieved at great cost: currently the fuel subsidies cost the government about $20 billion, equivalent to more than 5 per cent of GDP, and exceeding the government's entire social and capital works expenditure.[3] The subsidies make little sense on both efficiency and equity grounds. Oil consumption is growing rapidly, while production is declining, and is now one-third lower than it was in 2000. On the equity impacts, it is estimated that the top 10 per cent of households receive 45 per cent of the subsidy, while the bottom 10 per cent receive just 1 per cent (Bulman et al., 2008). In addition, as the world's third largest emitter of carbon dioxide (principally owing to rapid deforestation), the subsidies also complicate the country's international negotiating position on climate change, a not inconsequential consideration given that the country hosted the December 2007 global environment summit. Thus far the government has made relatively minor adjustments to domestic fuel prices, accompanied by compensatory packages for the poor.

The WTO report does not discuss developments in Indonesia's terms of trade and its exchange rate, and the implications for the trade regime. Indonesia has continued to enjoy a substantial windfall gain from high commodity prices. The country is a net energy exporter (though a net oil importer). It is also the world's largest exporter of palm oil, and a significant exporter of a wide range of minerals, including gold, copper and nickel. The prices of all these commodities have been at near record levels in 2007 and 2008.

---

[2] This sensitivity is well grounded in political history. The final trigger for the removal of Soeharto as president in May 1998, after 32 years in power, was his decision to increase domestic fuel prices.
[3] If global prices were to be in the mid-2008 range of $140–$150 per barrel, and there was no adjustment to prices, the subsidy would increase to about $30 billion.

FIGURE 1
Indonesia's Real Effective Exchange Rate (2001–08)

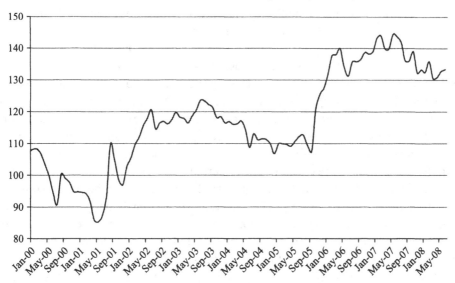

These effects have been felt particularly in the resource-rich regions off Java, as indicated by the strong growth in credit and wages. But they also, of course, have economy-wide effects. Indonesia's real effective exchange rate (REER) has appreciated significantly since 2001, by almost 50 per cent (Figure 1). This has occurred mainly as a result of an inflation rate consistently higher than that of its major trading partners, as well as a slight nominal appreciation. Increased capital inflows following the restoration of investor confidence over this period have also exerted upward pressure on the exchange rate.

The relationship between the exchange rate and the trade regime has been well established in the literature (see Corden, 1997). Earlier work by the authors demonstrated this proposition empirically for Indonesia in the period through to the mid-1990s (Basri, 2001; see also Basri and Hill, 2004). An appreciation of the REER lowers the price of tradables compared to non-tradables, other things being equal, and therefore increases the competitive pressures on the former. These pressures may be ameliorated by increased productivity, labour market adjustments, the provision of more efficient inputs (e.g. in infrastructure), or similar REER trends in major export competitors. In Indonesia, none of these domestic factors has been in operation over this period, and thus the profitability of tradable goods activities has declined. In addition, margins have been squeezed by the continued strong export performance of major Asian producers, particularly China.

3. TRADE POLICY: PRINCIPLES AND PRACTICE

Chapters II–IV of the Trade Policy Review provide a comprehensive summary of Indonesian trade policy, which we summarise and assess in this section.

Indonesian trade policy over the past two decades has been dominated by two key considerations. The first, and most important, has been a preference for unilateral trade reform, in the context of a preference for a multilateral system of trade negotiations and liberalisation. In particular, the trade liberalisations of the mid and late 1980s were significant and effective. For example, Fane and Condon (1996) showed that the weighted average rate of effective protection for manufacturing (excluding the special case of oil and gas processing) declined from 59 per cent to 16 per cent over the period 1987–95 (with most of the gains concentrated in the first half of the period), while the dispersion (standard deviation) fell from 102 to 39. The coverage of non-tariff barriers (NTBs) fell even faster: the percentage of non-oil manufacturing value added affected by NTBs declined from 77 per cent to 17 per cent. Indonesia's multilateral credentials are further illustrated by the fact that, unlike several of its Southeast Asian neighbours, it did not sign up to a bilateral preferential trade agreement (PTA) until 2008, when it signed an Economic Partnership Agreement with Japan, where arguably the principal concession offered to Indonesia is a modest expansion in employment opportunities for its semi-skilled workers.

The second general observation concerns Indonesia's membership of the Association of Southeast Asian Nations (ASEAN) since the body's establishment in 1967. ASEAN is the developing world's most durable and successful regional grouping. Although initially established with the intention of promoting peace and cooperation in a region then subject to considerable conflict and political uncertainty, over time several economic initiatives have become increasingly important. In 1992, an ASEAN Free Trade Area (AFTA) was enacted, with various targets for the unhindered flow of goods within the region, leading eventually to the possibility of some sort of economic union. Although ASEAN still falls well short of the textbook model of such a union (Lloyd, 2005), over time its economic cooperation measures have been intensified, leading to the 2007 announcement of a proposed Asian Economic Community (see Hew, 2007). In this context, it is important to recognise a key feature of ASEAN not widely understood beyond the region (including in the WTO report). This is that, while in principle the AFTA appears to be a preferential arrangement, in practice its discriminatory elements are relatively minor. This is because most of the concessions offered as part of the scheme have been multilateralised. In turn, two main factors explain this outcome. First, about 70 per cent of intra-ASEAN trade is through, to or with zero-tariff Singapore. Second, protection in the region continues to decline anyway, and hence the margin of preference offered by AFTA is falling. It is estimated that over 90 per cent of trade within ASEAN

TABLE 2
Structure of Indonesia's MFN Tariff, 2002–06 (per cent)

	2002	2003	2004	2005	2006	Final Bound[a]
1. Bound tariff lines (% of all tariff lines)	n.a.	n.a.	n.a.	n.a.	n.a.	93.2
2. Simple average applied rate	7.2	7.2	9.9	9.9	9.5	37.5
Agricultural products (HS01–24)	8.6	8.6	11.6	11.8	11.4	47.3
Industrial products (HS25–97)	7.0	7.0	9.6	9.6	9.2	35.8
WTO agricultural products	8.6	8.6	12.1	12.2	11.8	47.7
WTO non-agricultural products	7.0	7.0	9.6	9.6	9.2	35.8
Textiles and clothing	10.5	10.5	10.8	10.8	10.9	29.3
3. Domestic tariff 'peaks' (% of all tariff lines)[b]	1.6	1.6	5.0	5.0	5.1	0.5
4. International tariff 'peaks' (% of all tariff lines)[c]	3.6	3.6	10.7	10.4	10.6	90.7
5. Overall standard deviation of tariff rates	11.2	11.2	15.4	15.4	13.7	12.7
6. Coefficient of variation of tariff rates	1.5	1.5	1.6	1.6	1.5	0.3
7. Duty-free tariff lines (% of all tariff lines)	21.9	21.8	20.9	21.1	22.0	1.7
8. Non-*ad valorem* tariffs (% of all tariff lines)	0.2	0.2	0.2	0.2	0.2	0.0
9. Non-*ad valorem* tariffs with no AVEs (% of all tariff lines)	0.0	0.0	0.0	0.0	0.0	0.0
10. Nuisance applied rates (% of all tariff lines)[d]	0.0	0.0	0.0	0.0	0.0	0.0

Notes:
n.a. Not available.
[a] Based on 1998 tariff schedule in HS96 nomenclature. Calculations are based on 6,893 bound tariff lines (representing 93.2% of total lines), of which 6,717 (93.2%) are fully bound and 176 (2.4%) are partially bound. Implementation of the UR was achieved in 2005.
[b] Domestic tariff peaks are defined as those exceeding three times the overall simple average applied rate.
[c] International tariff peaks are defined as those exceeding 15%.
[d] Nuisance rates are those greater than zero, but less than or equal to 2%.
Calculations include AVEs for specific rates provided by the authorities.
The 2002 and 2003 tariff schedules are based on nine-digit HS02 nomenclature consisting of 7,532 tariff lines. The 2004, 2005 and 2006 tariff schedules are based on 10-digit HS02 nomenclature consisting of 11,151, 11,159 and 11,161 lines, respectively.

Source: WTO (2007, Table III.2).

does not avail of these preferences, owing to their limited value, in addition to the bureaucratic complexity of availing of such concessions.

Table 2, reproduced from WTO (2007, p. 41), summarises Indonesia's tariff structure over the period 2002–06. Several features warrant emphasis. First, tariffs are the main instrument of trade policy, but they account for only about 4 per cent of total government revenue. Owing to the introduction of a reasonably effective value-added tax in the 1980s, revenue considerations now play a minor role in trade policy, thus freeing policy makers from a traditional constraint governing trade policy. Second, tariffs are generally quite low: more than 75 per cent of tariffs fall within the range 0–10 per cent. Third, over 93 per cent of tariff lines are bound, but at a high average of 37.5 per cent. Thus tariff bindings, and hence indirectly any concessions as part of any WTO negotiations, are largely irrelevant. The biggest gap between applied and bound rates is in agriculture, and this is also the sector where the most serious NTBs are found (see below).

Fourth, over 99 per cent of applied tariffs are *ad valorem*, which contributes to their transparency. Nevertheless, the structure of tariffs remains complex in some instances, as there are 16 *ad valorem* rates and three specific rates. There is also some tariff escalation by degree of processing, in practice designed to support some heavy industry sectors, principally those that are state-owned.[4]

In addition to tariffs, the report discusses other aspects of government policy that affect trade policy. First, government procurement remains an important instrument of industry policy, and over the years the government has employed it, particularly in assigning preferences to enterprises that are owned by indigenous (so-called *'pribumi'*) interests. In fact, Indonesia has yet to sign the WTO Agreement on Government Procurement, thus signalling the government's reluctance to relinquish this industrial policy instrument. Second, Indonesia remains a relatively active user of anti-dumping measures, mainly for base metals and chemicals. Since these are also among the most heavily protected sectors, and mainly state-owned, it is reasonable to infer that this is a *de facto* trade policy instrument. Third, national standards are generally formulated in accordance with international standards, and the report concludes that SPS regulations are strictly enforced.[5] There have also been periodic attempts to enforce Intellectual Property Rights. Fourth, the report refers to, but does not attempt to systematically measure, NTBs. It notes that there are a considerable number of export restrictions, affecting coffee, textiles, rubber and certain wood products. There are also measures that restrict or affect trade in certain ways for selected 'sensitive' goods. These include rice, alcoholic beverages, sugar, hot- and cold-rolled iron coil, and steel products. Fifth, the report also notes that domestic prices are affected by other aspects of government policy. Two in particular are mentioned. One is administered prices for petrol, electricity, cement and some transport services. As noted above, domestic petrol prices are well below international levels. Another is an official commitment to competition policy, since the establishment in 1999 of a competition commission, known by its Indonesian acronym KPPU. The report regards this institution as 'significant in improving competition in the economy'. Such a judgment was warranted at the time of writing. However, developments since late 2007 suggest that the KPPU may have become an instrument of political patronage to some extent.[6]

---

[4] Although state enterprises have always been an important feature of the Indonesian economy, and the source of much protectionist pressure, the report's estimate that they account for 'up to 40 per cent' is probably a considerable over-estimate. In fairness, no accurate estimate of their size is available.

[5] This is now perhaps a point of controversy. Indonesia has recorded the largest number of fatalities due to bird flu, and there is some concern that the enforcement of health regulations may not be up to international standards.

[6] This assessment arose owing to the KPPU's judgment in late 2007 that Singapore interests had to divest from a major telecommunications company, even though they were minority partners in two companies that are majority state-owned. That is, if there is a 'competition problem', it is to do with the majority, state-owned, partner. See Kong and Ramayandi (2008).

As noted, the report refers to the existence of NTBs, but concludes that they are generally unimportant. This may be so, but it would have been useful if there had been more discussion of them, their likely incidence and their political economy. As Basri and Patunru (2007) observe, while tariff rates have gone down, or at least been maintained, some NTBs have proliferated since 2000. In agriculture, 'sensitive' products such as rice, cloves, sugar, corn and soybeans have been subject to special import licensing; in the case of the former three, exclusive import rights have been granted to domestic producers. Indonesia also continues to ban the import of chicken parts, in addition to imposing quantitative restrictions on the import of meat and poultry products. We discuss this further in the next section.

This somewhat discordant approach to trade policy – generally low tariffs combined with ever-present pressure for NTBs – is in part an institutionalised feature of the country's trade policy regime.[7] Specifically, tariff policy is under the control of the Ministry of Finance, which is generally predisposed towards open economic policies. However, line ministries have influence in setting NTBs, in concert with the Ministries of Finance and Trade. While the latter two ministries are run by highly able economists, the Ministries of Agriculture and Industry are avowedly protectionist, and also captured by vested producer interests. Hence trade policy is a continuous battleground, and a change of key ministerial personalities could easily result in a more protectionist trade policy regime.

One consequence of these incomplete reforms in Indonesia is the growing popularity of special export zones, which are supposed to offer simpler administrative procedures and (sometimes) freer trade. Their proliferation in recent years should be interpreted as reflecting the difficulty policy makers have in achieving further first-best, economy-wide liberalisation. The only zone of any significance is that located on the island of Batam, adjacent to Singapore. This zone's modest success derives from the fact that firms within it effectively operate as part of Singapore's custom zone, and thus the regulatory and logistical impediments to their operation are minimised.[8]

The report is evidently too polite to discuss smuggling, both technical and physical. With its 13,000 islands, proximity to the very open economies of Singapore and Malaysia, and a corruption-prone customs service, smuggling has been an ever-present feature of Indonesian commercial life. While accurate estimates are by definition not available, a widely adopted rule of thumb in the business community is that tariffs in excess of 15–20 per cent will attract illegal trade.[9]

---

[7] See also Bird et al. (2008) on this issue.

[8] For example, firms in Batam are also included in the Singapore–US free trade agreement.

[9] This is the main reason why, for most of its independent history, Singapore has not published its trade data with Indonesia, preferring to avoid the political embarrassment of large discrepancies between the two countries' official statistics.

The country's major decentralisation of 2001, which saw the transfer of significant resources to the approximately 510 sub-national governments, has also emboldened certain local authorities in strategic geographical locations (mainly in coastal proximity to Singapore and Malaysia) to in effect establish their own custom agencies, in contravention of national law. Particularly for goods that are easily tradable, this reality effectively constrains the country's trade policy.

4. ADDITIONAL COMMENTS AND ISSUES

This chapter concludes with a brief discussion of three pertinent trade policy issues that are not discussed in the report.

A major political economy question is why Indonesia has stayed largely open over the past decade.[10] Such an outcome may appear surprising, given the importance of the forces in favour of protectionism. At least four such forces may be identified. First, there has been a strong anti-globalisation sentiment in the public policy debates since the economic crisis of 1997–98, triggered in part by the country's perceived unjust treatment at the hands of the International Monetary Fund (IMF) and western donors. It is remarkable how little prominence is given to liberal economic policy opinion even in the country's 'quality' media. Second, as noted, the principal source of protectionist pressure now emanates from the agriculture sector, in contrast to earlier periods when manufacturing was the main beneficiary. With democratisation, rural votes matter, and politicians are able to exploit this factor along with appeal to sentimental notions of food self-sufficiency. Moreover, it is now easier to introduce protection for agriculture than manufactures owing to various loopholes (such as quarantine) and to the fact that the OECD North is extremely slow to liberalise its own agricultural protection. Third, democracy brings with it the imperative for political party funding, and with it the potential for 'buying votes'. Although much of that funding emanates from non-tradable sectors, particularly construction, in the last (2004) general election at least some of the vote buying was connected to increased protection. Fourth, as noted the country has experienced a mild Dutch disease since 2002, propelled by rising commodity prices. This has resulted in an appreciating currency, and hence increased pressure on profitability in the tradables sector. An additional complication is the more rigid labour market regulatory environment since 2000, which has had the effect of locking in this competitive disadvantage.

The explanation for Indonesia remaining open appears to rest on the following factors. First, in the immediate post-crisis period, the IMF Letter of Intent (LOI) played a role, and some of the dismantled protection (e.g. the notorious national

---

[10] See Basri and Hill (2004), Basri and Soesastro (2005), Basri and Patunru (2007) and Bird et al. (2008) for discussion of this issue.

car project and the clove monopoly, both run by one of Soeharto's sons) was popular. Second, the very large depreciation of the rupiah in 1997–98 provided some exchange rate protection for tradables, even if the effects had washed out by the early 2000s. Moreover, in the earlier period recovery was dependent on the growth of the export sector, which for a period was politically empowered, and of course opposed to protection. Third, finance ministries are typically central to the resolution of a crisis, and these now more powerful agencies are generally more likely to favour lower protection. This has certainly been a factor in Indonesia when, for most of this period, the position was occupied by an economist of high technical competence and integrity. Fourth, the major 1980s liberalisations were still a recent memory at the time of the crisis, for policy makers and the business community alike, and thus an unwinding of successful reforms was likely to be resisted. Fifth, the global trend towards liberalisation now has strong intellectual appeal, particularly with the example of the increasingly open Asian giants, China and India, and in contrast to the earlier appeal of Northeast Asian-style 'guided', export-oriented, industry policy. Sixth, Indonesia has had an unhappy experience with industry policy. Former technology minister and president, B. J. Habibie, had little to show for the estimated $3 billion allocated to his prestige, high-tech projects over two decades (although in fairness there was a significant training element). Finally, at the margin, Indonesia is a signatory to various regional trade agreements – WTO and AFTA in particular – which provided a mild barrier to increased protectionism.

The second issue not discussed in the WTO report is that, although NTBs remain contained thus far, there is a constant danger that they will proliferate. The case of rice, the country's most politically sensitive commodity, illustrates this danger. There has been a long history of intervention in the sector (see McCulloch and Timmer, 2008), even though domestic prices have generally followed international trends. In the wake of the 1997–98 economic crisis, as part of the IMF LOI, imports were liberalised and the import monopoly of the state food logistics agency, known as Bulog, was removed. However, from 2000 specific tariffs were re-imposed, initially set at Rp430/kg. In 2003, the tariff was increased to Rp750/kg, effectively raising the *ad valorem* equivalent tariff from 25 per cent to 45 per cent. The policy was further tightened in 2004 when the Minister for Trade and Industry issued a decree that effectively prohibited the import of rice unless explicitly authorised by the Minister. As a result, domestic prices began to exceed international prices by a significant margin, and smuggling ensued. The ban was in principle supposed to be administered on a seasonal basis, and to allow imports during the off-season. However, in practice it amounted to a complete ban, and the policy remained in place until 2006, when it was partially liberalised.

The third issue concerns Indonesia's export performance since 2000, a period of buoyant commodity prices and strong global economic growth. The country's export growth has lagged its neighbours (including even the Philippines), and also that of the pre-crisis period.

Table 3 clearly demonstrates the slowdown in export growth since the 1990s by decomposing the data into price and volume effects with the aid of sectoral deflators. In the pre-crisis period, 1990–96, real exports grew at 12.2 per cent per annum. However, since 1996 real export growth has slowed to less than half that rate, at 4.8 per cent, in spite of the major exchange rate depreciation in the late 1990s.[11] The slowdown in non-oil export growth was even sharper, from 20 per cent to 7.4 per cent. Most important of all, for the key labour-intensive manufactures segment, growth collapsed, from 23.5 per cent to 4.7 per cent. This applied to all major sub-sectors – garments, textiles, footwear (with negative growth) and furniture – suggesting the causes were economy-wide rather than sector-specific. There were some marginally negative price effects for these commodities over the period 1996–2006, presumably reflecting increased competition from China and other newly emerging exporters, but these effects explain only a small proportion of the declining growth.

Exports of electronics have also slowed sharply. This partly reflects the very high growth rates in the earlier period starting from the small initial base, and also the global slowdown in the industry in the early 2000s. However, Indonesia lags behind its neighbours in this, the most important export sector for developing country manufacturing. For example, the share of electronics parts and components in Indonesia's exports is about 9 per cent, compared to 21 per cent and 36 per cent for Thailand and Malaysia, respectively.

These slower growth rates result from the fact that Indonesia has not participated extensively in the rapidly expanding East Asian production and buying networks, especially in the electronics and automotive industries. The key here is for host countries to link to these highly competitive global production factories and networks. For countries to get into the loop they need commercial policy regimes and logistics systems which enable goods (and services) to flow seamlessly across international boundaries. Specifically, this requires open trade and investment regimes, and the removal of other trade frictions, through high-quality 'factory to market' logistics and smooth customs procedures (see Kimura, 2006; Athukorala and Hill, 2008). In these respects, Indonesia lags behind most of its East Asian neighbours. Foreign direct investment into Indonesia was negative over the period 1998–2004, and the country has always been ambivalent towards majority-owned FDI, the usual practice in these MNE-dominated, vertically integrated production networks. Customs procedures are slower than regional norms, while port productivity and other infrastructure provision are also weaker. Therefore,

---

[11] See also Athukorala (2006) who demonstrates that, after the immediate post-crisis export response, most of Indonesia's export growth has come from favourable world prices rather than volume expansion.

TABLE 3
Indonesia's Export Growth and Price Effect

Categories	1990	1996	2006	Constant Prices		Current Prices		Price Effect	
				1990–96	1996–2006	1990–96	1996–2006	1990–96	1996–2006
Oil/Gas	13.1	15.1	9.3	2.4	-4.7	8.4	6.2	6.0	10.9
Agriculture Commodities	3.7	5.4	13.0	6.5	9.1	15.3	8.4	8.8	-0.8
Fish and Shrimp	1.0	1.3	2.1	5.5	4.8	9.7	0.6	4.2	-4.3
Rubber	0.9	1.4	2.3	8.4	5.1	18.7	9.2	10.3	4.0
Palm & Palm Kernel Oil	0.4	0.8	5.1	12.9	20.4	27.4	17.3	14.5	-3.0
Coffee & Cocoa	0.7	0.9	1.3	4.6	4.1	12.9	4.2	8.4	0.1
Minerals	2.1	4.3	10.1	13.0	8.8	19.4	14.0	6.4	5.2
Copper	0.4	1.9	2.5	28.7	3.0	27.8	12.0	-1.0	9.0
Coal	0.1	1.0	5.4	39.0	18.8	37.3	17.2	-1.7	-1.6
Nickel & Tin	0.4	0.5	1.3	6.2	9.1	4.9	14.3	-1.3	5.1
Forestry Products	1.0	5.7	6.6	33.6	1.4	46.2	0.1	12.6	-1.3
Plywood	0.2	3.0	1.4	63.1	-7.4	80.5	-7.9	17.4	-0.5
Paper & Paper Products	0.1	1.4	2.5	48.3	6.2	35.6	10.5	-12.7	4.3
Pulp & Waste Paper	0.1	0.5	1.3	42.1	10.4	33.8	9.1	-8.3	-1.3
Manufactured Products	4.3	17.7	38.4	26.5	8.0	29.5	5.9	3.0	-2.1
Textiles & Footwear	2.2	8.0	12.1	23.6	4.2	23.3	1.6	-0.3	-2.6
Textile Fabric	0.5	1.8	2.5	22.1	3.2	16.2	-1.4	-5.9	-4.7
Textile Fibre & Thread	0.1	0.9	2.3	53.9	9.6	50.4	6.0	-3.5	-3.5
Garments	1.0	3.3	6.0	20.9	6.3	20.5	3.9	-0.4	-2.4
Footwear	0.6	2.0	1.3	23.0	-4.1	30.2	-4.0	7.2	0.0
Electronics & Computer Parts	0.2	3.4	8.6	61.6	9.7	90.2	8.1	28.6	-1.6
Other Manufactured Products	1.9	6.3	17.7	22.2	10.8	27.9	8.6	5.7	-2.3
Chemicals	0.2	1.5	5.4	34.9	13.8	34.8	11.1	-0.1	-2.7
Furniture	0.2	0.8	1.8	22.4	8.5	24.5	5.6	1.0	-2.9
Machinery	0.1	0.4	2.4	41.0	18.3	53.3	15.8	12.3	-2.5
Tyres & Rubber Products	0.1	0.2	0.7	26.4	11.6	28.9	11.3	2.5	-0.3
Total Exports	24.2	48.3	77.3	12.2	4.8	16.3	6.7	4.1	1.9
Total Non-Oil/Gas	11.1	33.2	68.0	20.0	7.4	26.3	6.8	6.4	-0.6
Labour-intensive Manufactured Exports									
Textiles & Footwear	2.2	8.0	12.1	23.6	4.2	23.3	1.6	-0.3	-2.6
Furniture	0.2	0.8	1.8	22.4	8.5	23.5	5.6	1.0	-2.9
Total Labour-intensive Manufacture	2.5	8.8	13.9	23.5	4.7	23.3	2.1	-0.2	-2.6

Source: Basri and Papanek (forthcoming), using BPS data from Tim Buehrer and the World Bank. * 2006 estimates.

as with labour-intensive manufactures more generally, the country's slower export growth is primarily associated with problems on the supply side, with demand-side constraints being generally minor. This indifferent export performance in turn weakens the constituency for a more liberal trade regime.

REFERENCES

Athukorala, P.-C. (2006), 'Post-crisis Export Performance: The Indonesian Experience in Regional Perspective', *Bulletin of Indonesian Economic Studies*, **42**, 2, 177–211.
Athukorala, P.-C. and H. Hill (2008), 'Asian Trade and Investment: Patterns and Trends', paper presented to workshop on 'Emerging Trends and Patterns of Trade and Investment in Asia', Brisbane, February.
Basri, M. C. (2001), 'The Political Economy of Manufacturing Protection in Indonesia, 1975–1995', unpublished doctoral dissertation, Australian National University, Canberra.
Basri, M. C. and H. Hill (2004), 'Ideas, Interests and Oil Prices: The Political Economy of Trade Reform during Soeharto's Indonesia', *The World Economy*, **27**, 5, 633–56.
Basri, M. C. and G. Papanek (forthcoming), 'Dutch Disease and Employment in Indonesia', Working Paper, LPEM, University of Indonesia, Jakarta.
Basri, M. C. and A. A. Patunru (2007), 'How to Keep Trade Policy Open: The Case of Indonesia', paper prepared for conference on 'Globalisation, Asian Economic Integration, and National Development Strategies: Challenges to Asia in a Fast-changing World', August.
Basri, M. C. and H. Soesastro (2005), 'The Political Economy of Trade Policy in Indonesia', *ASEAN Economic Bulletin*, **22**, 1, 3–18.
Bird, K., H. Hill and S. Cuthbertson (2008), 'Making Trade Policy in a New Democracy after a Deep Crisis: Indonesia', *The World Economy*, **31**, 7, 947–968.
Bulman, T., W. Fengler and M. Ikhsan (2008), 'Indonesia's Oil Opportunity', *Far Eastern Economic Review*, **171**, 5, 14–18.
Corden, W. M. (1997), *Trade Policy and Economic Welfare*, 2nd edn (Oxford: Oxford University Press).
Fane, G. and T. Condon (1996), 'Trade Reform in Indonesia, 1987–1995', *Bulletin of Indonesian Economic Studies*, **32**, 3, 33–54.
Hew, D. (ed.) (2007), *Brick by Brick: The Building of an ASEAN Economic Community* (Singapore: Institute of Southeast Asian Studies).
Higgins, B. (1968), *Economic Development: Problems, Principles, and Policies*, rev. edn (New York: W. W. Norton).
Kimura, F. (2006), 'International Production and Distribution Networks in East Asia: 18 Facts, Mechanics, and Policy Implications', *Asian Economic Policy Review*, **1**, 346–47.
Kong, T. and A. Ramayandi (2008), 'Survey of Recent Developments', *Bulletin of Indonesian Economic Studies*, **44**, 1, 7–32.
Lloyd, P. (2005), 'What is a Single Market? An Application to the Case of ASEAN', *ASEAN Economic Bulletin*, **22**, 3, 251–65.
McCulloch, N. and C. P. Timmer (2008), 'Rice Policy in Indonesia', *Bulletin of Indonesian Economic Studies*, **44**, 1, 33–44.
Manning, C. (2008), 'SBY's Dilemma: Jobless Growth?', Working Paper, Australian National University, Canberra.
WTO (2007), *Trade Policy Review – Indonesia 2007* (Geneva: World Trade Organization).

3

Missed Opportunities: The WTO Trade Policy Review for the East African Community

Oliver Morrissey and Chris Jones

1. INTRODUCTION

ALTHOUGH the East African Community (EAC), comprising Kenya, Tanzania and Uganda (with Burundi and Rwanda having applied to join), came into force on 7 July 2000 (replacing the East Africa Cooperation of 1993–99), the Common External Tariff (CET) was only established in January 2005. As the CET represented an asymmetric change in members' tariff structures – Kenya and Tanzania essentially reduced tariffs whereas Uganda increased them – this Trade Policy Review (TPR) of the EAC (WTO, 2007) is timely, especially insofar as all three countries had sustained significant trade liberalisation since the mid to late 1980s. As is typical of TPRs, WTO (2007) brings together a considerable amount of information on trade and tariff structures, export, sector and trade-related policies. One weakness is that although the TPR concerns the EAC, most of the report discusses each country separately; of the total of 276 pages, excluding minutes and reports by the EAC members, only 25 relate specifically to the EAC.

This focus on the individual countries rather than the EAC itself is limiting in a number of respects. First, to assess the effect of changes under the EAC on individual members one has to search through the country sections. Second, and more generally, the TPR does not bring together information on the countries relevant to the possible impact of the EAC. Third, and following, it is difficult to find relevant information to assess the future prospects of the EAC. Specifically, although changing relations with the European Union (EU) is probably the single most important policy issue facing the evolution of the EAC, this is not specifically discussed (although it is of course mentioned). In these respects the TPR is a missed opportunity to document the issues most relevant to the future of the EAC.

This lack of focus on integration is common in TPRs for sub-Saharan African (SSA) countries, as typically they cover only one country; since the start of 2006, there have been eight TPRs on individual countries, and although there was a TPR of Cameroon and Gabon in October 2007, both countries were treated independently. For SSA countries, integration is rarely a major issue. McKay (2005) notes that regional integration, given its very slow pace in West Africa, has been of no evident benefit to the Gambia; Milner (2004), in his review of the 2003 TPR of Burundi, does not even mention the potential of regional integration (although it is only recently that Burundi has started negotiations to join the EAC with Rwanda). This neglect may understate the true importance of intra-regional trade, either because such trade is not recorded across the porous borders common in SSA (McKay, 2005) or because prevailing protection undermines potential intra-regional trade (Panagariya, 2003).

However, it seems reasonable to expect that a TPR of the members of a regional integration agreement should address intra-regional trade. The only other recent TPR covering all the members of a regional integration agreement was on the Organisation of Eastern Caribbean States (OECS) in November 2007. Although the report argued for the benefits of further integration, within the OECS and between it and CARICOM, detail was presented separately for each member state and no collated statistics were provided on intra-regional trade. Arguably, this is not very important for the OECS, but it is potentially quite important for the EAC. Kirkpatrick and Watanabe (2005) use a gravity model to examine the effects of regional trade cooperation in East Africa over the period 1970–2001, and find that episodes of regional integration increased intra-regional trade (notably, intra-regional trade was greater in the 1970s and since the mid-1990s, compared to the intervening period when cooperation was suspended). 'The results of the empirical analysis are sufficiently robust to support the conclusion that regional trade cooperation can support the expansion of trade between the three economies' (Kirkpatrick and Watanabe, 2005, p. 157). It is unfortunate that such potential is not addressed in the TPR.

The Cotonou Agreement between the EU and Africa, Caribbean and Pacific (ACP) countries proposed the establishment of a series of economic partnership agreements (EPAs), under which the EU and regional groupings of ACP countries offer reciprocal trade preferences to each other. Negotiations between the EU and ACP regional groups began in 2003 and entered the final stage in March 2007, with EPAs to be implemented from 2008 (in fact, it is only negotiations on the details of agreements that are now taking place). In addition to enhancing the trade preferences offered to the ACP by the EU, and rendering preferences compatible with WTO rules, EPAs also have an objective of promoting regional integration amongst ACP countries, and this may offer the greatest benefit (Hinkle and Schiff, 2004). To this end, individual groups of ACP countries were expected to form regional integration agreements among themselves, and these regional groups would negotiate a reciprocal arrangement with the EU. Initially, Kenya and Uganda negotiated with the Eastern and Southern Africa (ESA) group; Tanzania was a member of this group and also the separate Southern Africa group. However, on 27 November 2007 the EAC itself signed a framework EPA with the EU (and Burundi and Rwanda are likely to be incorporated into this). Little attention is paid to this in the TPR, but as it is such an important future trade policy issue for the EAC, much of this chapter addresses related concerns.

As EPAs require the EAC to eliminate tariffs on 'substantially all' imports from the EU (in the Framework Agreement, the EAC commits to phased liberalisation of 82 per cent of imports from the EU in 2006 values by 2032), the impact will depend primarily on the structure of a country's imports. There are benefits for products where there are few or no competing domestic producers – consumption gains from increased cheaper imports and potential welfare gains in sourcing imports from more efficient EU producers. There are potential welfare losses, or adjustment costs, where cheap imports from the EU undermine domestic production or displace more efficient producers in the rest of the world. There are also implications for intra-regional trade, as tariff-free imports from the EU may displace the regional market share of current intra-regional exporters. It is unfortunate that the TPR did not address these issues in a coherent manner.

The remainder of the chapter is organised as follows. Section 2 provides the background context by reviewing trade policy reform in East Africa since the mid-1980s, with a comparison to SSA patterns, and relating this to trade performance. Section 3 then discusses some of the information provided in the TPR, focusing on the change in tariffs due to the CET, export promotion policies and investment policies. We note that whilst each member country has its own export and investment incentive policies, the EAC missed the opportunity to consolidate these into a regional policy. Section 4 considers the major trade policy issues facing the EAC in the future, in particular export diversification and EPAs.

2. TRADE POLICY REFORM IN EAST AFRICA IN THE 1990s

The East African countries, in common with sub-Saharan Africa (SSA) generally, have liberalised imports significantly since the 1980s (Ackah and Morrissey, 2005; Morrissey, 2005). As a consequence, effective protection due to trade policy has been reduced by half, to about 15 per cent across sectors in East African countries on average in the early 2000s compared to around 30 per cent in the early 1990s (Morrissey, 2007). Effective protection did increase for some sectors (e.g. clothing in Kenya, manufactured food in Tanzania and chemicals in Uganda).

Table 1 provides a broad picture of trade policy reform based on changes in average unweighted tariffs comparing 1990–95 and 2000–02 for SSA regions and the EAC members. Although no more than indicative, it is evident that

TABLE 1
Tariff Changes in Sub-Saharan Africa, 1990–2002

	Average Tariffs		
	1990–95	*2000–02*	*Percentage Change*
West Africa (15)	23	14	−39
Central Africa (9)	22	17	−23
Southern Africa (9)	20	13	−35
East Africa (7)	28	16	−43
Kenya	33	17	−49
Tanzania	28	16	−43
Uganda	17	9	−47

Notes:
Tariffs are the simple mean of countries for which average scheduled tariff data were available (number of countries in parentheses).

Source: Regional data adapted from Morrissey (2005, Table 2); country data from Ackah and Morrissey (2005).

average tariffs have been reduced significantly, by more than a third on average in SSA over some 10 years. East Africa (here broadly defined) reduced tariffs the most, by 43 per cent on average. Southern Africa has consistently had the lowest tariffs but still reduced tariffs further by 35 per cent (largely due to reductions in South Africa). West Africa reduced tariffs by 39 per cent and Central Africa by 23 per cent, the lowest proportional regional change. Although starting from, and hence ending at, quite different average rates, the three EAC countries reduced tariffs by very similar percentage proportions, all equal to or slightly above the East Africa average. Nevertheless, by the early 2000s (and prior to the CET), Kenya and Tanzania had average tariffs almost twice the level in Uganda.

Table 2 shows that there is no consistent relationship between tariff reductions and trade performance, measured by percentage change in imports and exports (both relative to GDP), although the periods are not identical (trade share changes are during the 1990s). The trade trends may of course be related; given other sources of foreign exchange (mostly aid), export growth is required to finance import growth. Furthermore, the percentage change refers to quite different starting points, as imports are typically a much higher share of GDP than exports (the table also shows percentage point changes). For SSA on average, in 1990–92 imports represented 39 per cent of GDP whereas exports were only 26 per cent, the gap being largely financed by aid; by the end of the decade, imports had grown by 9 per cent on average and exports by 19 per cent on average (Morrissey, 2005, p. 1141). Shares of GDP imports increased by just below four points, whereas exports rose by over five points.

TABLE 2
Trade Changes in Sub-Saharan Africa in the 1990s

	Percentage Change		Percentage Point Change	
	M	X	M	X
West Africa (15)	14.0	13.0	5.0	3.3
Central Africa (9)	21.5	58.5	7.9	13.0
Southern Africa (9)	−3.0	1.2	−1.6	0.4
East Africa (7)	5.4	18.7	1.8	4.0
Kenya	14.9	−4.5	4.3	−1.2
Tanzania	−30.7	17.8	−11.3	2.1
Uganda	4.1	35.9	0.9	2.8

Notes:
Percentage changes in imports (M) and exports (X), both measured as shares of GDP, and percentage point changes are the average for countries computed over 1990–92 to 1998–2000 (number of countries in parentheses).

Source: See Table 1.

For SSA, export growth during the period was driven largely by Central Africa (resource-led in a few countries), but was only relatively low in Southern Africa (an economically large, exporting region). While tariffs were reduced proportionally the most, imports rose by far less in East Africa than in the other regions except Southern Africa (where imports actually fell), and export growth was slightly below the SSA average. Perhaps more relevant is that the percentage point increase in exports was greater than in imports, implying a reduction in the trade deficit (this also applied to Central and Southern Africa). West Africa had a relatively large reduction in tariffs and a relatively large increase in imports, that exceeded export growth; this is the only region where there is any suggestion that import liberalisation increased the trade deficit. Central Africa had the lowest reduction in tariffs, but the largest increase in imports (due to the export growth). This shows that tariff reductions are only one factor determining import and export growth, and in SSA they may not be the most important (Morrissey, 2005).

There is a marked contrast between the three EAC countries. Kenya experienced above-average import growth (to 33 per cent of GDP by the end of the 1990s), but exports actually declined (to about 25 per cent of GDP). In Tanzania, imports fell quite dramatically (to just over 25 per cent of GDP by the end of the 1990s), and note that we show below that, although tariffs fell over the full period, they were increased in 1997; exports grew, albeit to only 14 per cent of GDP. In Uganda, imports grew only slightly (to 23 per cent of GDP) and the apparent rapid export growth is in the context of a very low base, such that it was only just over 10 per cent of GDP by the end of the decade. As discussed

TABLE 3
Tariff Structure in Kenya and Uganda

Distribution (% lines)	Kenya		Uganda	
	1994	2000	1994	2002
Tariff = 0%	3.63	4.15	4.27	16.13
1 to 10%	0.10	21.88	46.54	45.53
11 to 20%	10.40	38.57	23.78	38.34
21 to 30%	7.55	14.75	25.29	0.00
31 to 40%	43.12	20.53	0.00	0.00
41 to 50%	34.99	0.05	0.00	0.00
>50%	0.21	0.07	0.11	0.00
Average tariff (eight-digit)	35.12	17.71	17.07	8.94
CV (eight-digit)	0.38	0.65	0.53	0.60
Tariff bands	12	10	5	3

Notes:
The distribution gives the percentage of tariff lines in different rate bands. Average is the mean unweighted scheduled tariff and CV is the Coefficient of Variation (standard deviation divided by the mean). For Kenya, figures are based on 5,761 eight-digit tariff lines in 1994 and 5,924 in 2000; for Uganda, 5,306 eight-digit tariff lines in 1994 and 5,271 in 2002.

Source: Authors' computation from data in Jones (2008).

below, it is evident that export performance is very varied and largely independent of domestic trade (tariff) policy reforms.

a. Tariffs in the East African Community

Before considering the impact on the introduction of the CET by the EAC, it is useful to review the pattern of tariffs in each of the member countries in the 1990s. Table 3 provides an overview of changes in the tariff structure for Kenya (in 1994 and 2000) and Uganda (1994 and 2002). In Kenya, the number of tariff bands fell from 12 to 10, and the average unweighted tariff (based on data at the eight-digit level) fell over the period (by 65 per cent). In Uganda, which had already liberalised considerably by 1994, the number of tariff bands was reduced further and the average tariff also fell over the 10 years (by 48 per cent). The coefficient of variation rose in Kenya despite the large fall in the percentage of tariff lines that are over 30 per cent. Although the spread was greater in 1994, the proportion of tariffs further from the mean is greater in 2000. This can be seen in Figure 1 which reports the percentage of products (at the eight-digit HS level) subject to each tariff rate in 1994 and 2000 (and illustrates the significant reduction in tariffs). Although there is some bunching at 40 per cent (about 12 per cent of products), the main bunching is at 15 per cent in 2000 (just over 40 per cent of tariffs) compared to at 30 per cent and 50 per cent in 1994 (together about two-thirds of products).

FIGURE 1
Distribution of Tariffs in Kenya, 1994 and 2000

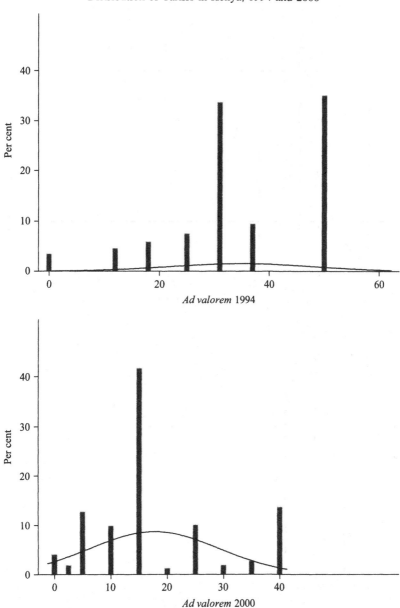

Tariff dispersion (CV) also increased, albeit only slightly, in Uganda: although tariffs above 20 per cent were eliminated by 2002, the proportion in the range 1–10 per cent remained stable while the proportion at 0 per cent and in the range 11–20 per cent increased. This is illustrated in Figure 2; the greater dispersion in

FIGURE 2
Distribution of Tariffs in Uganda, 1994 and 2002

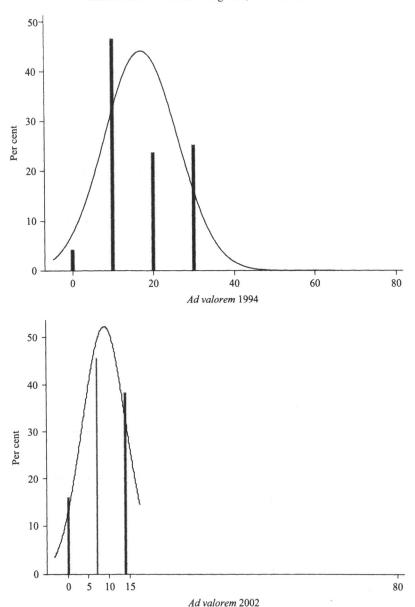

Ad valorem 1994

Ad valorem 2002

1994 is seen to be spread around the mean, whereas there is skewness to the left in the compressed spread of tariffs in 2002 (more than 80 per cent of products were at either 7 per cent or 15 per cent).

Table 4 shows the pattern of Tanzania's tariff structure for 1993, 1998 and 2000; the intervening year is included to illustrate a case where tariffs tended to

TABLE 4
The Tanzanian Tariff Structure, 1993–2000

Distribution (% lines)	1993	1998	2000
Tariff = 0%	9.95	15.87	2.36
1 to 10%	26.18	15.27	37.76
11 to 20%	43.48	17.01	20.28
21 to 30%	0.26	33.90	39.60
31 to 40%	20.02	17.93	0.00
41 to 50%	0.00	0.01	0.00
>50%	0.10	0.00	0.00
Average tariff (eight-digit)	19.47	22.12	16.19
CV (eight-digit)	0.62	0.64	0.56
Tariff bands	7	9	5

Notes:
Average is the mean unweighted scheduled tariff and CV is the Coefficient of Variation (standard deviation divided by the mean). Figures based on 5,798 eight-digit tariff lines in 1993, 7,499 eight-digit tariff lines in 1998 and 5,286 in 2000.

Source: Authors' computation from data in Jones (2008).

increase. The number of tariff bands increased from seven in 1993 to nine in 1998 before declining to five rates in 2000. The average tariff increased by 14 per cent between 1993 and 1998, but then fell by 27 per cent by 2000. The coefficient of variation fluctuated but decreased over the full period. This is illustrated in Figure 3: despite peak frequency at the average in 1993 (the 20 per cent rate), there was a long tail to the right, whereas by 2000 the compressed distribution resembled two peaks at either side of the mean (5 per cent and 25 per cent).

Although there were clear differences in the extent, timing and specific pattern of tariff reform in the three countries, there was a degree of convergence by the early 2000s: Kenya and Tanzania had comparable average tariffs (17 per cent and 16 per cent), although Uganda had a far lower average tariff (9 per cent). The major trade reforms implemented in all three countries were tariff reductions (and, similarly, the major policy impact of the EAC to date is the change in tariffs represented by the CET). As is evident from the foregoing discussion, the pattern of tariff changes varied across products. It is worth considering how tariffs on selected import commodities compare with the mean tariffs during the period of reform. As we are not concerned with considering the effect of tariff reductions on imports, the focus here is on important import commodities in 2000 (either because they had relatively high or low tariffs, or were a large share of imports).

Table 5 reports average tariffs and import shares for selected (two-digit) import sectors for Kenya in 1994 and 2000. The liberalisation discussed above is clearly exhibited. Tariffs fell considerably for all sectors, although there are relevant

FIGURE 3
Distribution of Tariffs in Tanzania, 1993 and 2000

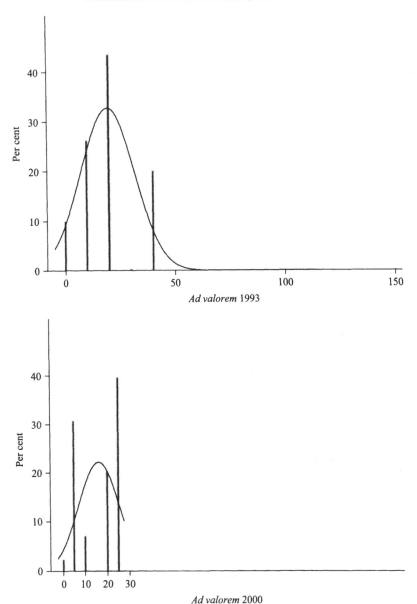

Ad valorem 1993

Ad valorem 2000

differences in the proportional changes (even if the relative pattern of protection is preserved). Tariffs on cereals were reduced by over two-thirds to a relatively low level, suggesting the importance of imports for consumption in a country often threatened by food production shortfall where cereals can be a relatively

TABLE 5
Selected Imports and Tariffs in Kenya

Code	Product Description	Sector Tariff		Import Share
		1994	2000	2000
10	Cereals	17.44	5.83	6.18
11	Products of Milling	41.32	17.11	0.17
15	Animal/Vegetable Fats	37.00	18.54	3.70
17	Sugars (and Confectionery)	30.39	10.24	1.23
25	Salt	27.96	12.77	0.25
27	Mineral Fuels	16.82	6.75	22.26
31	Fertilisers	0.00	0.00	2.47
44	Wood	37.48	25.07	0.12
69	Ceramic Products	39.29	24.86	0.32
72	Iron and Steel	23.23	11.10	3.68
87	Vehicles and Rolling Stock	30.59	18.76	5.96
96	Misc. Manufactured Articles	46.13	29.58	0.31
	Two-digit mean tariff	36.20	17.10	

Notes:
Sector tariff is the mean unweighted scheduled tariff for the eight-digit products in the two-digit sector. Import share is the percentage of import value accounted for by the sector.

Source: Authors' computation from data in Jones (2008).

large share of imports (note that fertilisers, an important input for the more commercial producers, faced zero tariffs). Tariffs on sugar were also reduced by about two-thirds, and on salt by over a half, both to relatively low (below-average) levels, although both are minor shares of imports. Other foods experienced reductions by about a half, but tariffs remained relatively high for fats and products of milling (the latter implying greater protection for domestic processors than for farmers, and it is relevant that imports are very low). Certain manufactures face relatively high tariffs (wood, ceramics and miscellaneous), but account for small shares of imports, suggesting that the sectors have domestic production to protect. The relatively low tariff on iron and steel is consistent with it being an input to some manufacturing sectors, whereas the high tariff on vehicles may reflect the luxury nature of some imports.

Table 6 lists average tariffs and import shares for the same sectors in Tanzania and Uganda. Compared to Kenya, both had relatively (to their average) higher tariffs on foods but comparable relative tariffs on the same manufactures; in broad terms, the sectors were of similar import importance for all three countries. In Tanzania, tariffs remained high on products of milling and sugars, suggesting a preference to protect domestic processing sectors, and relatively high in cereals (protecting domestic farmers). Although tariffs were generally lower in Uganda, the pattern of relatively high tariffs on foods is maintained. As with Kenya,

TABLE 6
Selected Imports and Tariffs in Tanzania and Uganda

Code	Tanzania			Uganda		
	Sector Tariff		Imports	Sector Tariff		Imports
	1993	2000	2000	1994	2002	2002
10	20.00	14.11	5.16	13.33	7.13	5.22
11	20.00	24.21	0.62	28.86	12.94	1.42
15	19.62	15.61	3.51	22.83	11.70	4.02
17	13.33	25.00	2.37	22.00	15.00	1.50
25	19.88	6.82	0.39	14.30	8.51	3.32
27	9.83	5.63	18.73	9.32	8.49	16.40
31	0.00	0.00	1.05	0.00	0.00	0.60
44	23.43	19.72	0.21	27.14	13.47	0.21
69	14.06	21.03	0.54	21.29	14.45	0.59
72	13.14	15.23	2.71	11.96	6.96	4.87
87	8.70	11.53	11.21	16.00	10.19	10.05
96	21.86	24.90	0.29	27.04	11.08	0.31
Mean	21.10	17.30		19.20	10.80	

Notes:
See Table 5.

Source: Authors' computation from data in Jones (2008).

fertiliser was subject to a zero tariff in both countries; iron and steel faced a higher tariff in Tanzania but lower in Uganda. The single major import commodity, mineral fuels (petroleum) ultimately faced a low tariff in all three (but would be subject to excise duties).

What we have shown in this section is that, from the early 1990s to the early 2000s, the three EAC countries implemented a similar degree and pattern of tariff reductions. As Uganda started from a lower average it ended at a lower average, whereas Kenya and Tanzania ended at a similar average. All three offered similar relative levels of tariff protection to the same manufacturing and food processing sectors, although Tanzania and Uganda offered relatively greater tariff protection to food producers than Kenya. The first issue to address in the next section is how the introduction of the CET affected the pattern of protection.

3. TRADE POLICY IN THE EAC

The most obvious effect of the establishment of the EAC is the Common External Tariff that came into force in January 2005. This introduced a very simplified structure that effectively increased Uganda's tariffs but reduced those

TABLE 7
Broad CET Compared to Country Tariffs

Average Tariffs (2000)	Kenya	Uganda	Tanzania	CET (2005)
Country	17.1	10.8	15.1	12.9
Manufacturing	17.5	10.2	14.0	12.8
Agriculture	15.9	12.6	18.3	17.3

Notes:
All tariffs are simple average applied MFN.

Source: Jones (2008) for countries; WTO (2007) for CET.

TABLE 8
EAC CET by Selected Sectors

Product Description	Applied 2006 Tariff		Import Share (%, 2004)		
	Average	Range	Kenya	Tanzania	Uganda
Live Animals	23.2	0–25	0.02	0.14	0.07
Dairy Products	42.5	25–60	0.06	0.12	0.14
Coffee, Sugar etc.	24.6	0–100	2.24	2.75	3.41
Grains	28.3	0–75	4.03	7.57	6.66
Chemicals	4.5	0–25	12.84	12.12	13.33
Textiles and Clothing	21.4	0–50	3.50	4.05	5.46
Transport Equipment	7.3	0–25	10.04	10.04	9.54

Notes:
Products based on WTO definitions.

Source: Derived from Table III.3 (WTO, 2007, p. 20).

of the other members, as illustrated in Table 7. 'Some 99% of all tariff lines carry rates of 0%, 10%, or 25%, with 25% being the modal rate and applying to 40% of tariff lines' (WTO, 2007, p. 17). The simple average tariff overall and on manufactures is 13 per cent (an increase only for Uganda), but is 17 per cent on agriculture commodities (only for Tanzania is this a decrease). Most of the sensitive products subject to high tariffs are also agricultural, such as milk (60 per cent), rice (75 per cent), maize (50 per cent), wheat (35 per cent) and sugar (35 per cent or 100 per cent), but also includes various linens (50 per cent) and some other products (WTO, 2007, pp. 18–19).

Recalling that the average CET is 13 per cent and 25 per cent is the standard maximum, Table 8 confirms that the high tariffs are mostly on agriculture or sectors where there is domestic production to protect (textiles and clothing, especially linens). It is interesting to note the broad similarity in the import shares of the selected sectors for all three countries. Live animals and dairy products are quite minor shares of imports but generally attract high tariffs, especially milk. This is true to a lesser extent for grains (although imports are quite variable, and sometimes much higher for Kenya) and textiles and clothing. Although Kenya has a much larger manufacturing sector, the three countries share quite a similar production structure, with a strong bias towards agriculture. This is reflected in the CET structure. Imports that offer little competition to domestic producers, such as chemicals and transport equipment, bear quite low tariffs.

Insofar as the CET to a large extent consolidates the tariff reductions that each country had implemented from the early 1990s, it is unlikely to have an appreciable effect on the pattern, or even level, of protection afforded to domestic sectors, with the exception that there is some increase for Uganda. The EAC itself has not represented noticeable liberalisation with respect to extra-regional imports.

Surprisingly, the TPR devotes no specific attention to the possible impact on intra-regional trade. As most of the TPR text comprises a discussion of each country individually without an attempt to highlight trade flows between the countries, one has to search through appendix tables to find information from which to draw inferences. This is a regrettable oversight (given that substantially all the TPR does is compile information); while intra-regional trade is small relative to the total trade of the member countries, it can be quite significant in particular sectors and is large by SSA standards. It transpires that in certain respects intra-regional trade is quite significant. It is possible to discern from the Appendix tables on origin of imports that in 2004 Kenya accounted for 21 per cent of Ugandan imports and Tanzania less than 1 per cent (page A3-276); Kenya accounted for 5 per cent of Tanzania's imports, Uganda is not separately identified (page A2-207); only 1.8 per cent of Kenya's imports were from SSA, and neither Tanzania nor Uganda are identified (page A1-14). Thus, the EAC provides over 20 per cent of Uganda's imports, over 5 per cent of Tanzania's but less than 2 per cent of Kenya's.

This understates the importance to Kenya. Considering the tables on destination of exports, in 2004 Uganda accounted for 10 per cent of Kenyan exports (excluding re-exports) and Tanzania 6.9 per cent (page A1-113). For Tanzania, 6.4 per cent of exports went to Kenya and about 1 per cent to Uganda (page A2-206). For Uganda, 12 per cent of exports went to Kenya and 1.9 per cent to Tanzania (page A3-275). This is a general pattern that has persisted for some three decades: 'exports of Kenya to regional partners account for 14.2 per cent of total exports during the 1970–97 period, whereas for the same period the figure is 3.1 per cent for Tanzania and 2.4 per cent for Uganda. Overall, intra-EAC trade has averaged 9.5 per cent over the period 1970–97' (Kirkpatrick and Watanabe, 2005, p. 145). This underestimates the intensity of intra-regional trade: relative to their total trade, intra-regional trade is highly concentrated in East Africa, more so than in the rest of SSA (Kirkpatrick and Watanabe, 2005, p. 146). Thus, the EAC is actually an important destination for exports of the member countries, accounting for some 17 per cent of Kenyan exports, over 7 per cent for Tanzania and about 14 per cent for Uganda in the mid-2000s. Unfortunately, the TPR offers no insight into how the EAC may affect these non-negligible export shares, and is particularly remiss in not attempting to identify the specific products concerned.

In general, Kenya supplies light manufactures and some processed foods to Tanzania and Uganda, whereas the latter mostly supply foods to the others (we surmise, as it is not documented). Kenya accounts for by far the greater share of intra-regional trade and, unlike the other countries, supplies manufactures or semi-processed goods. This does not imply that there are no potential gains for Tanzania and Uganda, as opportunities for them to supply food to the regional market could be beneficial. Intra-regional trade in food (which is likely to be under-recorded in official statistics) provides an outlet for local (seasonal) surpluses, especially in regions closer to neighbouring countries than their own urban markets (given the low level of regional market integration); could encourage crop diversification and the development of traders and distribution networks; and could help to smooth regional and seasonal price instability (Poulton et al., 2006, p. 252).

It is clear that intra-regional trade does not involve the major export commodities for each country. Using the tables on the structure of exports, taking 2004 figures, we can shed light on this. Kenya's main exports include tea (22 per cent), horticultural products (13 per cent), vegetables (8 per cent), coffee (5 per cent), and a variety of manufactures accounting for about 25 per cent (page A1-111); only some of the latter and petroleum re-exports are likely to be intra-regional. Tanzania mainly exports fish (8 per cent), nuts (5.2 per cent), coffee (3.7 per cent), tobacco (4.2 per cent), cotton (5.5 per cent), mining (8.5 per cent) and various manufactures accounting for 10 per cent (page A2-203). Uganda exports primarily coffee (20 per cent), fish (11 per cent), gold (10 per cent), agricultural raw materials (14 per cent) and a wide variety of simple manufactures accounting for 14 per cent of exports (page A3-273). The TPR helps to show that intra-regional trade is non-negligible but largely unrelated to each country's main exports, but does not help identify the sectors where the EAC may have an impact in each country. We return to this issue in the final section when considering the implications of an EPA on intra-regional trade.

a. Export Policies

No common EAC export assistance regime has been established, although member states are allowed 'to establish manufacturing under bond [MUB], export processing zones [EPZ] and duty drawback schemes' (WTO, 2007, p. 25). All three countries have duty drawback schemes, export promotion bodies, export credit schemes and zero-rated exports for VAT, but otherwise have quite different incentive schemes.

Kenya (pages A1-61–63) requires a licence for the export of most agricultural and mineral products, especially foods where self-sufficiency is a concern, and has no export quotas. Incentives under the EPZ, which mostly covers garments and apparel exported to the US under the African Growth and Opportunity Act (AGOA), include duty and VAT exemptions for imports of machinery and raw materials, a 10-year tax holiday (for corporate, income and withholding taxes) and 100 per cent investment allowances. Under the MUB, firms exporting all of their output enjoy similar benefits (there is no indication of how many firms are covered or in what sectors). Although textiles and clothing accounted for only about 2 per cent of total exports in 2004, the EPZs were estimated to account for 16 per cent of manufacturing employment and about 2 per cent of GDP; about 85 per cent of EPZ companies are owned by foreigners. There is an Export Promotion Council that supports mostly horticulture, traditional exports (tea and coffee), fish, livestock, and textiles and clothing.

Tanzania (pages A2-159–62) restricts exports of cereals, beans and unprocessed fish on food security grounds, imposes taxes on exports of cashew nuts, raw hides and skins, and requires licences to export foods, fish, forestry products, wildlife and minerals/gems. The MUB provides tariff-free imports of capital equipment and inputs for the production of exports. Mainland Tanzania introduced an EPZ scheme in 2002 for manufacturing (including agri-processing, textiles and clothing, fish processing, leather and wood products) with limited tax exemptions (Zanzibar has a longer established scheme with more attractive incentives, mostly for garments and fish processing). By 2005, the EPZ had attracted over $80 million in investment, about two-thirds from domestic sources.

Uganda (pages A3-238–41) prohibits exports of whole fresh fish and timber, but appears to require less licensing than the other countries. There are taxes on exports of coffee (1 per cent), cotton (2 per cent), and raw hides and skins (20 per cent). Uganda has no EPZ scheme (there appear to be plans to introduce one), although the MUB offers duty-free imports for firms producing only for export.

The extent of export-incentive and promotion schemes is roughly in line with the importance of exports for each country. Kenya has the most developed and extensive schemes, reflecting its position as a relatively significant and diversified exporter (exports are about 25 per cent of GDP). In Tanzania, exports are about 15 per cent of GDP and the schemes are more limited. In Uganda, where exports are a little over 10 per cent of GDP, the schemes are very limited. One implication is that the individual countries are not doing much to expand diversified exports, and so far the EAC offers little on this. We return to this in the final section.

b. Investment Measures

A major constraint on growth in SSA countries generally, including EAC, is low levels and especially low productivity of investment. The Commission for

Africa (2005) places considerable emphasis on investment as essential for a 'big push' to invest in people (especially health and education) and infrastructure. Regional integration agreements such as the EAC can have potential beneficial effects on investment, especially foreign investment, by including measures to support regional public infrastructure (UNCTAD, 2006a), trade facilitation (such as coordinating customs procedures) and improving the 'business environment' more generally. They can also have a more direct impact on foreign direct investment (FDI) by including investment provisions and incentives (UNCTAD, 2006b), to stimulate regional investment cooperation and promotion and grant national and most favoured nation (MFN) treatment to foreign firms (te Velde and Fahnbulleh, 2006). Even if regional integration agreements do not include provisions for investment, their trade effects may influence investment, by increasing the market size and encouraging new export opportunities. The EAC offers little for market size or exports, and includes no common policy on investment measures (although there is a proposal for an EAC Competition Committee). Thus, we limit attention to the policies of the member countries.

Perhaps surprisingly, since the mid-1990s FDI to Kenya has been lower than that to the other countries, 'e.g. during 1997–02, Kenya's FDI was about 26% of Uganda's and 19% of Tanzania's' (page A1-43). Inflows varied considerably from year to year but averaged about $56 million per annum over 2000–03, equivalent to about 0.5 per cent of GDP or less than 3 per cent of total investment, and were concentrated in horticulture. Kenya has bilateral investment treaties (BITs) with the Netherlands and Germany. In addition to the incentives for exporting, especially the EPZs, there are tax holiday and investment allowance incentives. In its own report, Kenya stresses renewed policies to enhance the investment environment and notes an increase in FDI in 2005, with China and the UK emerging as the major sources (page 289).

Privatisation (especially in communication services) and new mining opportunities (notably gold) attracted FDI in excess of $400 million per annum to Tanzania over 2000–04 (equivalent to almost 5 per cent of GDP), accounting for over 20 per cent of total investment and bringing the FDI stock to almost 50 per cent of GDP by 2005 (page A2-140). South Africa was the major source, accounting for almost half of FDI. Tanzania has BITs, with varying coverage, with nearly 20 countries, mostly EU or SSA (but not with South Africa). Tanzania offers a variety of tax incentives, usually including duty exemptions and VAT deferrals, especially for capital goods and inputs/equipment for agriculture, mining and tourism (hotels and tour operators).

FDI to Uganda was also quite healthy at around $200 million per annum over 2000–04 (page A3-223), equivalent to over 3 per cent of GDP and 14 per cent of total investment. The main sectors were manufacturing (especially food processing), water and energy, and real estate, and the sources were diverse. Uganda has signed BITs with 17 countries, including South Africa, Switzerland

and seven EU countries. Incentives are available, especially allowances on investment capital and depreciation, VAT exemptions or deferrals (especially in agri-business).

Given the broad compatibility of the investment incentive regimes in each country, but differences in the activities attracting most FDI, the absence of a coordinating investment regime in the EAC is an oversight. The problems EAC countries, especially Kenya currently, face in respect of FDI are that the level is generally very low and concentrated in particular sectors, with low levels of technology transfer and low linkages or spillovers for the rest of the economy. The reasons for low FDI are quite similar to those for low private investment: relatively small markets hence few investment opportunities, corruption, bureaucracy and weak property rights. Regional integration and associated regulatory reforms provide an opportunity for the EAC to attract higher levels of more diversified FDI: lower transactions costs associated with trade and investment and a more favourable business environment.

Investment protection provisions, such as limiting the threat of expropriation or supporting the security of property rights, encourage foreign investment because investors prefer a secure and predictable investment climate. Such provisions are most effective if there is also a stipulated dispute settlement mechanism, especially if this allows for some regional or international panel or an independent arbitrator (te Velde and Fahnbulleh, 2006). While such provisions exist in the Common Market for Eastern and Southern Africa (COMESA), of which the EAC countries are also members, these are weak to the extent that integration within COMESA is quite limited. It would have been relatively easy to embody these provisions in the EAC, perhaps with investor–state dispute settlement procedures (these are generally considered stronger than the state–state procedures in COMESA, perhaps because the investor has a more direct role in the process). Established dispute settlement procedures also support investment guarantees against non-commercial risks.

There are three particular areas of regulatory reform that could be incorporated into the EAC to promote a more attractive investment climate. First, trade facilitation, such as measures to coordinate and streamline customs and port clearance procedures, reduces transactions costs and this encourages production and investment. Second, measures that make it quicker and easier to establish a business or make an investment. In general, this means reducing red tape; for example, in Uganda 12 steps are required for a foreigner to establish a business (page A3-230). While some are standard (health and safety clearance, registering with utilities, obtaining land and building approval), at least seven different licences or clearance registrations are required. It seems likely that such a system could be streamlined to encourage foreign investors. Third, improvements in the legal system to make property rights more secure, e.g. contract enforcement and investor protection. These are particularly suited to incorporation as EAC provisions.

4. PROSPECTIVE ISSUES FOR EAC TRADE POLICY

Finally, we explore further two issues that are not really touched on in the TPR: the underlying reasons for poor export performance and the potential implications of an EPA. Trade liberalisation, even if limited to tariff reductions, increases the return to exports relative to import-competing products so exports should increase. As SSA countries such as EAC face numerous constraints on export supply response, the benefits of liberalisation have been slow to materialise, although overall export growth in SSA was quite strong during the 1990s, with the export/GDP ratio increasing by almost a fifth (Morrissey, 2005, p. 1141). The EAC countries are no exception to this trend and, as seen above, have only had limited policies to promote export growth and diversification. An EPA may help to address this by providing enhanced market access to the EU.

a. Export Diversification

Developed countries have, at least in principle, tried to stimulate SSA exports by providing preferential market access. The EU has provided trade preferences to the ACP countries since 1975 under successive Lomé conventions. However, these preferences have been of limited value (Langhammer, 1992), and trade preferences in general have not provided significant benefits to SSA (Brenton and Ikezuki, 2007). One reason is the restricted conditions under which preferences were granted, limiting the products eligible for full preferences (frequently to the exclusion of products of particular benefit to SSA) or imposing very restrictive Rules of Origin requirements (thus limiting opportunities for diversification). Another reason is the structure of production and policy-induced distortions in SSA; incentives for product diversification are weak, exacerbating the problem of export dependence on a narrow range of primary commodities. To address this, it is argued that achieving sustained growth in Africa requires implementing policies to expand and diversify exports away from dependence on a narrow range of (largely unprocessed) primary commodities (Commission for Africa, 2005). Trade preferences can play a role in encouraging such diversification. There is evidence that the AGOA supported an increase in 'new' exports for many SSA countries (Frazer and van Biesebroeck, 2007). As mentioned above, Kenya's EPZs have been oriented towards AGOA, and there has also been investment in garment factories in Uganda. The EPAs being negotiated with the EU also offer potential improvements in market access, at least to the extent that Rules of Origin requirements will be relaxed compared to existing regimes.

However, an emphasis on 'preferences for export diversification' can divert attention away from what is required to enhance the competitiveness of existing producers, whether import-competing or traditional exports (Morrissey, 2005), especially in agriculture (which remains a very important sector in the EAC countries). Before considering the potential implications of EPAs for the EAC, it is useful to review the underlying reasons for poor export performance.

There are a number of reasons why exports may not increase following trade liberalisation, in particular constraints on production and export supply response that are widespread in SSA. For example, McKay et al. (1999) show that export crop production in Tanzania is not evidently responsive to changes in export prices; production volumes have largely followed a declining secular trend over time. The implication is that producers came to expect long-run declining real prices, discounting the effect of temporary increases. The effect of declining export prices was to increase relative returns to and production of food crops. Similar concerns apply to the other EAC countries: while traditional cash crops remain important, they are unlikely to be viewed as opportunities for future growth. There are incentives to shift into more promising crops, typically food (for the domestic market) in Tanzania and Uganda and horticulture in Kenya. The difficulties of exporting traditional or non-traditional crops are exacerbated by relatively high transport costs, reflecting poor infrastructure and inefficient institutions (such as in customs and distribution), which provide 'natural protection' against imports but are an effective tax on exports (Milner et al., 2000). Much of the poor growth performance of SSA countries over the period 1970–95, in particular the absence of export-led growth, can be explained by the combination of primary commodity dependence, high protection and high transport costs (Morrissey, 2007), especially as traditional primary exports have high unit transport costs relative to value. The EAC is no exception.

One reason for the weak trade response in the EAC is that the reduction in trade barriers was not accompanied by a similar reduction in natural barriers; for example, overall transport costs have not fallen since the mid-1990s. Remoteness, whether being landlocked or located far inland in a large country, in the context of poor transport and distribution infrastructure is clearly damaging to trade because it raises trade costs. Uganda faces the highest transport costs; although land freight costs fell for imports, reflecting the decline in costs in Kenya (Kiringai, 2006), this was largely offset by an increase in sea freight costs (Rudaheranwa, 2006). In Tanzania, in contrast, land (rail) freight costs rose but sea freight costs fell, because of investment and efficiency improvements in the port of Dar-es-Salaam (Kweka, 2006). Effective protection due to transport costs remained about 15 per cent on average, and transport costs became more important than trade policy as a source of protection. The situation for exports is worse: effective taxation of exports due to transport costs was around 40 per cent on average for all three countries in the early 2000s (Morrissey, 2007). Extra-regional export growth for the EAC requires diversification; Kenya has had success moving into horticulture, although prospects for future growth in this sector may be limited; Tanzania and Uganda have relied on luck, as the recent appearance of mining (especially gold) exports may be all that has prevented total exports from declining. Luck is not a good strategy for the future, but the EAC offers some opportunities, which we consider in the context of EPAs.

b. Economic Partnership Agreements

In principle, EPAs offer potential benefits to the EAC countries beyond what was available under Lomé conventions, although these are quite limited. As least developed countries, Tanzania and Uganda are entitled to largely free access to the EU without offering any reciprocity; only Kenya stands to gain a preference as the EPA would be tariff-free and the alternative is less preferential access. However, all three should benefit from less restrictive Rules of Origin requirements. An underlying premise is that the EAC, as with any regional integration among groups of ACP countries as a precursor to EPAs, should derive benefit from enhanced regional integration. The intra-regional trade benefits may be limited (although, as alluded to above, they may be significant for specific sectors), but there are potential benefits from regional economic cooperation. For example, coordinated and streamlined customs and port clearance procedures could reduce trade costs and facilitate trade, enhancing the business environment to both attract investment and promote exports.

When negotiating EPAs, ACP countries were expected to form themselves into regional groups. Some of the six groups that emerged were relatively integrated or at least regionally inclusive – the Caribbean, Pacific, and Southern Africa – but others have no inclusive integration agreement and are quite diverse – East and Southern Africa (ESA), Central Africa and West Africa. As mentioned above, the EAC decided to sign an EPA with the EU itself, although it is likely that subsequent negotiations will be at least cognisant of ESA negotiations, if not with the broader region. The African experience with regional integration arrangements has not been encouraging; most have been weak, have proved politically difficult to sustain and have generated few clear economic benefits (Lyakurwa et al., 1997). The general problem has been that most of the benefits accrue to the largest and richest member, Kenya in the EAC case (as it accounts for most intra-regional trade), and few economic benefits accrue to the poorest members. This is exacerbated under EPAs because the richer country is not least developed whereas the poorer countries are. The former stands to gain from enhanced access to the EU market whereas the latter are entitled to this anyway. It is therefore relevant to assess the impact of the reciprocity, the effect of offering tariff-free access to imports from the EU.

McKay et al. (2005) conducted such an exercise for Tanzania and Uganda within the EAC (data were unavailable for Kenya at the time). The potential costs of tariff-free access to imports from the EU in addition to the loss of tariff revenue is that increased import competition from the EU will displace domestic production, and may capture some of the market in intra-regional trade (a particular concern for Kenya). Whether the loss of domestic production implies a welfare loss depends on the potential efficiency of domestic producers compared to EU competitors. Furthermore, the revenue losses should not be exaggerated; tariffs have already been reduced, countries have at least 10 years to phase in tariff elimination and can continue to exclude a range of designated 'sensitive products' (thus there is time to plan for revenue substitution).

McKay et al. (2005) assume that the EPA would require the full liberalisation of trade flows in both directions; this represents a 'long-run' outcome and would tend to overstate the impact. There are three general trade effects: an increase in cheaper imports from the EU (a consumption gain), displacement by the EU of imports from the rest of the world (a potential welfare loss), and EU displacement of intra-regional trade (which may benefit the importing member to the cost of the exporting member). Tanzania and Uganda could, in principle, benefit from the EPA by being able to avail of cheaper imports of intermediate and raw material inputs from the EU. Kenya also gets these benefits, but these should be offset against losses of regional market share to EU imports (this effect would be negligible for Tanzania and Uganda). In respect of exports to the EU, Tanzania and Uganda only obtain improved access if relaxed Rules of Origin benefit them (this would be limited unless export diversification is encouraged). Kenya, however, requires the EPA to maintain its preferences and could benefit more from less restrictive Rules of Origin.

The results of estimating the impact of an EPA, albeit using data from the mid-1990s, are informative. Although the two countries are in many respects quite similar, McKay et al. (2005) find that Tanzania experiences a small welfare loss but Uganda experiences a small welfare gain. This arises because in Uganda the increase in imports from the EU either relates to products where the EU is already the dominant supplier (a clear consumption gain) or tends to displace relatively inefficient imports from Kenya (implying a consumption welfare gain), whereas in Tanzania there is a greater tendency to displace relatively efficient imports from the rest of the world (implying a welfare loss). By implication, Kenya would experience a welfare loss associated with the loss of regional market share in addition to any losses to domestic producers facing increased competition from EU imports. Tanzania and Uganda will also suffer the latter losses, but to a lesser extent given their domestic production structure. It must be acknowledged that these welfare gains will be less visible than any losses, either in tariff revenue (not insignificant) or from increased competition faced by domestic producers (especially in Kenya). The simple point is that the EPA will have effects on domestic producers, revenue and intra-regional trade and any losses will not necessarily be offset by gains in market access to the EU. On the other hand, the liberalisation with respect to the EU will be implemented over a long period (Kiguta, 2008): excluding the sensitive products (the almost 20 per cent of imports from the EU that will not be liberalised), raw materials and capital goods facing a zero CET and accounting for almost two-thirds of imports from the EU are *de facto* liberalised; intermediate products (the 10 per cent CET) accounting for 16 per cent of imports from the EU are to be liberalised over 2015–22 and finished products (25 per cent CET) over 2020–32 (accounting for only 2 per cent of imports).

5. CONCLUSION

The specific effect of the establishment of the EAC is the CET. Although this has reduced tariffs in Kenya and Tanzania and increased tariffs in Uganda, it largely preserves the established sectoral pattern of tariff protection. The TPR does a good job of documenting this, when complemented with detail on the countries' pre-CET tariffs. In this sense, the EAC is unlikely to significantly affect the pattern of extra-regional imports. The regional integration embodied in the EAC, in particular the elimination of tariffs on trade between the members (although not yet fully implemented) may affect intra-regional trade. The TPR offers little on this issue. In general, the TPR provides considerable information on trade and related policies in each of the EAC countries but, other than the CET, limited information on the EAC itself. This reflects the limited scope of the EAC to date; as it is little more than a Customs Union, the TPR only covers what is in the EAC. In this review we have tried to go further, considering the EAC both in the context of the members' prior tariffs and prospects for the future.

From a forward-looking perspective, the EAC is deficient. There appears to have been no attempt to consolidate or coordinate export promotion or investment policies, and little if any attention to intra-regional trade. This represents a missed opportunity as regional agreements are appropriate places to incorporate investment provisions and export diversification strategies, especially as all three members have a need to address where future exports and investment will come from, and indeed to coordinate some investment into prospective export sectors. In part this requires attention to products where there is potential to expand intra-regional trade. In part it also requires attention to the implications of an EPA with the EU, and some of the issues were discussed above. It is perhaps a little surprising that the TPR and comments by members in the Report included nothing on how the EAC views negotiating an EPA, given that this is the single most important issue on the horizon.

REFERENCES

Ackah, C. and O. Morrissey (2005), 'Trade Policy and Performance in Africa since the 1980s', Economic Research Working Paper No. 78 (Tunis: African Development Bank).

Brenton, P. and T. Ikezuki (2007), 'The Value of Trade Preferences for Africa', in R. Newfarmer (ed.), *Trade, Doha and Development: A Window on the Issues* (Washington, DC: The World Bank).

Commission for Africa (2005), *Our Common Interest: Report of the Commission for Africa* (London: Commission for Africa).

Frazer, G. and J. van Biesebroeck (2007), 'Trade Growth under the African Growth and Opportunity Act', NBER Working Paper No. W13222 (Cambridge, MA: NBER).

Hinkle, L. and M. Schiff (2004), 'Economic Partnership Agreements between Sub-Saharan Africa and the EU: A Development Perspective', *The World Economy Global Trade Policy 2004*, **26**, 9, 1321–34.

Jones, C. (2008), 'The Political Economy of Trade Policy in Africa', unpublished PhD Thesis submitted to the University of Nottingham.

Kiguta, P. (2008), 'The EAC Interim Agreement', *Trade Negotiations Insights*, **7**, 2, 6 (March), at http://www.ictsd.org/tni.

Kiringai, J. (2006), 'Trade and Transport Costs in Kenya', School of Economics, University of Nottingham, CREDIT Research Paper 06/11.

Kirkpatrick, C. and M. Watanabe (2005), 'Regional Trade in Sub-Saharan Africa: An Analysis of East African Trade Cooperation, 1970–2001', *The Manchester School*, **73**, 2, 141–64.

Kweka, J. (2006), 'Trade and Transport Costs in Tanzania', School of Economics, University of Nottingham, CREDIT Research Paper 06/10.

Langhammer, R. (1992), 'The Developing Countries and Regionalism', *Journal of Common Market Studies*, **30**, 2, 211–31.

Lyakurwa, W., A. McKay, N. Ng'eno and W. Kennes (1997), 'Regional Integration in Sub-Saharan Africa: A Review of Experiences and Issues', in A. Oyejide, I. Elbadawi and P. Collier (eds.), *Regional Integration and Trade Liberalisation in Sub-Saharan Africa* (Vol. 1) (London: Macmillan), pp. 159–209.

McKay, A. (2005), 'Trade Policy Issues in a Small African Economy: The Trade Policy Review of The Gambia 2004', *The World Economy Global Trade Policy 2005*, **28**, 9, 1197–210.

McKay, A., O. Morrissey and C. Vaillant (1999), 'Aggregate Agricultural Supply Response in Tanzania', *Journal of International Trade and Economic Development*, **8**, 1, 107–23.

McKay, A., C. Milner and O. Morrissey (2005), 'Some Simple Analytics of the Welfare Effects of EU–ACP Economic Partnership Agreements', *Journal of African Economies*, **14**, 3, 327–58.

Milner, C. (2004), 'Trade Policy in Burundi: Reform without Political Stability', *The World Economy Global Trade Policy 2004*, **27**, 9, 1363–78.

Milner, C., O. Morrissey and N. Rudaheranwa (2000), 'Policy and Non-policy Barriers to Trade and Implicit Taxation of Exports in Uganda', *Journal of Development Studies*, **37**, 2, 67–90.

Morrissey, O. (2005), 'Imports and Implementation: Neglected Aspects of Trade in the Report of the Commission for Africa', *Journal of Development Studies*, **41**, 4, 1133–53.

Morrissey, O. (2007), 'Trade Policy and Transport Costs: What can the EU do to Promote Export Growth in East Africa?', in W. Hout (ed.), *EU Development Policy and Poverty Reduction: Enhancing Effectiveness* (Aldershot: Ashgate), pp. 47–65.

Panagariya, A. (2003), 'South Asia: Does Preferential Trade Liberalisation Make Sense?', *The World Economy Global Trade Policy 2003*, **26**, 9, 1279–92.

Poulton, C., J. Kydd and A. Dorward (2006), 'Overcoming Market Constraints on Pro-poor Agricultural Growth in Sub-Saharan Africa', *Development Policy Review*, **24**, 3, 243–78.

Rudaheranwa, N. (2006), 'Trade and Transport Costs in Uganda', School of Economics, University of Nottingham, CREDIT Research Paper 06/09.

te Velde D. W. and M. Fahnbulleh (2006), *Investment and Economic Partnership Agreements*, Brussels: EU–ACP Project Management Unit (PMU), EU–ACP Negotiations in Focus Briefing Paper, 25 October.

UNCTAD (2006a), *The Least Developed Countries Report 2006: Developing Productive Capacities* (New York and Geneva: United Nations).

UNCTAD (2006b), *Investment Provisions in Economic Integration Agreements* (New York and Geneva: United Nations).

WTO (2007), *Trade Policy Review for East African Community 2006* (Geneva: Bernan Associates for World Trade Organization).

4

Liberalising Trends in Israel's Trade Policy: Trade Policy Review of Israel

Alfred Tovias

1. TARIFF BARRIERS

SINCE 1991 Israel has moved slowly but steadily towards a very open trade regime. Endeavours in this direction include, among others, increased transparency of its tariff system. Unilateral tariff liberalisation between 1991 and 1998 was meant to bring maximum most favoured nation (MFN) tariff rates for most products to a range of 8–12 per cent over a period of six years. All major political parties accepted a gradual liberalisation of trade policy in order to increase the efficiency of the regulated economy in which the level of public expenditure was unusually high for a developed country. The plan thus required a gradual reduction of tariffs, when as a first step tariffs replaced non-tariff barriers (NTBs) such as licences and quotas. The reduction process was postponed to 2000 for the textile industry, but market forces proved to be very strong, so that by the beginning of 2000, most of Israel's textile plants had closed down and moved production to neighbouring countries such as Jordan and Egypt.

Since 1998–2000, Israel has continued to implement trade liberalisation reforms, albeit at a somewhat slower pace than in the previous six-year period. The average applied MFN tariff has fallen from 10.8 per cent in 2000 to 8.9 per cent in 2005, with a maximum rate of 560 per cent on fresh or dried dates(!), and high tariff dispersion (with a coefficient of variation of 2.8). About 48.5 per cent of all tariff lines now carry the zero rate, up from 45.1 per cent in 2000 (WTO, 2006). Other frequent tariff rates are 12 per cent (2,094 lines), 10 per cent (614

This chapter draws from a report submitted to the FEMISE Network in December 2007. It has been duly updated. The author wishes to acknowledge the helpful assistance of Emmanuelle Blanc and Yonatan Rotem.

lines), and 8 per cent (603 lines). Some 46.4 per cent of the tariff lines carry duties between zero (excluded) and 15 per cent (included).

MFN tariff rates on non-agricultural products (WTO definition) are generally lower (5.1 per cent on average), with the highest rates (ranging up to 34.4 per cent) applying to fish and fishery products and textiles and clothing. MFN tariffs on agricultural products (WTO definition) remain high, with an average tariff of 32.9 per cent, and rates varying considerably among product groups. Tariffs are particularly high on dairy products (with an average rate of 124.4 per cent), fruit and vegetables (54.0 per cent), and live animals and products thereof (50.4 per cent) (see later). Tariffs are relatively low on chemicals and photographic supplies (with an average rate of 2.2 per cent), mineral products (3.6 per cent) and transport equipment (3.6 per cent).

Low tariffs mean that tariff escalation almost does not exist, with a higher range, close to 8 per cent for final and semi-processed products and a lower range for unprocessed products. This system usually provides a greater degree of protection for the local manufacturing sector, but in recent years tariff escalation has not been maintained in all stages of processing.

Coverage of an additional tariff, called the 'safeguard levy', has also been substantially reduced and phased out, from the equivalent of 2.7 per cent of the tariff lines in 1992 to 0.8 per cent in 1999 to nil at present. The main difference between MFN tariffs and the safeguard levy is that any change in the former requires approval by the Knesset (the Israeli Parliament), while the levy did not. This fact had introduced a certain element of uncertainty to tariff protection and, following strong protestations by the United States, had to be phased out. Another aspect of uncertainty for importers results from the fact that Israel has bound rates on just half of its tariff lines. These are often above applied MFN rates, giving Israel the opportunity to unilaterally raise its applied tariffs. This issue might be solved by narrowing the gap between bound and applied rates, as well as by increasing the coverage of tariff bindings.

However, the significance of MFN tariff schedules is limited. The bulk of Israel's imports to supply local consumers is conducted within the framework of free trade agreements with the European Union (now covering 27 countries), the United States, EFTA, Canada, Mexico, Turkey and Mercosur;[1] a partial preferential agreement with Jordan[2] and the Customs Union Agreement with the Palestinian

---

[1] On 17 December 2007, Israel signed a landmark trade agreement with Mercosur, the first ever free trade agreement signed by Mercosur with a country outside Latin America. See http://www.mfa.gov.il/MFA/MFA+events/Around+the+world/Israel+signs+free+trade+agreement+with+MERCOSUR+18-Dec-2007.htm?DisplayMode=printhttp://www.mfa.gov.il/MFA/MFA+events/Around+the+world/Israel+signs+free+trade+agreement+with+MERCOSUR+18Dec-2007.htm?DisplayMode=print.

[2] This agreement is being implemented gradually. For instance, in early 2007, the Israeli press was reporting that Jordan was reducing tariffs on Israeli imports for the third time.

Authority (PA). Thus, in practice, most importers do not pay the MFN applied tariff, since less than a quarter of Israel's total imports in 2007 took place under MFN agreements. For instance, the EU-27 and the United States (which in 2007 together represented more than 50.3 per cent of Israel's merchandise imports) export their goods within the ambit of their respective bilateral trade agreements and receive either duty-free status or their exports are taxed less than the MFN rate. Note that many tariff preferences are subject to quotas. It is also to be noted that, in contrast to all EU member states, including the new ones, Israel does not intend to apply generalised preferences to developing countries in the foreseeable future.

2. NON-TARIFF BARRIERS

Because of the limited role that tariffs (and in the event preferential tariffs) play nowadays in Israel's trade policy, but with the exception of the special case of agricultural and food imports (see below), attention must be turned briefly to non-tariff barriers (NTBs).

As an integral part of its strategy to become an open economy, Israel abolished many NTBs that used to exist decades ago. The trade agreement between the European Union and Israel, for example, prohibits import restrictions except under strict conditions for safeguard or balance-of-payment reasons. However, NTBs such as import licences, standards and quality controls still exist.

The oldest NTB in Israel is the kosher certificate requirement. The Jewish religion, which in Israel is not separated from the State, demands that almost every product entering the country must be kosher. Over the last decade, with the massive influx of immigrants from Russia, who brought with them a new and more liberal culture and also began to import non-kosher products, the restriction became less rigorous, although officially nothing has changed. In December 1994, Israel restated a ban on imports of non-kosher meat and meat products. And, more generally, because of the power of the Rabbinate, any overseas exporter who aims to reach unlimited market access and significant share in Israel must comply with kosher requirements and therefore bear the additional cost of carrying out the 'kosher' process. The EU has occasionally protested the lack of transparency with which the law is applied.

One of the main NTBs in the Israeli economy originates from its centralistic structure regarding imports. While in most countries, especially those with open economies, many firms may import identical products, in Israel only one firm is allowed to import a certain label. For example, a study conducted in Israel in 1988 discovered that three main importers hold more than half of the import market in 75 per cent of imported products (Brezis, 1999). Since the study was carried out, the situation has improved dramatically, but the issue of the high concentration in imports has not been resolved altogether.

Two main setbacks continue to characterise the structure of the import market: an importer imports a certain label exclusively and usually imports a number of labels from the same sector, i.e. cars, alcohol or perfumes. There are almost no parallel imports, leading to a situation in which foreign producers who did not sign agreements with the 'exclusive importer' in Israel are denied access to the market. While the phenomenon might be acceptable in heterogeneous products, in homogeneous (standardised) products such as cement, for example, it is not.

The reason for a lack of parallel imports is mostly historical and goes back to the period when Israel had low foreign exchange reserves. Because of this, the government tried to restrict imports by restricting the number of authorised importers (Brezis, 1999, p. 7). Until 1991, Israeli importers received a licence only if they had the ability to cover imports with their private foreign exchange reserves or via barter deals. This policy became one of the main NTBs and created a large number of import monopolies, which exist even today. The best examples are vehicle importers (Karasso, Lubinsky, Meir) as well as importers of wheat (Zanziper) and some cosmetic products (Shastovich).

The Israeli government has been trying in recent years to remedy this situation and some publications reveal that it might approve parallel imports in the vehicles sector shortly. Yet several years ago, all import licensing still covered 8.5 per cent of tariff lines, down from 19.2 per cent in 1992. Most of the remaining licences are related to safety and security concerns (WTO, 1999). Additionally, in 1998 the Ministry of Industry, Trade and Labour changed the law regarding import licences for products with spare parts to allow parallel imports (Brezis, 1999). This type of product previously also fell under restrictions forbidding parallel imports.

Special licensing regimes have prevailed until very recently for countries that did not have an MFN agreement with Israel, such as Albania, Indonesia and Cambodia. All imports from these countries were traditionally subject to licensing. More generally, since July 2003, Israel has lifted its general prohibition on imports from WTO members that had no diplomatic relations with it or prohibited imports from Israel, e.g. Bahrain, Bangladesh, Brunei, Chad, Cuba, Kuwait, Malaysia, Morocco, Pakistan, Tunisia and the United Arab Emirates. However, a licensing requirement remains in place for eight other countries that prohibit imports from Israel, and some prohibitions of imports according to origin still prevail. In that respect, clearly, the largest anomaly in Israel's import trade policy is the prohibition of imports from two of its neighbours, Syria and the Lebanon. To that should be added the non-application of the Customs Envelope Agreement of September 1994 with the PA since at least the year 2000, because of the security situation. Normalisation of trade relations with these three immediate neighbours in the future could make a clear difference for the Israeli consumer. Because of the importance of transport costs on trade in fresh, perishable and bulky products, the huge MFN tariffs applied by Israel on many food imports (see below) are prohibitive. They would turn to non-prohibitive for a large range of products if they could be freely imported from Syria, the Lebanon and the PA.[3] No preferential trade agreements with neighbours would actually be needed to promote the latter's exports. They should in fact be prevented from emerging, as this would imply discriminating in favour of Arab countries in the Israeli local market against other developing economies with the implied cost of trade diversion which the 1991 unilateral trade liberalisation strategy was trying to prevent.

3. STANDARDS AND PROCUREMENT

Another NTB is standardisation and quality controls. All products entering Israel must comply with local standards, as determined by the Standards Institution of Israel and the Ministry of Industry, Trade and Labour. A first type of standard, called 'Israeli Standard', relates to the quality of the product, but is not binding. A second type, called 'Official Israeli Standard', is mandatory and products cannot enter the local market without this official mark given by the Ministry of Industry and Trade.

While standardisation is customary in many Western countries in order to protect local customers from low-quality products, in Israel its origin is quite different. In the past standards were set in such a way as to protect local producers and prevent imports of competing products. In the last decade, particularly since the adoption of the Standards Law of 1998, the Ministry of Industry, Trade and Labour has been working for the phasing out of many official standards aimed at preventing imports. Some 250 of 540 official standards were dropped, among them marks for the length of simple matches and a standard to determine a minimal number of ventilator speeds (Brezis, 1999). More generally, the Israeli government has been moving over time in the direction of bringing its standards into line with international ones and completely abolishing some anachronistic local standards. This is also the case regarding electronic products.[4] Currently, one-quarter of the mandatory standards emulate international standards.

Protectionism through the use of government procurement has plagued the Israeli economy since independence in 1948, as the State and its agencies have played a dominant role in developing the economy in the first 40 years after independence and in defending its citizens to this very day. In other words, public expenditure is unusually high for an OECD-type economy, with the Army and the Ministry of Defence playing a central role. A clear sign of protectionist

---

[3] A good example are dates where the MFN tariff rate is currently 560 per cent and which probably protects local production by kibbutzim in the Jordan Valley and by Bedouin tribes in the Negev desert.
[4] http://www.sii.org.il/siisite.nsf/Pages/MtiNews022007#cot13 (in Hebrew).

intent in that respect is that while Israel has been for years party to the plurilateral Agreement on Government Procurement (GPA), it has always invoked developing country status, allowing it to implement offset arrangements. For instance, the decision adopted by the Committee on Government Procurement in December 2004 allows Israel to require offsets for up to 20 per cent of a contract. Government agencies and state-owned companies are required even today to follow an offset policy, designed to promote national manufactures (Mandatory Tenders Regulation (Preference for Israeli Products and Mandatory Business Cooperation) of 1995). All international public tenders with a value of US$0.5 million or above must include a clause on 'industrial cooperation' (IC) with Israeli entities in the amount of at least 35 per cent (30 per cent in tenders covered by the GPA) of the value of the contract. To satisfy the IC offset requirement, a foreign supplier can subcontract to local companies, invest in local industries, undertake a know-how transfer, or acquire goods made in Israel or from work or services performed in Israel.

Foreign governments, particularly the United States, have been complaining for years about the lack of transparency in Israeli practices. For instance, there is the problem of the language. Officially, only for tenders under the GPA, the information must be published in an English newspaper (either the *Jerusalem Post* or the *International Herald Tribune-Ha'aretz*). Even so, the office of the United States Trade Representative has been claiming a lack of transparency and lengthy procedures, as well as arbitrary awards of contracts. For example, although some Israeli government entities make a point of notifying the US government on tenders valued at over US$50,000, many do not. Notifications, say US authorities, are often received shortly before deadlines and only in Hebrew. Complex technical specifications and kosher certification requirements discourage foreign participation in government tenders for food (US Department of Agriculture, 2005). For tenders not covered by the GPA, Israel's tendering regulations award price preferences to local suppliers, certain regions and local subcontracting. The price preferences are up to 15 per cent for Israeli companies. And it suffices to organise a closed tender for procurement of goods up to an amount of 312,000 NIS (about 56,000 euros at current (2008) exchange rates) by any government Ministry (except the Defence Ministry where the amount is limited to half this).

Invoking the status of developing country for applying Uruguay Round resolutions has not been limited to the domain of government procurement, but to other highly relevant issues, such as TRIPS, where Israel was given until 2000 to change its law on intellectual property. In fact, Israel continues to invoke this status at the same time as it is conducting negotiations to accede to the OECD after having been invited by the latter in May 2007, together with Russia, Estonia, Chile and Slovakia. Once a member, Israel will clearly have difficulty in justifying 'infant industry–infant country' status, allowing for disguised protectionism.

On the other hand, according to local independent experts on the matter, treatment of anti-dumping duties, a once complex and very long process, has been accommodated to WTO provisions.[5]

4. INTER-SECTORAL DIFFERENCES

There are huge inter-sectoral differences in the levels of protectionism applied by Israel. Agriculture is a case in point. Since the inception of the State, the agricultural sector has been defined as one of the vital parts of the economy, and the first Zionist settlers at the beginning of the previous century dedicated themselves to its development, despite the fact that climatic conditions are not favourable to most crops.

For the last few decades the economy's focus has switched from agriculture to other areas of expertise, mostly high-tech; agriculture represents only 1.6 per cent of GDP, down from 2.5 per cent in 2001 (HSBC, 2004). However, in absolute terms agricultural output has grown almost without interruption since 1948 and reached US$3.3 billion in 2000. The irony is that Israel's agricultural sector even today satisfies most of the country's food needs and around 20 per cent of the yearly production designated for export (Tovias, 2003). This impressive trade performance is feasible through a combination of high levels of tariff protection with export promotion policies. The only exception to agricultural self-sufficiency is feed grains such as wheat and soybeans, where Israel is a net importer. This is only possible, because, as happens in the European Union and the United States, the agricultural sector is still highly protected, especially in comparison to industrial goods.

Despite the general process of lowering MFN tariffs on most imports, MFN tariffs on agricultural products did rise more than 2.5 times from 1993 to 1999 with the adoption by the GATT's Marrakech Agreement of 1994 of the principle of *tariffication* (WTO, 1999). According to WTO (2006), Israeli farmers still benefit from relatively high tariff protection. In 2005, the average MFN applied tariff (including the *ad valorem* equivalents of specific, compound and alternate duties) on agricultural products (ISIC Revision 2 definition) is 41 per cent. Around 40 per cent of agricultural goods enter Israel duty free compared with around 51 per cent of non-agricultural products. MFN applied tariffs are higher than the overall average rate in six subsectors: live animals (with an average tariff of 29.0 per cent), meat products (64.6 per cent), dairy products (120.6 per cent), edible vegetables (63 per cent), edible fruit (87.1 per cent), and preparations of cereals, flour, starch or milk products (42.3 per cent). The average MFN applied tariffs on these products, and on vegetable plaiting materials, sugars and sugar confectionery,

---

[5] http://www.reader.co.il/article/7463/ (in Hebrew).

and edible preparations have increased since the previous TPR of Israel in 1999.
Note that tariff rates on imports of fruit (87.1 per cent on average), vegetables
(63 per cent) and related products are relatively high, having increased substantially
since 1999. This in spite of the fact that Israel says it has a comparative advantage.
Within these groups there is also high dispersion due to tariff peaks on certain fruit
(560 per cent) and vegetables (344 per cent). Applied MFN tariffs are generally
relatively low on cereal and oilseed products (average of about 10 per cent), with
the exception of wheat (50 per cent) and certain vegetable seeds (tariff peaks of
up to 114 per cent). Tariff protection for dairy and meat products is high and has
also increased since 1999. Applied MFN tariffs on meat average 64.6 per cent.
One of the ironies is that these tariffs protect all local producers, including those
kibbutzim and Arab meat producers which are allowed to supply non-kosher meat.

Imports of milk products are still subject to high applied MFN tariffs of between
zero and 212 per cent. Imports of cheese are subject to relatively high tariff rates
and tariff quotas. Bound rates on fresh, grated or blue cheese ranged between 185
per cent and 290 per cent in 1995, and between 157 per cent and 247 per cent
in 2004. These horrendous rates are there to protect not only small family
farms but also *moshavim* (production cooperatives) and *kibbutzim* (communes).

Tariff quotas apply to 12 product groups although for most of these products the
in-quota tariff rate is above the MFN applied rate, thus rendering the quota
redundant (WTO, 2006). When it is not, there is obviously some scope for
lobbying the Ministries of Agriculture and Rural Development (for agricultural
products and fresh food) and Industry, Trade and Labour (for processed food) which
are the ones in charge of the administration of those quotas. They apply among
others to imports of prunes, walnuts, sweetcorn and concentrated citrus fruit.

Another protection measure for agriculture was traditionally the variable
import levy, which was applied to imports of basic products such as sugar, pasta,
sunflower seeds, jams, fruits, wine, cheese and frozen fish (WTO, 1999). At the
end of the 1990s, in accordance with the WTO Agreement on Agriculture, all
variable levies were eliminated. Now, Israel applies tariff quotas to 12 product
groups (nuts, corns, orange juice, sheep and goats' milk and cheese). 'However,
for most of these products the in-quota tariff rate is above the MFN applied rate,
thus rendering the quota redundant.[6] As a result, these tariff quotas are in general
overfilled' (WTO, 2006, p. 63). On the other hand, note that some of the PTAs
signed by Israel with third countries offer the latter some tariff preferences (generally
within a quota). For instance, in 1996 Israel and the United States signed an
agricultural trade accord aimed at including the remaining goods not covered by
the 1985 US–Israel FTA. Accordingly, agricultural imports from the United
States were entitled to a preference of 10 per cent (US Department of Agriculture,

---

[6] In principle 'in-quota' tariff rates should be below MFN rates in order to enable a minimum level
of imports to a protected market.

2005). This implies, of course, devastating trade diversion against non-preferred countries, such as Argentina.

A second sector deserving particular attention covers food, beverages and tobacco industries. In 2002, it accounted for about 15 per cent of industrial production; it was the second largest employer in the industrial sector with more than 16 per cent of industrial employment in 2004. The sector exhibits an oligopolistic market structure, especially in the case of tobacco products, soft drinks, fresh juices and wines. According to political economy models, oligopolistic structures favour the emergence and operation of lobbies. The industries are mostly oriented towards the domestic market, with exports representing only 6 per cent of production or less. The simple average MFN for the sector has increased from 20.5 per cent in 1999 to 25.5 per cent in 2005. According to WTO (2006), average tariffs have increased for food manufacturing and preparations, but decreased for the beverage and tobacco industries. MFN tariffs are particularly high on dairy products (112.7 per cent on average), manufacture of bakery products (60.9 per cent) and meat products (50.3 per cent). Tariff rates also feature a high dispersion, ranging from zero to 340 per cent in the food industry and fruit and vegetables canning.

Finally, it is interesting to note that, regarding textiles and wearing apparel, the simple average applied MFN tariffs are at present 'only' 7.7 per cent (down from 12.5 per cent in 1999) and 11.3 per cent (down from 31.2 per cent in 1999), respectively. As noted in much of the literature on Israel's trade policy, Israel has accepted for at least a decade that if textile and clothing firms are to survive under Israeli ownership and management they had to be 'de-localised' to neighbouring countries such as Jordan and Egypt and some less developed East European countries (such as Romania). The process has taken place in an orderly way and is now almost complete. It is remarkable to note that whereas such a move has been accepted as a second-best option for the textiles and clothing industry, such is not the case either for the agricultural or for the food sectors. Apart from the old conventional argument that population dispersion is a defence imperative, something which was also true regarding textiles and clothing, there are two other possible reasons. One might be that small protected farms are partly in the hands of settlers in the West Bank, including the Jordan Valley (and until 2005 in the Gaza Strip). They have had a lot of clout in certain key political parties. Another reason for high tariffs might be the fear of the government that lowering protection might leave the very poor Arab-Israeli population in the Negev desert, made up of Bedouin tribes, without alternative employment. Such a move could lead to a nationalist uprising in Israel or to massive migration to urban suburbs in the centre of the country. So here the lobby in favour of maintaining protection would be the defence establishment and the intelligence services.

However, the oligopolistic structure of the food industry has probably also played a role in lobbying for higher levels of protection. Up until the mid-1990s there were only three companies controlling the food market, one of them being the largest agricultural manufacturer (Tnuva). In some sectors, there were monopolies (dairy products, poultry, pasta, dry products such as soup powder, etc.). The agricultural manufacturer mentioned above, was responsible until 2000 for purchasing 90 per cent of the poultry, for example, from the growers bound by exclusive agreements with the company. Be that as it may, both the Ministry of Agriculture and the Ministry of Trade and Industry have been joining hands in trying to convince other countries in the context of the Doha Round negotiations that the agricultural sector is important and sensitive to Israel and that is why it needs special protection. They have been asking openly that Israel should be authorised to keep a large degree of flexibility in the way protection is to be given to this particular sector.[7] On the other hand, Israel seems much less reluctant in liberalising its agricultural trade with the European Union on a reciprocal basis. Negotiations have been taking place for several months on this subject but they are not yet concluded.

5. CONCLUSION

To sum up, it seems that the Israeli government has been efficient – especially in comparison to those other Mediterranean countries which are non-EU members – in implementing gradual, mostly unilateral, liberalisation of its trade policy regime. Agriculture and related activities are the only major exception to the liberalisation tendency. This trend reflects mainly a broad consensus among major political parties in Israel in pursuing liberal trade policy reforms. On the other hand, it may mean that protectionist pressures from organised sectoral lobbies were either weak or inefficient.[8]

REFERENCES

Brezis, A. (1999), 'Structure of Israel's Trade System: Concentration of Imports', *Israel Tax Quarterly*, No. 104, Jerusalem, Israel (in Hebrew).
HSBC (2004), *Israel: Business Profile*, 2nd edn (London: HSBC).
Tovias, A. (2003), 'Mapping Israel's Policy Options Regarding the Future Institutionalised Relations with the European Union', Working Paper No. 3 (Brussels: CEPS).
US Department of Agriculture (2005), *Israel: Grain Trade Policy* (Washington, DC: Foreign Agricultural Service).
WTO (1999), *Trade Policy Review: Israel*, Report by the Secretariat, WT/TPR/S/58 (Geneva: WTO).
WTO (2006), *Trade Policy Review: Israel*, Report by the Secretariat, WTR/S/157/Rev.1 (Geneva: WTO).

---

[7] Press Release of 27 July 2006, http://www.moit.gov.il/NR/exeres/7E8342B4-9248-40AE-A937-6BFBC51DD38F.htm.
[8] Once again with the exception of the agricultural lobbies.

5

United Arab Emirates
Trade Policy Review

Wasseem Mina

1. INTRODUCTION

THE United Arab Emirates (UAE) is an important player in world trade. In 2006, the UAE was ranked the 23rd and 27th world leading merchandise exporter and importer, respectively.[1] It has also been the most important Middle East trade partner for the European Union, the United States, Japan and Canada, with imports amounting to nearly $50 billion in 2006. Compared to the other Gulf Cooperation Council (GCC) countries, the UAE is considered the most open economy, with merchandise trade accounting for 136 per cent of GDP in 2004.[2]

Ten years after it joined the World Trade Organization (WTO), the UAE had its first Trade Policy Review in 2006. Similar to the International Monetary Fund's surveillance of monetary and exchange rate policies of member countries, the WTO conducts surveillance of member countries' trade policies through a trade policy review mechanism. This aims to improve adherence of member countries to the rules, disciplines and commitments made under the WTO's multilateral trade agreements, through regular evaluation of trade policies and practices. The evaluation is conducted against the background of economic and developmental needs, policies and objectives of the member concerned, and the member's external environment, as mentioned in the preface to the review. Being a multilateral trading system review mechanism, the trade policy review also examines the impact of a member's trade policies and practices on the multilateral trading system.

Trade policies of WTO member countries are subject to periodic reviews, depending on their world trade share. The four largest trading entities are reviewed every two years, the 16 next largest every four years, and other members every six years. A longer period may be fixed for least developed countries. Based on its ranks as a leading merchandise exporter and importer, the UAE

---

[1] See WTO (2007).
[2] The GCC countries are Bahrain, Kuwait, Oman, Qatar, Saudi Arabia and the UAE.

61

could have possibly had its first trade policy review six years after its member-ship, but the review has likely been delayed in consideration of the ongoing institutional development of the emerging UAE economy.[3]

A Trade Policy Review is composed of two documents: a policy statement by the member country and an evaluation report by the WTO Secretariat. The UAE laid down its policy statement in four sections covering: (a) economic develop-ment, (b) trade policy developments, (c) sectoral developments, and (d) future objectives and needs. The WTO Secretariat report is also in four sections: (a) the economic environment; (b) trade and investment regimes; (c) trade policies and measures affecting imports, exports, and production and trade; and (d) trade policies affecting the different sectors.

The WTO Secretariat has raised a number of concerns, which can be grouped into two main areas: foreign investment, and domestic competition in goods and labour markets. These two areas influence the degree and speed of the integration of the UAE economy into the world economy, which are means to diversifying and restructuring the economy. Concern has also been raised about recent inflationary pressures, which reduce trade and investment competitiveness.

In the area of foreign investment, concerns were raised about the limits on foreign equity participation, the obligations on branches of foreign companies to recruit a local agent, and reserving import activities and distribution services exclusively for national agents. In the area of domestic competition, concerns were raised about the absence of competition legislation, the policy of employ-ment of UAE nationals through a quota system known as 'emiratisation' policy, and the separation of the regulatory functions of state enterprises from their commercial activities.

Questions were raised about preparations for the GCC currency union expected in 2010, including the type of exchange rate regime envisaged, schedule of GCC policies harmonisation, and UAE reconciliation of bilateral free trade agreement negotiations with its GCC membership. Clarifications have also been sought on trade-related issues, including the procurement regime of non-federal public bodies, the UAE standards and technical regulations, free trade zones, protection of geographical indications, well-known marks, enforcement of legislation on intellectual property, and ending the state monopoly in telecommunications.

Finding a convincing approach to reviewing the trade policy review has not been an easy task in this chapter. This is the first trade policy review for the UAE and therefore one cannot evaluate the performance of trade policies over time, as Ramasamy and Yeung (2007) did in the case of Malaysia. Taking an approach similar to Ludema (2007), in which the impact of US trade issues on the global economy

---

[3] The UAE approached the International Monetary Fund in 2005 for technical assistance on statistics improvement, especially in coordination among the seven emirates' main data-producing agencies.

and the multilateral trading system is examined in the US 2006 Trade Policy Review, is not applicable to the case of the UAE. Despite its large degree of trade openness and significant economic growth, the UAE is still considered a small economy.

This chapter's approach is to elaborate on concerns that were not adequately developed, given the breadth of the Review's coverage. The first is domestic property rights protection and the contracting of investment treaties to strengthen property rights protection and promote foreign direct investment. The second is barriers to competition. The chapter uses free trade zones to make the case that in the absence of foreign investment and competition barriers, which free trade zones epitomise, foreign investment is promoted.

In the following section, the UAE economic performance, achievements and future challenges are discussed based on the UAE policy statement and WTO Secretariat evaluation report. In Section 3, the chapter focuses on domestic property rights protection and investment treaties, which are important in the promotion of foreign direct investment (FDI). Despite the importance of investment treaties for FDI promotion, this issue was mentioned only briefly in the Trade Policy Review. Free trade zones, in which barriers to foreign investment and domestic competition do not exist, are discussed in Section 4. In Section 5, FDI performance is discussed. The question of whether bilateral investment treaties and free trade zones promote FDI is raised. Preliminary statistical evidence suggests that FDI is encouraged by investment treaties and free trade. Section 6 concludes.

2. ECONOMIC DEVELOPMENTS AND CHALLENGES

The UAE has experienced high growth in the first four years of the third millennium. Between 2001 and 2004, the economy grew annually by more than 14 per cent. This growth rate is attributed to trade openness, largely free market policies and regulations, an enabling business environment, economic diversification away from oil to non-oil industries, and to the enhanced role of the private sector as contributor to growth over the long run.

The UAE is the most open economy in the GCC region. Between 2000 and 2006, merchandise imports and exports both grew at an annual rate of 19 per cent. In the period 2003–05, trade amounted to nearly 160 per cent of GDP and to US$39,288 per capita, the highest in the region.[4] UAE's share of world merchandise exports and imports amounted to about 1.2 per cent and 0.8 per cent, respectively.[5,6]

---

[4] The next most open GCC economy is Qatar with trade amounting to 150 per cent of GDP and to US$38,076 per capita during the period 2003–05.

[5] See WTO (2007).

[6] In comparison, Saudi Arabia's shares of world merchandise exports and imports amounted to 1.73 per cent and 0.53 per cent, respectively, in 2006.

The UAE is also an important participant in global capital markets, attracting inward FDI and exporting capital abroad, whether in FDI or portfolio investment. Several UAE investment institutions undertake these outward investments. These include, among others, the Abu Dhabi Investment Authority, the Dubai Ports Authority, Dubai Holding, and the Abu Dhabi International Petroleum Investment Corporation.

On the trade policy front, the UAE believes in free trade as a necessary condition for increased competitiveness and enhanced productivity in the long run. Against this, the UAE has signed bilateral trade agreements with some Arab countries, including Iraq, Jordan, Lebanon, Morocco and Syria. It started bilateral trade negotiations with Australia and the United States in 2005, and signed a framework agreement on economic, trade, investment and technical cooperation with China in 2004, an initial step to launch negotiations on a free trade agreement. At the regional level, the UAE is a member of the GCC customs union established in January 2003, in which a common external tariff of 5 per cent or 0 per cent applies on 85 per cent of tariff lines, and of the Greater Arab Free Trade Area, which eliminated most tariffs among its member countries in January 2005. It also has an interest in greater non-agricultural market access and further trade liberalisation of the Doha Development Agenda. At this point, the GCC countries, including the UAE, are undertaking negotiations on a free trade agreement with the European Union.

As far as the fiscal, monetary and exchange rate policies are concerned, the UAE holds a balanced budget stance conducive to long-run economic growth. The UAE has a fixed exchange rate regime, in which the UAE dirham is pegged to the US dollar at a rate of AED 3.67 per US dollar. Due to the weakening US dollar and the significant increase in the UAE price level, the UAE government has been under immense pressure from the business community to revalue the dirham and switch the peg from the US dollar to a basket of currencies as in the case of Kuwait, or fundamentally switch to a floating exchange rate regime. In light of the adopted fixed exchange rate regime, the UAE monetary policy is of limited effectiveness.

Diversification into industry and services and away from oil is a government priority. Availability of basic infrastructure and communications within industrial zones, proximity to suppliers of raw materials, and availability of private capital are location advantages, which encourage the development of manufacturing. In its efforts to liberalise the telecommunications sector, the government has established an independent Telecommunications Regulatory Authority. A second mobile phone operator started operation in 2006. Tourism has been successful and the expansion of facilities and attractions, such as shopping malls, museums and golf courses is currently under way in several emirates. In banking, the UAE is expanding Islamic banking and has plans to export it in the future to other countries, mainly in the Middle East. Air and maritime transportation have also expanded recently.

The UAE envisages a number of future challenges regarding the regulatory environment, market structure, expansion of electronic government services, emiratisation of the labour force, and the synergy between multilateral and bilateral trade agreements. The investment framework should be more conducive to expanded foreign ownership, which helps in the diversification of the economy. In order to protect consumers from a less-than-competitive market structure, the government has considered the introduction of a competition law and consumer protection authority. More efforts will be exerted to develop electronic government services to serve businesses and citizens. With the largely expatriate-dominated private sector, the government proposes to protect the employment of nationals through an emiratisation programme, which would establish a minimum quota system for the employment of nationals in banking and certain sectors, and improve education and training for nationals. Committed to trade liberalisation globally, regionally and individually with leading trade partners, the UAE believes that the international economic system will prosper most if regional and bilateral agreements fit within the WTO rules framework.

3. PROPERTY RIGHTS PROTECTION AND BILATERAL INVESTMENT TREATIES

In order to encourage FDI, the UAE has contracted a number of bilateral investment treaties since 1990. Between 1990 and 2006, the UAE signed treaties with 30 countries, of which 23 have been ratified, as shown in Table 1. Bilateral investment treaties are legal instruments under international law between two contracting countries, which identify the circumstances under which expropriation can take place and the associated compensation standards, and establish investment dispute settlement mechanisms, which facilitate foreign investment in the presence of imperfect domestic property rights protection institutions. They externally commit the contracting countries to honouring the property rights of the partner country's investors, to reducing host country political risks, and thereby increasing foreign investors' confidence and promoting foreign investment (Ginsburg, 2005; Hallward-Driemeier, 2003; Neumayer and Spess, 2005; UNCTAD, 1998). Bilateral investment treaties are therefore contracted in order to strengthen property rights protection.

But what is the degree of strength of property rights protection in the UAE and how does it compare to other institutional functions? In evaluating this for the UAE, the International Country Risk Guide's (ICRG) political risk index components are used. Of the different components, investment profile, which refers to investment risks arising from contract expropriation, profits repatriation and payment delays, is the most property rights related component. Other components are: law and order; government stability; corruption; bureaucracy

TABLE 1
UAE Contracted Bilateral Investment Treaties (concluded as at 1 June 2007)

Contracting Partner	Dated Signed	Date Ratified
Turkey	2005	..
Belgium and Luxembourg	2004	..
Mozambique	2003	..
Korea	2002	2004
Austria	2001	2003
Mongolia	2001	..
Sudan	2001	..
Yemen	2001	2001
Algeria	2001	2002
Belarus	2000	2001
Sweden	1999	2000
Morocco	1999	2002
Switzerland	1998	1999
Turkmenistan	1998	1999
Lebanon	1998	1999
Germany	1997	1999
Egypt	1997	1999
Syria	1997	2001
Finland	1996	1997
Tunisia	1996	1997
Italy	1995	1997
Pakistan	1995	..
Tajikistan	1995	..
Czech Republic	1994	1995
China	1993	1994
Romania	1993	1996
Poland	1993	1994
United Kingdom	1992	1993
France	1991	1992
Malaysia	1991	1992

Source: http://www.unctad.org/sections/dite_pcbb/docs/uae.pdf

quality; and democratic accountability.[7] Table 2 provides averages for these over
the period 1984–2004. Because the maximum points for each of the six components
vary, the averages are normalised by the maximum risk points in order to obtain
an institutional strength ratio. Also because the ICRG index is constructed in

---

[7] Law and order refer to the strength and impartiality of the legal system and popular observance
of law. Government stability refers to government's ability to carry out its declared programme(s)
and its ability to stay in office. Corruption refers to corruption within the political system and in
business; corruption in business takes the form of demands for special payments and bribes
connected to economic activity, such as trade licences, exchange controls, tax assessments, police
protection and loans. Bureaucracy quality refers to the degree of strength and expertise of the
bureaucracy to govern without drastic changes in policy or interruptions in government services.
Democratic accountability refers to government responsiveness to its people.

TABLE 2
Property Rights Protection and Relevant Domestic Institutions

	ICRG Political Risk Index Components					
	Investment	Bureaucracy	Stability	Democracy	Law	Corruption
Average	7.6	2.4	7.7	2	3.6	2.4
Maximum	12	4	12	6	6	6
ISR	0.63	0.60	0.64	0.33	0.60	0.40
ISR Rank	2	3	1	5	3	4
	Governance Indicators					
	Quality	Effectiveness	Stability	Accountability	Law	Corruption
Average	0.7	0.7	0.8	−0.8	1	0.9
Maximum	2.5	2.5	2.5	2.5	2.5	2.5
ISR	0.28	0.28	0.32	−0.32	0.4	0.36
ISR Rank	4	4	3	5	1	2

Notes:
ICRG political risk index components and governance indicators are averaged over the periods 1984–2004 and 1996–2004, respectively. ICRG's political risk index components in the top panel are, in order: investment profile; bureaucracy quality; government stability; democratic accountability; law and order; and corruption. Governance indicators in the lower panel are, in order: regulatory quality, government effectiveness, political stability and absence of violence, voice and accountability, rule of law, and control of corruption. ISR is institutional strength ratio.

such a way that the higher the index, the lower the risk, the same applies to the institutional strength ratio: the higher (lower) the ratio, the lower (higher) the risk and the better (worse) the institutional performance becomes. Ranking of the different institutional strength ratios suggests that property rights protection is among the best performing of UAE's institutional functions; investment profile, a proxy for property rights protection, ranks second after government stability and above the other institutional functions.

A different institutional performance evaluation, however, is obtained using the six governance indicators developed by Kaufmann et al. (2007). These indicators are: voice and accountability; political stability and absence of violence; government effectiveness; regulatory quality; rule of law; and control of corruption. Of relevance to property rights protection is regulatory quality, which measures the government ability to formulate and implement policies and regulations promoting private sector development.[8] Ranking indicator averages over the period 1996–2004, as Table 2 shows, suggests that regulatory quality, as a proxy for property rights protection, lags behind law and order, control of corruption and political stability.

[8] Regulatory quality builds on ICRG's investment profile. Government effectiveness, political stability, voice and accountability, rule of law, and control of corruption build on ICRG's bureaucracy quality, government stability, democratic accountability, law and order, and corruption, respectively.

Based on the evaluation of the degree of property rights protection using the political risk index components and governance indicators, it is clear that property rights protection is not the best performing institution, although it is among the best according to the political risk index. Therefore bilateral investment treaties, as an external commitment mechanism to property rights protection, may have been contracted to strengthen domestic property rights protection as an institutional function. In fact, the UAE treats bilateral investment treaties as legally superior to and *substitutes* other domestic legal instruments. This point is mentioned clearly in the summary observations section of the WTO Secretariat evaluation report of the review, which notes, 'Once ratified, treaties/international agreements *prevail* over domestic legal instruments. These comprise the Constitution, followed by laws, decree-laws, ordinary decrees, and regulations'. It therefore follows that bilateral investment treaties are contracted to improve property rights protection and encourage inward FDI.

4. FREE TRADE ZONES

The UAE government has created and recently expanded the number of free trade zones, in parallel with the contracting of bilateral investment treaties, in order to encourage FDI. Currently there are 23 free trade zones in the UAE, according to the Trade Policy Review, which are characterised by 100 per cent foreign ownership and no income taxes.[9] In the free trade zones, the barriers to foreign investment and domestic competition, i.e. the concerns raised by the WTO Secretariat evaluation report, do not exist. There are no limits on foreign equity participation, no obligations on branches of foreign companies to recruit a local agent, and no reserved import activities and distribution services exclusively for national agents. In addition, companies are not subject to the emiratisation policy of (minimum) quota employment of UAE nationals. Anecdotal evidence seems to suggest that, in the absence of these barriers, a great deal, if not the majority, of non-oil FDI takes places in the free trade zones. This may have in turn encouraged the proliferation of free trade zones, as a barrier-free economic enclave, in the different UAE emirates.

5. FDI PERFORMANCE

The next logical question is whether bilateral investment treaties and free trade zones have succeeded in promoting inward FDI, much desired as an important

---

[9] Outside the free trade zones, foreign ownership currently stands at 49 per cent, though this restriction is changing under UAE commitments to the WTO.

TABLE 3
UAE FDI Performance

	Inward	Outward
	FDI Stock (US$ million)	
1990	751	14
1995	1,770	710
2000	1,061	1,938
2001	2,246	2,152
2002	3,552	2,564
2003	7,808	3,555
2004	17,812	5,764
2005	28,712	9,514
2006	37,098	11,830
	Growth Rate (per cent)	
1990–2006	27.6	52.2
1990–95	18.7	118.4
1995–2000	−9.7	22.2
2000–06	80.8	35.2
2004–06	44.3	43.3
	FDI Performance Index	
2004–06	3.316	0.938
2003–05	4.315	1.157
	FDI Performance Rank	
2004–06	33	25
2003–05	18	24

source of technology transfer and as a driver of economic diversification in the UAE. In fact, the UAE inward FDI performance has been impressive over time. In 2006, the date the UAE Trade Policy Review was issued, the stock of inward FDI the UAE has attracted amounted to $37 billion from less than $1 billion in 1990, as Table 3 shows. Between 1990 and 2006, FDI has grown at an annual average rate of 27.6 per cent, while in the 2000s the annual growth rate amounted to nearly 80 per cent. At a global level, the UAE inward FDI performance index for the period 2004–06 amounts to about 3.3 and is ranked the 33rd among 141 countries. The index suggests that the UAE's share of world inward FDI is more than triple its share of world GDP. Among the GCC countries, Bahrain's index and rank exceed the UAE's at about 5.5 and at the 11th position, respectively.

It is useful to also have a look at the UAE outward FDI to assess the importance of the UAE in global capital markets.[10] The stock of outward FDI reached about $12 billion in 2006 from $14 million in 1990, with an average annual growth rate of 52.2 per cent between 1990 and 2006, while in the 2000s the growth rate

---

[10] This may not be related to barriers to foreign investment and competition.

TABLE 4
Inward FDI, Bilateral Investment Treaties and Free Trade Zones (correlation coefficients)

	FDI Stock	FDI Stock (Per cent of GDP)	FDI Stock (Log form)	FDI Stock (Per cent of GDP – log form)
Signed treaties	0.879*	0.738*	0.903*	0.697*
Ratified treaties	0.871*	0.703*	0.873*	0.655*
Free trade zones	0.905*	0.752*	0.904*	0.718*

* Statistically significant at the 5 per cent level.

amounted to 35 per cent. At a global level, the UAE outward FDI performance index for the period 2004–06 amounts to about 0.9, suggesting that the UAE's share of outward FDI is nearly equal its share of world GDP, and is ranked in 25th position.[11]

Can we possibly conclude that bilateral investment treaties and free trade zones encourage inward FDI in the UAE? The results of analysis conducted by the author on panel data for the six GCC countries are suggestive.[12] Specifically, the author finds no impact of either signed or ratified bilateral investment treaties on FDI flows using a difference generalised method of moments (GMM) estimator (Mina, 2007a), a surprisingly negative impact of ratified bilateral investment treaties on FDI stocks also using a difference GMM estimator in Mina (2007b), and a mixed impact of ratified bilateral investment treaties using an instrumental variables approach (Mina, 2008).

Preliminary evidence for the UAE, as shown by the correlation coefficients provided in Table 4, suggests that the stock of inward FDI is highly correlated with contracted bilateral investment treaties, whether signed or ratified, and with free trade zones. Initially this may lend support to the importance of commitment to property rights protection to FDI. It may also lend initial support to the concerns raised by the WTO Secretariat evaluation report on the barriers to foreign investment and domestic competition.

6. CONCLUSION

The first Trade Policy Review for the UAE issued in 2006 has raised a number of concerns about barriers to foreign investment and competition. In reviewing the UAE Trade Policy Review, this chapter has elaborated on concerns that were not adequately dealt with, given the breadth of the Trade Policy Review coverage.

[11] The outward FDI performance index for Bahrain and Kuwait exceeds the UAE's at about 3.6 and 3.2, respectively.
[12] Equally they may not.

The chapter has focused on bilateral investment treaties and free trade zones, which encourage FDI.

Property rights protection is not perceived as the strongest domestic UAE institutional function. Therefore contracting bilateral investment treaties has taken place in order to strengthen property rights protection. The proliferation and geographical expansion of free trade zones in the UAE, which seem to attract a great deal if not the majority of FDI, reflect the success of free trade zones in attracting FDI. It should be clear to UAE policy makers that the success of free trade zones most likely reflects the barriers that investors face outside these zones, a point the Trade Policy Review highlights. Preliminary statistical evidence suggests that FDI is positively associated with bilateral investment treaties and free trade zones, which renders initial support to the Trade Policy Review concerns.

REFERENCES

Ginsburg, T. (2005), 'International Substitutes for Domestic Institutions: Bilateral Investment Treaties and Governance', *International Review of Law and Economics* **25**, 1, 107–203.

Hallward-Driemeier, M. (2003), 'Do Bilateral Investment Treaties Attract FDI? Only a Bit . . . and They Could Bite', World Bank Policy Research Working Paper 3121.

Kaufmann, D., A. Kraay and M. Mastruzzi (2007), 'Governance Matters VI: Aggregate and Individual Governance Indicators 1996–2006', World Bank Policy Research Working Paper 4280.

Ludema, R. (2007), 'Allies and Friends: The Trade Policy Review of the United States, 2006', *The World Economy*, **30**, 8, 1209–21.

Mina, W. (2007a), 'Impact of BITs on FDI – The GCC Experience', Paper presented at Singapore Economic Review Conference, Singapore (2–4 August 2007).

Mina, W. (2007b), 'BITs Contracting and FDI in GCC Countries', Paper presented at the 14th Annual Conference of Economic Research Forum, Cairo, Egypt.

Mina, W. (2008), 'External Commitment Mechanisms, Institutions, and FDI in GCC Countries', *Journal of International Financial Markets, Institutions and Money* (forthcoming) (doi10.1016/j.intfin.2008.02.001) .

Neumayer, E. and L. Spess (2005), 'Do Bilateral Investment Treaties Increase Foreign Direct Investment to Developing Countries?', *World Development*, **33**, 10, 1567–85.

Ramasamy, B. and M. Yeung (2007), 'Malaysia – Trade Policy Review 2006', *The World Economy*, **30**, 8, 1193–208.

UNCTAD (1998), *Bilateral Investment Treaties in the Mid-1990s* (Geneva: UNCTAD).

WTO (2007), *International Trade Statistics 2007* (Geneva: WTO).

6

Conceptualising Globalisation
A Symposium for the
World Economy

Edited by John Whalley

Foreword:

The three chapters in this symposium were presented at summer meetings of the CESifo summer institute held in Venice in August 2004 and 2005. They are grouped around the theme of conceptualising globalisation and published here as a contribution to the growing literature on globalisation.

Chapters:

'International Organisations: The Challenge of Aligning Mission, Means and Legitimacy'	**Robert Z. Lawrence**
'Defining Globalisation'	**Jan Aart Scholte**
'Globalisation and Values'	**John Whalley**

7

International Organisations:
The Challenge of Aligning Mission,
Means and Legitimacy

Robert Z. Lawrence

1. INTRODUCTION

SINCE its founding at the end of the Uruguay Round, the WTO has become an increasingly controversial institution. On the one hand, it has been assailed for having gone too far. Some critics, typically reflecting the concerns of many developing countries, claim that by adopting rules such as TRIPs and TRIMs, the WTO has strayed beyond its basic mission and forced many of its members to accept obligations that are not in their interest and beyond their implementation capacities. On the other hand, the WTO has also been assailed for not going far enough. Other critics, typically reflecting the concerns of developed countries, have sought to broaden and deepen its coverage by negotiating new disciplines on issues such as investment, labour standards, competition and the environment.

At the Cancún Ministerial Meeting these conflicts came to a head when the meeting ended in an impasse over efforts to launch negotiations on the so-called Singapore Issues (Investment, Competition, Transparency in Government Procurement and Trade Facilitation) and that failure was preceded by other unsuccessful efforts such as the negotiations for a Multilateral Agreement on Investment at the OECD, and the US efforts to introduce labour standards into the WTO at the ministerial meetings held at Marrakech in 1994 and Seattle in 1999.

In this chapter, I will argue that these recent controversies at the WTO are not an accident; they are the predictable result of the fundamental governance problems

This chapter was prepared for the Venice Institute on Global Economy organised by CESifo. The author is grateful to participants in the seminar and to two anonymous referees for extremely helpful comments.

faced by many international organisations. In this chapter I will describe, in general terms, the nature of these problems and illustrate how they apply in the case of the WTO and then provide an approach that might help deal with these problems. My argument is straightforward: to be effective, an international organisation must obviously have the means to accomplish its mission. In addition, however, it must only be charged with those missions and means that are compatible with a high degree of legitimacy. Ensuring these conditions are met is not easy because there is an inherent tendency for many international institutions to experience 'mission creep', particularly when accountability for burden sharing is weak. This in turn leads to failures of one of two types: either having inadequate means to carry out the mission or problems of legitimacy. In my view, the best way for the WTO to deal with its problems would be to adopt an approach built on a more variable geometry.

2. THE DILEMMA OF INTERNATIONAL ORGANISATIONS

There is a large unmet demand for international public goods. Economic growth and technological developments in communications and transportation have dramatically increased global interdependence and created huge pressures for international cooperation. As part of the response, international organisations have been created to tackle problems in areas such as economic underdevelopment and poverty, protectionism, financial instability, environmental degradation, disease, war, insecurity and violations of human rights.

a. Mission Creep

Given the immensity of the problems they face, international organisations are subject to strong pressures to expand their missions. One relates to the weak links between costs and benefits that are often associated with joint action. If a country can have an international organisation devote resources to a goal, it may have to spend less of its own resources on achieving it. For example, people eating out together may order more expensive items from the menu when they have agreed to split the bill equally than if the bill is split according to the charge for each item.

The argument here is well captured in game theory by the classic game of chicken. In one version of this game, two players can each choose to provide a good from which both of them will benefit. While both would benefit from providing the good in a joint fashion, there is an incentive for each to hold back and capture the benefits when the other provides it. Similarly, there is an incentive for participants in international organisations to try to get others to pay for worthy missions, and thus a strong tendency to propose these. When mechanisms to ensure and monitor compliance are relatively weak, there are incentives for countries to make commitments that they cannot be compelled to meet.

When large groups act together, it is difficult to assign responsibility for success or failure and the behaviour of international organisations often exemplify this problem. To be sure, domestic governments are also subject to continuous pressures to accept new obligations but the knowledge that their failures could be punished by the voters provides at least some discipline on their willingness to assume obligations they cannot adequately fulfil. Likewise, the knowledge they might have to find the resources also disciplines the acceptance of new commitments. However, performance in providing international public goods is hard to monitor, partly because of difficulties associated with measuring output and partly because of ensuring compliance. When governments undertake new missions collectively, therefore, they are aware that they can always blame others for failures. Under these circumstances, it will generally be easier to accept a mission and then perform poorly in carrying it out rather than reject new assignments when the capacity to carry them out is lacking.

Secondly, in many cases large bureaucracies generally develop independent interests of their own that are tied to the expansion of the organisation. International bureaucracies are particularly prone to such behaviour because these organisations often have greater scope for independent action. They are less subject to external scrutiny than their domestic counterparts. In addition, they develop traditions in which national origin rather than competence plays a key role in appointment and advancement. Under these circumstances, national governments may find it difficult to complain about the performance of or obtain the dismissal of the nationals of other countries thereby weakening accountability.

A third reason, particularly for organisations that are initially successful in what they do, is a variant of the Peter Principle which states that 'in a hierarchy people are likely to rise to their level of incompetence'. The logic is simple. Success at any particular task leads to advancement and people will be promoted until they are placed in a job they do poorly. Once this happens they will no longer be promoted. In the long run, therefore, most people will be found in the jobs they cannot do well. If bureaucrats are interested in expanding the size and scope of the organisation, they will be more successful in attracting new assignments. Thus the more successful is an international organisation in its missions, the more complicated the missions it is likely to be asked to perform. Eventually organisations will be tasked with missions they are unable to carry out.[1]

---

[1] 'In the UN with programs becoming increasingly fragmented among different subsidiary bodies and agencies, it has become almost impossible to monitor many activities, let alone to coordinate them. At one point in the second half of the 1980s, more than 150 committees, commissions, subcommissions and working groups were operating in the economic and social fields on more than 1,000 issue areas' (Simai, 1994, p. 323).

b. Inadequate Means

While there are difficulties in limiting the missions of such organisations, it is often the case they are not given the appropriate means and resources to carry out their missions. Thus the United Nations is told to keep the peace, but its soldiers are not allowed to fire their weapons. The International Monetary Fund is asked to solve financial crises but is not given powers to regulate borrowers before such crises break out and also not given sufficient resources to play the role of lender of last resort once they do. While national governments can tax and/or compel their citizens to provide the resources required to provide public goods, international organisations lack such mechanisms. As a result, their means will often be inadequate.

By their nature, the key feature of public goods (or bads) is that benefits (or costs) are not limited to single consumers (nations) or groups of consumers. (nations). As Samuelson (1954) pointed out, the efficient provision of public goods requires that the marginal cost of their production should equal the sum of the marginal benefits to *all* those that consume them.[2] While in principle, the shares in the costs of providing a public good should reflect individual demands for them, there are problems in having consumers actually reveal (and pay for) their true demands.[3] If exclusion is difficult or impossible, consumers will have an incentive to understate their needs in order to free-ride. In a domestic context, these problems are tackled in democratic societies by having voters choose representatives whose tax and spending preferences match their own. Since the state has the ability to enforce its decisions, consumers have an incentive to reveal their preferences more accurately. But in an international setting, when such enforcement is not possible, efficient provision is particularly problematic. International organisations (and collective action in many domestic institutions) will therefore be prone to 'common pool' problems. To be sure, as the existence of international organisations and agreements attests, these problems do not mean that cooperation will be absent – there are a variety of mechanisms states may use to induce others to comply such as tit-for-tat strategies – but it does imply that cooperation and resources for public goods are likely to be less than an omniscient planner might chose.

Indeed, this is a more general problem entailed by collective action. As Mancur Olson argued in his classic study:

> Even in the smallest groups, the members will not provide as much of the good as it would be in their common interest to provide. This tendency toward suboptimality is due to the fact that a collective good is, by definition, such that other individuals in the group cannot be kept from consuming it once any individual in the group has provided it for himself. Since an individual member thus gets only part of the benefit of any expenditure he makes to obtain more

[2] Samuelson (1954).
[3] See Musgrave and Musgrave (2003).

of the collective good, he will discontinue his purchase of the collective good before the optimal amount for the group as a whole has been obtained. In addition, the amounts of the collective good that a member of the group receives free from other members will further reduce his incentive to provide more of the good at his own expense.[4]

In particular, institutions making decisions on the basis of one country one vote will be particularly prone to free-riding behaviour. With majority voting, the preferences of the median voter nation will prevail, and there will be systematic pressures for these voters to try to obtain the goods from which they benefit while, at the same time, having others pay more of the costs. This was the experience at the United Nations. As noted by Simai:

> The history of the financial crisis of the United Nations illustrates the political roots of the financial problems that beset almost all Inter-Governmental Organizations. During the 1970s, especially the latter half of that decade, the developing countries mustered their collective voting power to initiate a number of resolutions designed to reshape the international economic order. Debates, even on technical matters, became increasingly politicized, and the developed countries and the Soviet bloc sought to curb the huge bureaucratic growth that the new programs threatened.[5]

Institutions making decisions based on unanimity can reduce the problem of cost shifting by free riders by giving all members veto rights.[6] However, this may make the organisation particularly susceptible to foot-dragging. The problem here is that institutions might not adequately provide public goods. One way to deal with the problem is to construct packages of agreements so that all can agree, but this may not always be possible.[7] Under these circumstances, of course, international organisations will be heavily criticised for inaction.

c. Legitimacy

Granting organisations more power and resources obviously makes it more likely that they will be able to carry out its mission. Indeed, as was noted above, nation states can in principle use voting and the ability to raise resources through taxation to supply national public goods in appropriate amounts. But the closer international organisations come to acting like nation states, the more likely that their legitimacy will be questioned.

---

[4] Olson (1977).

[5] Simai (1994, p. 325). In response to these problems, the United Nations altered the one country-one vote procedure with regard to budgetary issues requiring a consensus of the members of the responsible committee (Simai op. cit., p. 320).

[6] The virtues of the unanimity rule are explored and emphasised by Buchanan and Tullock (1974).

[7] The United Nations is based on the principle of one country one vote because of the sovereign equality of states. In budgetary issues, however, in the 1980s, the system was modified to require consensus. In the Bretton Woods institutions, countries' voting power reflects their financial contributions and allows for veto power for the largest contributors. UN resolutions are not binding, however, whereas those approved by the security council are.

Legitimacy, the acknowledged right of governors to govern, can be obtained through a variety of mechanisms. One source in today's era is through democracy – the rule by the people. But the right could also be secured on grounds of competence (technocracy), impartiality, adherence to rules and procedures and/or charismatic leadership.

All international organisations are inherently vulnerable to concerns that they are insufficiently democratic, particularly when held to the standards of the nation state. As Dani Rodrik has emphasised, there are basically two simple approaches to providing mass democratic decision-making: the nation state or global federalism.[8] Acting alone, however, increasingly nation states find they cannot provide the international public goods required to meet the needs and provide the full benefits from a global economy. Acting alone they cannot meet the functional or political requirements asked of global governance. Full global federalism permits eliminating the nation state and thus combining mass democratic politics and the ability to tax and enforce with an integrated global economy but it comes precisely at the expense of the nation state and few seem ready for this outcome.

So if the nation state is inadequate, and global federalism is not wanted, then intermediate approaches that reflect some compromises will have to be crafted. Inevitably these will be imperfect and vulnerable to criticism and thus the more powerful international organisations become the more opposition they will generate.

International organisations are vulnerable to charges that they lack legitimacy because the standards for legitimate governance are generally set by those of the nation state. Global governance is inevitably likely to be less democratic and thus less 'legitimate' than the nation state. In particular, international organisations derive their legitimacy in part from the notion that their members, national governments, accurately reflect the interests of their constituents. But this notion can be questioned either when there are other international non-governmental actors with claims to represent certain interests or when national governments are seen as insufficiently representative, or insufficiently informed and competent. In addition, international organisations are often set up to focus on a single purpose such as health, or trade or finance. This focus is particularly vulnerable to accusations that other factors are not being given sufficient weight.

As long as missions remain fairly limited and international organisations are restricted in their means, these potential problems may not be of great consequence. But the more ambitious the goals and the more intrusive the means, the more susceptible they will be to attacks on these 'democratic deficits'.

The problem is also less likely to be exposed as long as the international organisation engages in activities that are generally regarded to be 'win-win', i.e. provide benefits to all parties. But they are more likely to come to the fore, when issues are widely perceived as having major distributional implications among the members.

---

[8] Rodrik (2000).

This, then, is the basic dilemma facing global organisations:

> If missions are expanded, and organizations given insufficient means, they are likely to fail (or fall short of optimal behavior) and be criticized for ineffectiveness. However, the more extensive the means they are given, the more likely that their legitimacy will be questioned.

(i) GATT to WTO

The transition from the GATT to the WTO exemplifies some of these propositions. The mission of the GATT was fairly narrow. According to its Preamble it was

> to enter into reciprocal and mutually advantageous arrangements directed to the substantial reduction of tariffs and other barriers to trade and to the elimination of discriminatory treatment in international commerce.

After the United States was granted a waiver for agriculture in 1955, the GATT concentrated on reducing border trade barriers for industrial products. The GATT also sought to eliminate discriminatory treatment members through rules requiring most favoured nation (MFN) and national treatment. GATT did not seek to harmonise standards or policies; it simply required that domestic and imported goods be treated in the same way (GATT: Article III). Provided they respected this principle, countries remained free to implement any domestic policies or rules they desired. Policies relating to matters such as regulation, standards, intellectual property and subsidies were not covered by the GATT's disciplines.

The means the GATT used were fairly simple. Contracting parties met in multilateral negotiations to reduce their bound tariff rates. The negotiating power of powerful members was leveraged through the principle of MFN treatment to reduce tariffs for all. By and large, agreements were implemented by national governments and members did not require extensive institutional capabilities to meet their obligations. The GATT secretariat itself did not police compliance. Instead it offered assistance to contracting parties in settling disputes when parties felt that an agreement had been violated. But the settlement system itself was weak, since the consensus rule made participation by defendants voluntary. Even when they lost a case, parties were not required to give GATT rulings direct effect in their laws – the worst that could happen was that countries could face the suspension of concessions equivalent to their infraction and prior to the formation of the WTO this never happened.

Finally, although some disparaged the GATT efficacy and power – it was sometimes labelled the General Agreement to Talk and Talk and at other times even said to be dead – the GATT's legitimacy was generally accepted.[9] Essentially,

---

[9] One noteworthy exception related to the United States perspective on the GATT's origins. The GATT was negotiated by the United States under the 1945 extension of the trade agreements authority. US negotiators were not given the authority to negotiate an agreement establishing an organisation. See Jackson (1998).

members participated in and adhered to the GATT because they believed to do so was in their interest. Decision-making based on consensus ensured that in principle, every agreement made every party better off. Assuming that nations accurately represented their interests this practice ensured that every agreement was a Pareto improvement. Countries were not required to remove all their trade barriers or even to match the reductions of other parties. Instead, reciprocity was the guiding principle, but it required each party to agree to a volume of new imports that matched the volume of exports others would grant it. While this notion of reciprocity was never precisely enforced, it did serve as a guiding myth that helped create the perception that agreements were fair.[10] All told, most parties agreed that reducing some trade barriers was desirable and conforming to the rules was compatible with a significant space for divergent domestic policies.

The GATT was remarkably successful. Its membership grew and tariffs came down steadily. This success in reducing tariffs, however, led to additional demands. One set of demands came from developing countries that sought special preferences and differential treatment. Another was to extend the rules to cover non-tariff barriers and other practices that distorted international trade. Here already we see the dynamic of mission creep in operation.

The Tokyo Round agreement, concluded in 1977, therefore included an 'Enabling Clause' that created more scope for special and differential treatment. Special and differential treatment clearly and explicitly represents a departure from the principle of reciprocity. As long as developing countries are relatively small players in the world economy this may not be a matter of great concern. But once they become large, the myth of reciprocity becomes increasingly less tenable.

The Tokyo Round also concluded seven codes dealing with import licensing, technical barriers to trade, customs valuation, subsidies and countervailing duties, anti-dumping, civil aircraft and government procurement. However, the focus remained on rules and barriers that were clearly related to trade in goods. The fact that the GATT parties that did not sign agreements were not bound by them clearly aided their acceptance and legitimacy.

The codes represented an expansion in the WTO's mission to cover non-tariff barriers and rules governing fair trade, but the means to back up these rules were sometimes lacking. The codes had disparate and separate dispute settlement systems. Moreover, as the disputes between the US and the EU made clear, the combination of a weak dispute settlement system and opaque rules made it particularly difficult to impose disciplines on agricultural subsidies. In addition, parties resorted to extra-legal measures such as voluntary export restraints and unilateral retaliation that violated basic GATT principles such as avoiding discrimination and the use of quotas.

---

[10] For a more detailed discussion see Lawrence (2004).

The institution became much more controversial as a result of the Uruguay Round. This was because of a major expansion in the mission, an increase in the means and as a consequence increasing questions about legitimacy.[11]

The Uruguay Round agreement dramatically increased the organisation's mission by including General Agreement of Trade in Services (GATS), Sanitary and Phytosanitary Measures (SPS), Technical Barriers to Trade (TBT), Trade-related Investment Measures (TRIMS), Trade-related Intellectual Property (TRIPs) and a new agreement on Subsidies and Countervailing Measures (SCM). The TRIPs is particularly noteworthy since it requires countries to implement policy regimes that achieve a minimum level of intellectual property protection. Moreover, the WTO was a single undertaking in which most of the codes in addition to the new agreements were all made part of the same agreement. This dramatically increased the obligations of the members.

In addition to this large expansion in the WTO's scope, the Uruguay Round agreement also enhanced the power of the Dispute Settlement Body (DSB) to enforce trade rules. It required unanimity to prevent proceedings meaning that no one country could block the panel from hearing a dispute. The single undertaking meant that all WTO rules and most agreements were subject to dispute settlement understanding; WTO members therefore had the ability for cross-sectoral retaliation. For example, if a country violates the TRIPs agreement's intellectual property rules, it can be subject to the loss of other trade benefits, such as low tariffs on manufactured goods.

When trade policies cover only border barriers, they bring a fairly narrow group of producers and consumers into the political fray, but as they expand to constrain national regulatory policies, many more players will seek to enter the game. Some of these see trade agreements as an opportunity to further their agendas; others see trade agreements as a threat. One concern in particular is that trade officials will be allowed to decide among competing values.

What explains this expansion in the organisation's mission? It is important to understand that a major source of pressures for expansion is functional. As the world economy becomes more integrated, there is a growing need for greater governance. The more complex nature of cross-border economic activities, the more agents will require a secure framework in which to operate. As trading, financial and investment relationships deepen there are benefits from deepening the rules and making enforcement more effective. At the same time, as countries became increasingly interested in attracting foreign investment, they too had a growing interest in locking in their policies to give them greater credibility.

The second driver is political. The most important forces in our societies, business, labour and environmentalists, each find themselves competing with their

---

[11] For an excellent discussion of the challenge to WTO legitimacy see Keohane and Nye (2001).

counterparts in other countries and they all claim to seek level playing fields and to have their issues subject to international rules.

As it has responded to the growing demands for governance in the trade area and its rules have become more expansive and its enforcement more effective, it should be no surprise that the WTO has also become increasingly controversial. To be sure, since the Uruguay Round agreement was adopted on the basis of consensus, all WTO members indicated implicitly that they viewed the agreement, on balance, as in their interest. But since the rules had become increasingly complex, some members complained that they did not fully understand their implications. In other cases, even where national governments found the agreement beneficial, some of their important constituents did not.

(ii) WTO under fire

The Uruguay Round agreement and the establishment of the WTO has therefore generated friction. One set of criticisms has been that the purview of trade agreements has been extended too far. Developing countries complain about the TRIPs which channels rents to developed country inventors. Environmental groups argue that the WTO advantages trade at the expense of other considerations. Yet there are others who argue the WTO does not go far enough. Some have in mind extending the rules to deepen international integration by making international markets more contestable through liberalising investment, increasing disciplines on regulation, making government procurement more transparent and applying competition policies. Others believe that extending social rules relating to labour and environmental standards can help ensure that the benefits of globalisation are more equitably distributed. And many emphasise the need for additional measures such as capacity building to promote development.[12]

Yet questions can be raised about whether the organisation has the means to implement comprehensive agreements on all of these issues. The WTO relies on national implementation of agreements, but many developing countries lack the requisite resources and capacity. The WTO also relies on the dispute settlement system to police enforcement – yet many of the least developed countries have not found it easy to use the system. In addition, it should not be a surprise that

---

[12] A comparison between the chapeau of the GATT with that of the WTO reveals that whereas the GATT emphasises the importance of efficiently allocating the world's resources, the WTO calls in addition for 'sustainable development' and ensuring that trade leads to development. The WTO chapeau states '. . . while allowing for the optimal use of the world's resources in accordance with the objective of sustainable development, seeking both to protect and preserve the environment and to enhance the means for doing so in a manner consistent with their respective needs and concerns at different levels of economic development'. Recognising further that there is need for positive efforts designed to ensure that developing countries, and especially the least developed among them, secure a share in the growth in international trade commensurate with the needs of their economic development.

since market access negotiations are based on reciprocity, the agreements generally reflect the priorities of the nations with large markets. Since these are mostly developed countries and barriers have remained highest in the labour-intensive manufactures and agriculture.

While the mandate of the WTO has been enlarged considerably, as Richard Blackhurst has noted, it has not been given adequate resources to carry out the mandate. The WTO's budget and staff are extremely modest and far smaller than many other international organisations with much more modest mandates.[13]

For a number of reasons, therefore, the legitimacy of the organisation has been called into question. In many developing countries, trade liberalisation remains controversial; even more questionable are disciplines on domestic policies such as subsidies and selective government procurement that are viewed as placing excessive constraints on national development strategies. In addition, the associated difficulties of implementing such reasons are also a source of concern.

A second concern relates, paradoxically, to the fact that the dispute settlement system has become more effective. WTO agreements require consensus. Inevitably this means they are incomplete and imprecise and reflect the use of 'constructive ambiguity'. This becomes problematic for those called upon to adjudicate. One response could be for the dispute settlement process to fill in the blanks but this raises issues of legitimacy and is expressly prohibited. For this reason, the DSB is enjoined from adding to or subtracting from the obligations contained in the agreement. Despite considerable effort to hew closely to the texts of the agreements, there have been allegations that the DSB has been excessively activist and has undermined the decisions that sovereign governments have embodied in the agreements.[14]

A third complaint relates to the disparities among members when it comes to differences in the ability to use retaliation. The system is widely seen as inequitable since small, less powerful countries have less ability to retaliate. Indeed, while several members have been authorised to retaliate (e.g. Ecuador, Brazil and Canada) only the US and the EU have actually done so. This appears to violate the basic principle that all members should have equal rights.

A fourth set of concerns has been raised about the lack of representation in the institution for non-governmental actors, although it is unclear whether or not allowing such representation and participation would increase or decrease concerns about legitimacy.

Finally, there are issues relating to the organisation's alleged lack of transparency. On the one hand, many members are seeking to open up the process, whereas others feel this would be incompatible with the institution's fundamental role as an intergovernmental organisation.

---

[13] Blackhurst (1998).
[14] See Barfield (2001).

These controversies have placed the WTO in a difficult position. They confirm that more ambitious missions and enhanced power place pressures on perceptions of legitimacy. At the same time, however, there is also considerable evidence that global integration remains seriously incomplete and that there could be substantial additional benefits from deeper integration. Even when tariffs are removed, border effects continue to impede the free flow of goods and services. This was surely the experience of Europeans who concluded in the early 1980s that despite the virtual elimination of internal tariffs their markets remained fragmented. The considerable extent of fragmentation even among developed countries is documented by Bradford and Lawrence as are the large welfare benefits that could be enjoyed from price convergence that would result from the elimination of the obstacles that borders continue to present to increased international integration.[15]

As this account of the WTO recent problems underscores, however, it is important to proceed with caution and care. Success requires recognising the basic vulnerability of the system. It requires selecting only those missions that are strictly necessary (e.g. genuinely global public goods) which have the highest likelihood of the greatest payoffs and for which the institution has adequate means. Success also requires ensuring that agreements command a high degree of acceptance by those who sign them. One approach would simply be to reflect the lowest common denominator. But while this would help retain acceptance, it could also lead to frustration that the institution was not fully realising its potential. At the opposite extreme, even more ambitious rules and enhancement of the WTO's enforcement power could be contemplated. But as Cancún has demonstrated, this is not yet feasible. Accordingly, it appears that inevitably a middle course will have to be found. Let us turn therefore to evaluate the potential of an alternative approach to the single undertaking: having the WTO act as a club of clubs.

3. WOULD A CLUB OF CLUBS MAKE THE WTO A MORE EFFECTIVE INSTITUTION?

Several years ago, in the capstone of a volume of over 20 studies on Integrating National Economies undertaken by the Brookings Institution, Albert Bressand, Takatoshi Ito and I wrote *A Vision for the World Economy*.[16] In that monograph we argued that there was a need for new global institutions and agreements. However, we emphasised that these institutions needed to be developed with great care. In particular, whatever their purposes they needed to be crafted to achieve a balance between three desirable objectives: openness, diversity and cohesion. We argued that this balance could best be achieved through an

---

[15] See Bradford and Lawrence (2004).
[16] Lawrence et al. (1996). For an elaboration of how these clubs would operate see Lawrence (2006).

international architecture comprised of three different sorts of arrangements, which we called clubs.

We suggested that some of these clubs would be functional and devoted to single or related issues. Examples include the International Labour Organisation and the Bank of International Settlements. Other clubs could be regional and might contain several issues – such as APEC or the EU. In addition we advocated global coordinating clubs to deal with linkages among the functional and regional clubs. These we called the club of clubs. We pointed out that the United Nations, the WTO and the OECD already embodied elements of such an institution. In our proposal we envisaged a greater role for the 'clubs of clubs' in coordinating functional and regional organisations, initiating new clubs and encouraging dialogue and greater coherence among the clubs.

In this chapter, however, I will not be looking at the potential role for the WTO as an overarching organisation coordinating the relationships between organisations or clubs with agendas that are not directly related to trade, nor will I focus on the WTO's role as an institution that helps attain greater policy coherence between the Bretton Woods multilateral institutions. Instead, I will focus on the role that a club of clubs approach could play with respect to agreements that relate specifically to international trade. In what follows I will build on the ideas of the previous section to provided criteria for how issues should be chosen.

The WTO should only host clubs that are (a) related to its mission; (b) enforceable by the means available to the organisation and the members who join the club and (c) compatible with maintaining and enhancing legitimacy.

a. Mission

The Preamble of the WTO Agreement indicates that the WTO is an organisation which seeks to enhance welfare by (a) reducing barriers to trade (such as tariffs); (b) reducing discrimination in trade (e.g. requirements for MFN and national treatment), and (c) enhancing development through trade. Accordingly, the issues that are chosen should be trade-related in at least one of these respects and ideally in all of them. In this context, trade should be interpreted broadly to include international exchanges of goods and services and the movement and location of firms and people designed to accomplish such trade. The coverage should relate either to policies which directly affect market access (e.g. border barriers) or to the aspects of other policies which can materially affect such access. The aim is to a facilitate trade in both goods and services while at the same time preserving adequate scope for national policy differentiation. While there are many other issues that may be important subjects for international cooperation (e.g. environmental policies and human rights) and many other policies that could contribute to economic development (education, health etc.), trade-relatedness should be the *sine qua non* for inclusion. In addition, to the maximum extent possible, agreements should provide the maximum space for other functional international clubs to implement non-trade-related international agreements and for members to have considerable scope for differentiating their domestic policies to match their conditions and requirements. The issues contained in clubs should also not overlap with issues that are already part of the WTO's single undertaking.

b. Means

The WTO itself and members of the clubs must have, or be readily able to acquire, adequate means to carry out the missions. The WTO itself must have adequate expertise, resources and authority. For example, a competition policy agreement that envisaged the WTO club operating to provide consent on international mergers would have to be equipped with the expertise and resources and authority of the US Justice Department or the European Commission. However, a weaker agreement that entailed simply providing an opinion would need similar expertise but less power. In addition, since most clubs would rely heavily on national implementation, members should have, or be readily able to acquire, the necessary capacity. Only the able should be encouraged to join.

c. Legitimacy

The desirability of the issue as an item for inclusion in the WTO club framework should enjoy widespread acceptance by the membership. All members should view their obligations on each issue (or club) as welfare-enhancing. Even if members are themselves not ready to accept binding obligations and club membership there should be a consensus that the WTO is the appropriate institutional setting. Finally, the approach should minimise inhibitions on national autonomy required to achieve any given objective, i.e. subsidiarity should be a key element.

4. CONCLUSIONS

For all the talk of globalisation, the world economy remains highly fragmented as the economic effects of borders inhibit the realisation of more global economic integration. The WTO has a key role to play in helping nations to reap the full benefits of deeper integration but as its mission and means have expanded it has become more controversial. The organisation's legitimacy has been attacked from many quarters and efforts to add new issues to the rules have foundered, as many members have refused to accept new obligations on a variety of grounds that include problems in implementation, fears these could result in trade retaliation, and views that they will constrain the scope for differentiated domestic policies.

Supplementing the core WTO obligations with a club of clubs approach could help to promote deeper global integration while at the same time alleviate some of the WTO's institutional problems. The club of clubs offers a compromise in which diversity can co-exist with a more extensive set of commitments for willing members. Clubs would be chosen where they could help to promote the central missions: lowering barriers to trade; reducing the discriminatory effects of domestic policies and enhancing economic development through trade. All WTO members would participate in negotiating club rules, but members would be free not to join. Clubs would use the DSB to deal with disputes but suspension of concessions in the event of violations would be confined to the provisions of the same club in which the violation occurred.

The club of clubs approach might reduce the ability of some members to obtain agreements by packaging them in a single undertaking. It could also reduce the power of retaliation as an enforcement mechanism for certain obligations. But the approach could also enhance the legitimacy of the WTO by helping members to avoid undertaking obligations they did not view as in their interest. It would thereby ensure a better alignment between mission, means and legitimacy, the keys to a more effective international organisation.

REFERENCES

Barfield, C. E. (2001), *Free Trade, Sovereignty, Democracy: The Future of the World Trade Organization* (Washington, DC: American Enterprise Institute, AEI Press).

Blackhurst, R. (1998), 'The Capacity of the WTO to Fulfill its Mandate', in A. Krueger (ed.), *The WTO as an International Organization* (Chicago: University of Chicago Press), Chapter 1.

Bradford, S. and R. Z. Lawrence (2004), *Has Globalization Gone Far Enough? The Costs of Fragmented Markets* (Washington, DC: Institute for International Economics).

Buchanan, J. M. and G. Tullock (1974), *The Calculus of Consent: Logical Foundations of Constitutional Democracy* (Ann Arbor, MI: University of Michigan Press), Chapter 7.

Jackson, J. (1998), *The World Trading System* (Cambridge, MA: MIT Press), Chapter 2.

Keohane, R. O. and J. Nye (2001), 'The Club Model of International Cooperation', in R. B. Poret, P. Sauve, A. Subramanian and A. B. Zampetti (eds.), *Efficiency, Equity and Legitimacy: The Multilateral Trading System at the Millennium* (Washington, DC: Brookings Institution Press), Chapter 12.

Lawrence, R. Z. (2004), *Crimes and Punishments: Retaliation under the WTO* (Washington, DC: Institute for International Economics), Chapter 2.

Lawrence, R. Z. (2006), 'Rule Making amidst Growing Diversity: A Club of Club Approach to WTO Reform and New Issue Selection', *Journal of International Economic Law*, 9, 4, 823–35.

Lawrence, R. Z., A. Bressand and T. Ito (1996), *A Vision for the World Economy: Openness, Diversity and Cohesion* (Washington, DC: Brookings Institution Press).

Musgrave, R. A. and P. B. Musgrave (2003), 'Prologue', in I. Kaul, P. Conceicao, K. Le Goulven and R. U. Mendoza (eds.), *Providing Global Public Goods: Managing Globalization* (Oxford: Oxford University Press), xii–xv.

Olsen, M. (1977), *The Logic of Collective Action: Public Goods and the Theory of Groups* (Cambridge, MA: Harvard University Press).

Rodrik, D. (2000), 'Governance of Economic Globalization', in J. S. Nye and J. D. Donahue (eds.),

Governance in a Globalizing World (Washington, DC: Brookings Institution Press, Visions of Governance for the 21st Century).

Samuelson, P. A. (1954), 'The Pure Theory of Public Expenditure', *Review of Economics and Statistics*, **36**, 4, 387–89.

Simai, M. (1994), *The Future of Global Governance: Managing Risk and Change in the International System* (Washington, DC: United States Institute of Peace).

8

Defining Globalisation

Jan Aart Scholte

1. INTRODUCTION

DEFINITION is not everything, but everything involves definition. Knowledge of globalisation is substantially a function of how the word is defined. The dissection of globalisation must include a careful and critical examination of the term itself. A muddled or misguided core concept compromises our overall comprehension of the problem. In contrast, a sharp and revealing definition promotes insightful, interesting and empowering knowledge, an understanding that helps us to shape our destiny in positive directions.

Notions of globalisation have grabbed many an intellectual imagination over the past two decades. In academic and lay circles alike, many have pursued an intuition that this concept could provide an analytical lynchpin for understanding continuity and change in contemporary society. 'Globalisation' is not the only (or necessarily the best) entry point for such an enquiry, of course, but it has generated a lot of provocative and sometimes highly insightful commentary on present times.

Yet what lies in this word? The present chapter develops a definition in four main steps. Section 2 traces the rise of the vocabulary of globalisation in academic and lay thinking. Section 3 identifies several analytical culs-de-sac with respect to globalisation, that is, definitions that generate redundant and in some respects also unhelpful knowledge. Section 4 sets out a conceptualisation of globalisation as the spread of transplanetary and, in present times more specifically, supraterritorial social relations. To stress that this analysis does not succumb to globalist exaggerations, Section 5 adds half a dozen key qualifications to this definition, including, for example, that territorial geography continues to have importance alongside the new supraterritoriality. Section 6 concludes the chapter.

Much of this chapter appears in Jan Aart Scholte, *Globalization: A Critical Introduction*, first published in 2005 by Macmillan Press Ltd., reproduced with permission of Palgrave Macmillan.

2. RISE OF THE G-WORD

Although the term 'globalisation' was not coined until the second half of the twentieth century, it has a longer pedigree. In the English language, the noun 'globe' dates from the fifteenth century (derived from the Latin *globus*) and began to denote a spherical representation of the earth several hundred years ago (MWD, 2003; and Robertson, 2001, p. 6254). The adjective 'global' entered circulation in the late seventeenth century and began to designate 'world scale' in the late nineteenth century, in addition to its earlier meaning of 'spherical' (OED, 1989, VI, p. 582). The verb 'globalise' appeared in the 1940s, together with the term 'globalism' (Reiser and Davies, 1944, pp. 212, 219). The word 'globalisation', as a process, first surfaced in the English language in 1959 and entered a dictionary two years later (Schreiter, 1997, p. 5; and Webster, 1961, p. 965). Notions of 'globality', as a condition, began to circulate in the 1980s (Robertson, 1983).

The vocabulary of globalisation has also spread in other languages over the past several decades. The many examples include the terms *lil 'alam* in Arabic, *quanqiuhua* in Chinese, *mondialisation* in French, *globalizatsia* in Russian, *globalización* in Spanish and *utendawazi* in Swahili. In minor languages, too, we now find *globalisaatio* in Finnish, *bishwavyapikaran* in Nepalese, *luan bo' ot* in Timorese, and so on.

When new vocabulary gains such wide currency across continents and cultures, can it just be explained away as fad? Or does the novel word highlight a significant change in the world, where new terminology is needed to discuss new conditions? For example, when Jeremy Bentham coined the word 'international' in the 1780s (1789, p. 326; and Suganami, 1978), the concept caught hold because it resonated of a growing trend of his day, namely, the rise of nation-states and cross-border transactions between them. The current proliferation of global talk also seems unlikely to be accidental. The popularity of the terminology arguably reflects a widespread intuition that contemporary social relations have acquired an important new character. The challenge – indeed, the urgent need – is to move beyond the buzzword to a tight concept.

As a deliberately fashioned analytical tool, notions of the global appeared roughly simultaneously and independently in several academic fields around the early 1980s. In Sociology, for example, Roland Robertson began to 'interpret globality' in 1983 (Robertson, 1983). Concurrently, in Business Studies, Theodore Levitt wrote of 'the globalization of markets' (Levitt, 1983). These years also saw some researchers in International Relations shift their focus to 'global interdependence' (Rosenau, 1980). Economists, geographers and others picked up the concept later in the decade.

Since the 1990s globalisation has become a major academic growth industry. The problem is now explored across disciplines, across continents, across theoretical approaches, and across the political spectrum. Countless academics have rushed to claim the cliché of the day. The number of entries for 'globalisation' in the United States Library of Congress multiplied from 34 in 1994 to 5,245 in 2005 (Waters, 1995; and LoC, 2005). A host of research institutes, degree programmes, course modules, textbooks and websites now focus on the problem. The recent appearance of several anthologies and the preparation of an *Encyclopedia of Globalization* further attest to the consolidation of a new field of enquiry (cf. Higgott and Payne, 2000; Lechner and Boli, 2000; Held and McGrew, 2003; and Robertson and Scholte, 2006). Since 2000 several new professional groups have also emerged: Global Studies Associations in Britain and the USA: and a Globalisation Studies Network with worldwide membership. Some theorists have even presented globalisation as the focal point for an alternative paradigm of social enquiry (Shaw, 1999; and Mittelman, 2002).

Yet ideas of globalisation tend to remain as elusive as they are pervasive. We sense that the vocabulary means something – and something significant – but we are far from sure what that something is. Anthony Giddens has observed that 'there are few terms that we use so frequently but which are in fact as poorly conceptualised as globalisation' (Giddens, 1996).

Persistent ambiguity and confusion over the term has fed considerable scepticism about 'globaloney', 'global babble' and 'glob-blah-blah'. One critic has pointedly dismissed the idea of lending analytical weight to the notion of globalisation as 'folly' (Rosenberg, 2001). True, some of these objectors have had dubious motives, such as vested interests in orthodox theory, or an intellectual laziness that resists rethinking conceptual starting points. However, other doubters have quite rightly demanded clear, precise, explicit, consistent and cogent conceptualisation before they will treat globalisation as a serious scholarly category.

3. REDUNDANT CONCEPTS OF GLOBALISATION

Much if not most existing analysis of globalisation is flawed because it is redundant, failing to generate new understanding that is not attainable with other concepts. Four main definitions have led into this cul-de-sac: globalisation as internationalisation; globalisation as liberalisation; globalisation as universalisation; and globalisation as westernisation. Arguments that build on these conceptions fail to open insights that are not available through pre-existent vocabulary. Commentators who reject the novelty and transformative potential of globalisation in contemporary history have almost invariably defined the term in one or several of these four redundant ways. Moreover, these conceptions can also raise political objections.

a. Internationalisation

When globalisation is interpreted as internationalisation, the term refers to a growth of transactions and interdependence between countries. From this perspective, a more global world is one where more messages, ideas, merchandise, money, investments, pollutants and people cross borders between national-state-territorial units. For certain authors, like Paul Hirst and Grahame Thompson, globalisation is an especially intense form of internationalisation, so that the global is a particular subset of the international (1999, pp. 7–13). Many other analysts are less discriminating and simply regard the words 'global' and 'international' as synonyms to be used interchangeably.

Most attempts to quantify globalisation have conceived of the process as internationalisation. Thus, for example, Dani Rodrik has measured globalisation in terms of the current account as a proportion of GDP (Rodrik, 2001). Similarly, the globalisation indexes developed by A. T. Kearney consultants and *Foreign Policy* magazine since 2001 and by the Centre for the Study of Globalisation and Regionalisation since 2005 have been largely calculated with reference to amounts of cross-border activities between countries. That is, the scores mainly relate to foreign direct investment, international travel, membership in international organisations, international telephone traffic, etc. Moreover, the calculation measures and compares the indicators on a territorial basis, so that one country is said to be more, or less, globalised than another (Kearney/FP, 2001; and CSGR, 2005).

Ideas of globalisation-as-internationalisation are attractive insofar as they entail a minimum of intellectual and political adjustments. Global relations of this kind can be examined on the same ontological and methodological grounds as international relations. Global Economics can be the same sort of enquiry as International Economics. The study of Global Politics need not differ substantially from traditional International Politics, global culture is equivalent to international culture, and so on. Globalisation-as-internationalisation gives the comforting message that the new can be wholly understood in terms of the familiar.

Indeed, most accounts of globalisation-as-internationalisation stress that contemporary trends are replaying earlier historical scenarios. In particular, these analyses frequently note that, in proportional terms, levels of cross-border trade, direct investment and permanent migration were as great or greater in the late nineteenth century as they were a hundred years later (Hirst and Thompson, 1999; and O'Rourke and Williamson, 1999). The suggestion is that globalisation (read international interdependence) is a feature of the modern states-system and world economy that ebbs and flows over time. So today's social researchers can relax and carry on enquiries as previous generations have done.

Yet these very claims of familiarity and historical repetition constitute strong grounds for rejecting the definition of globalisation-as-internationalisation. If globality is nothing other than internationality – except perhaps larger amounts of it – then why bother with new vocabulary? No one needed a concept of globalisation to make sense of earlier experiences of greater international interaction and interdependence, and this notion is similarly redundant today.

Ideas of globalisation-as-internationalisation can also be politically objectionable. They readily imply that world social relations are – and can only be – organised in terms of country units, state governments and national communities. As such, the vocabulary of internationality tends to ignore, marginalise and silence other modes of organisation, governance and identity that exist and are highly valued by, for example, indigenous peoples, regionalists and various kinds of cosmopolitans.

b. Liberalisation

A second common analytical dead-end in discussions of globalisation has equated the notion with liberalisation. In this case, globalisation denotes a process of removing officially imposed restrictions on movements of resources between countries in order to form an 'open' and 'borderless' world economy. On this understanding, globalisation occurs as authorities reduce or abolish regulatory measures like trade barriers, foreign-exchange restrictions, capital controls and visa requirements.

Using this definition, the study of globalisation is a debate about contemporary so-called 'neoliberal' macroeconomic policies. On one side of this argument, many academics, business executives and policymakers have supported neoliberal prescriptions that worldwide liberalisation, privatisation, deregulation and fiscal restraint would in time bring prosperity, freedom, peace and democracy for all. On the other side, critics in the so-called 'anti-globalisation' movement have opposed neoliberal policies, contending that a *laissez-faire* world economy produces greater poverty, inequality, social conflict, cultural destruction, ecological damage and democratic deficits.

To be sure, large-scale globalisation and widespread economic liberalisation have frequently transpired concurrently in the past quarter-century. For example, average tariff rates for non-agricultural products have fallen to record low levels. Moreover, this wave of neoliberalism has often played a significant (albeit not necessary) facilitating role in respect of contemporary globalisation. However, it is quite something else to conflate the two concepts, so that globalisation and liberalisation become the same thing. Moreover, such an equation can carry the dubious – and potentially harmful – political implication that neoliberalism is the only available policy framework for a more global world.

Indeed, on cross-examination most 'anti-globalisation' protesters are seen to reject *neoliberal* globalisation rather than globalisation *per se*. True, some of these critics have adopted a rejectionist, mercantilist position that advocates 'de-globalisation' to a world of autarkic regional, national or local economies. However, most opponents of neoliberalism have sought different approaches to globalisation – or 'alter-globalisations' – that might better advance human security, social justice and democracy. Many in mainstream circles, too, have recently suggested that globalisation can be rescued with social, environmental and human rights safeguards. They have thereby also acknowledged that neoliberal policies are not intrinsic to globalisation.

In any case, the language of globalisation is unnecessary to rehearse arguments for and against *laissez-faire* economics. People have debated theories and practices of 'free' markets for several centuries without invoking talk of globalisation. For example, no one needed the concept of globalisation when the international economy experienced substantial liberalisation in the third quarter of the nineteenth century (Marrison, 1998). Likewise, globalisation-as-liberalisation opens no new insight today.

c. Universalisation

A third cul-de-sac appears in analyses of globalisation when the notion is conceived as universalisation. In this case, globalisation is taken to describe a process of dispersing various objects and experiences to people at all inhabited parts of the earth. On these lines, 'global' means 'worldwide' and 'everywhere'. Hence there is a 'globalisation' of the Gregorian calendar, tobacco, business suits, curry dinners, bungalows, Barbie dolls, shotguns, and so on. Frequently globalisation-as-universalisation is assumed to entail homogenisation with worldwide cultural, economic, legal and political convergence. For example, some economists have assessed globalisation in terms of the degree to which prices for particular goods and services become the same across countries (Bradford and Lawrence, 2004).

Yet this third type of conception, too, opens no new and distinctive insight. To be sure, some striking worldwide diffusion has transpired in contemporary history. Moreover, substantial cultural destruction in recent times has appeared to lend credence to the homogenisation thesis (although, as is elaborated later in this chapter, the dynamics of globalisation are actually more complex). However, universalisation is an age-old feature of world history. Indeed, Clive Gamble has written of 'our global prehistory', arguing that the transcontinental spread of the human species – begun a million years ago – constitutes the initial instance of globalisation (1994, pp. ix, 8–9). Various aptly named 'world religions' have extended across large expanses of the earth for centuries, and several of these faiths have held explicit universalistic pretensions. Transoceanic trade has distributed various goods over long distances on multiple occasions during the past millennium. No concept of globalisation was devised to describe universalisation in earlier times, and there is no need to create new vocabulary to analyse this old phenomenon now either.

Moreover, inasmuch as this approach carries misguided assumptions of globalisation-as-homogenisation, it can have unhappy political consequences. Cultural protectionists can be led to oppose globalisation *per se*, when they are in fact only against one of its possible results. Indeed, globalisation can, when handled in certain ways, promote cultural diversity, revival and innovation.

d. Westernisation

A fourth common conception of globalisation has defined it as westernisation. As such, globalisation is regarded as a particular type of universalisation, one in which social structures of Western modernity (capitalism, industrialism, rationalism, urbanism, etc.) are spread across all of humanity, in the process destroying pre-existent cultures and local self-determination. Globalisation understood in this way is often interpreted as colonisation, Americanisation and (in the vocabulary of the Iranian intellectual, Ale Ahmad) 'westoxification'. For these critics, talk of globalisation is a hegemonic discourse, an ideology of supposed progress that masks far-reaching destruction and subordination (Petras and Veltmeyer, 2001).

To be sure, a cogent case can be made that current large-scale globalisation has resulted mainly from forces of modernity like rationalist knowledge, capitalist production, technologies of automation and nation-states (Giddens, 1990). At the same time, early global consciousness arguably facilitated the onset of modernity, too (Robertson, 1992, p. 170). In turn, contemporary globalisation has often inserted patterns of modern, western social relations more widely and deeply across the planet. Sometimes this westernisation has involved violent impositions that could indeed warrant descriptions as imperialism. Moreover, it is true that governance institutions, firms, academics and civil society associations in Western Europe and North America have ranked among the most enthusiastic promoters of contemporary globalisation.

Yet it is one thing to assert that globalisation and westernisation have had interconnections and quite another to equate the two developments. After all, modernity and western civilisation have appeared in many other guises besides contemporary globalisation. Moreover – and it is politically important to acknowledge this – globalisation could in principle take non-western directions: e.g. Buddhist globalisation, Confucian globalisation, Islamic globalisation, or possible future postmodern globalisations. Also, it is by no means clear that globalisation is intrinsically imperialist, given that there are emancipatory global social movements as well as exploitative global processes.

In any case, westernisation, modernisation and colonisation have a much longer history than contemporary globalisation. Perhaps currently prevailing forms of globality could be analysed as a particular aspect, phase and type of modernity. On this reading, a definition of globalisation would need to specify what makes *global* modernity distinctive. Yet in this approach, too, westernisation and globalisation are not coterminous.

In sum, then, much talk of globalisation has been analytically redundant. The four definitions outlined above between them cover most current academic, corporate, journalistic, official and popular discussions of things global. Critics of 'globaloney' are right to assail the historical illiteracy that marks most claims of novelty associated with these conceptions of globalisation.

Of course, this is not to suggest that debates about international interdependence, neoliberalism, universalism-versus-cultural diversity, modernity and imperialism are unimportant. Indeed, a well-fashioned concept of globalisation could shed significant light on these problems. However, it is not helpful to define globalisation as – to treat it as equivalent to – internationalisation, liberalisation, universalisation or westernisation. Not only do we thereby merely rehash old knowledge, but we also lose a major opportunity to grasp – and act upon – certain key circumstances of our times.

4. A WAY FORWARD

Fortunately, the four definitions critiqued above do not exhaust the possible definitions of globalisation. Important new insight into historically relatively new conditions is available from a fifth conception. This approach identifies globalisation as the spread of transplanetary – and in recent times also more particularly supraterritorial – connections between people. From this perspective, globalisation involves reductions in barriers to transworld social contacts. People become more able – physically, legally, linguistically, culturally and psychologically – to engage with each other wherever on earth they might be.

In this usage, globalisation refers to a shift in the nature of social space. This conception contrasts with the other four notions of globalisation discussed above, all of which presume (usually implicitly rather than explicitly) a continuity in the underlying character of social geography. To clarify this crucial point, the following pages first note the general importance of space in social relations and then elaborate on the features of transplanetary and, more specifically, supraterritorial links between persons. The far-reaching methodological implications of this understanding of globalisation are also noted, although the final section of the chapter highlights several major qualifications to this definition.

To clarify the vocabulary, in the approach adopted here, the words 'global', 'transplanetary' and 'transworld' are treated as synonyms. They are therefore used interchangeably in the rest of this chapter. References to 'supraterritoriality' are made whenever that particular quality of globality comes into play.

a. Space

The term globality resonates of spatiality. It says something about the *arena* and the *place* of human action and experience: the *where* of social life. In particular, globality identifies the planet – the earth as a whole – as a field of social relations in its own right. Talk of the global indicates that people may interact not only in local, provincial, country and macro-regional realms, but also in transplanetary spaces where the earth is a single place.

Why highlight issues of space? Most social analysis takes the spatial aspect as an unexplored given. Yet geography is a defining feature of social life (cf. Lefebvre, 1974; and Brenner et al., 2003). Relations between people always occur somewhere: in a place, a location, a domain, a site. No description of a social circumstance is complete without a spatial component.

Moreover, no social explanation is complete without a geographical dimension either. Space matters. To take one ready example, geographical differences mean that desert nomads and urban dwellers lead very diverse lives. Space is a core feature – as both cause and effect – of social life. On the one hand, the geographical context shapes the ways that people formulate knowledge, relate to nature, undertake production, experience time, organise governance, construct identities and form collectivities. Concurrently, culture, ecology, economics, history, politics and psychology also shape the spatial contours of social relations.

Given these dense interconnections, a change of spatial structure affects society as a whole. A reconfiguration of social geography is intimately interlinked with shifts in patterns of production, governance, ecology, identity and knowledge. So a transformation of social space – like large-scale globalisation – is enveloped in larger dynamics of social change.

b. Globality: Transplanetary Relations and Supraterritoriality

Globality in the conception adopted here has two qualities. The more general feature, transplanetary connectivity, has figured in human history for many centuries. The more specific characteristic, supraterritoriality, is relatively new to contemporary history. Inasmuch as the recent rise of supraterritoriality marks a striking break from the territorialist geography that came before, this trend potentially has major implications for wider social transformation.

Globality in the broader sense of transplanetary ('across the planet') relations refers to social links between people located at points anywhere on earth. The global field is in these cases a social space in its own right. The globe, planet earth, is not simply a collection of smaller geographical units like regions, countries and localities. It is also itself a distinct arena of social life. We can therefore distinguish between 'international relations' (as exchanges between countries) and 'global relations' (as exchanges within a planetary realm).

Of course, this more general kind of globality – transplanetary connections between people – is by no means new to the past few decades. Long-distance and intercontinental domains have had age-old importance in human history. On the other hand, contemporary transplanetary links are denser than those of any previous epoch. More people, more often and more intensely engage with the planetary arena as a single social place. Volumes of transworld associations, communications, diseases, finance, investment, travel and trade have never been as great (for detailed indicators see Scholte, 2005, Ch. 3).

However, the distinctiveness of recent globalisation involves more than the quantity, frequency, scope and intensity of transplanetary social links. Qualitatively, too, much of today's global connectivity is different. Unlike earlier times, contemporary globalisation has been marked by a large-scale spread of supraterritoriality.

As the word suggests, 'supraterritorial' relations are social connections that substantially transcend territorial geography. They are relatively delinked from territory, that is, spatial domains that are mapped on the land surface of the earth, plus any adjoining waters and air spheres. Territorial space is plotted on the three axes of longitude, latitude and altitude. In territorial geography, place refers to locations situated on this three-dimensional grid; distance refers to the extent of territory separating territorial places; and border refers to a territorial delimitation of sections of the earth's surface.

Yet territorial locations, territorial distances and territorial borders do not define the whole geography of today's transplanetary flows. These global connections often also have qualities of *transworld simultaneity* (that is, they extend anywhere across the planet at the same time) and *transworld instantaneity* (that is, they move anywhere on the planet in no time). Thus, for example, on average 3,000 cups of Nescafé are reputedly drunk around the planet every second (Nescafé, 2003), and telephone links permit immediate communication across the ocean as readily as across the street. Global relations with supraterritorial features are not adequately mapped on a territorial grid.

Supraterritorial forms of globality are evident in countless facets of contemporary life. For instance, jet aeroplanes transport passengers and cargo across any distance on the planet within 24 hours. Telecommunications networks effect instantaneous links between points all over the earth, so that a call centre or data processing bureau for customers in North America may be located 12 time zones away in India. The global mass media spread messages simultaneously to transworld audiences. The US dollar and the euro are examples of money that has instantaneous transplanetary circulation. In global finance, various types of savings and investment instruments (e.g. offshore bank deposits and eurobonds) flow instantaneously in transworld domains. Ecologically, developments such as climate change, stratospheric ozone depletion, certain epidemics and losses of biological diversity unfold simultaneously on a global scale. Ideationally, many people have a supraterritorial concept of place, for instance, when watching televised moon landings and global sports events simultaneously with hundreds of millions of other people scattered across the planet. Global human rights campaigns do not measure their support for a cause as a function of the territorial distance and territorial borders that lie between advocates and victims.

With these and many more supraterritorial phenomena, current globalisation has constituted more than an extension of the compression of time relative to territorial space that has unfolded over a number of past centuries. In this long-term trend, developments in transportation technology like motor ships, railways and early aircraft progressively reduced the time needed to cover a given distance over the earth's surface. Thus, while Marco Polo took years to complete his journey across Eurasia in the thirteenth century, by 1850 a sea voyage from South East Asia to North West Europe could be completed in 59 days (PTT, 1951, p. 11). In the twentieth century, motorised ships and land vehicles took progressively less time again to link territorial locations. Nevertheless, such transport still required substantial time spans to cross long distances and moreover still faced substantial controls at territorial frontiers.

Whereas this older trend towards a shrinking world occurred *within* territorial geography, the newer spread of transworld simultaneity and instantaneity takes social relations substantially *beyond* territorial space. In cases of supraterritoriality, place is not territorially fixed, territorial distance is covered in no time and territorial boundaries present no particular impediment. The difference between territorial time-space compression and the rise of supraterritoriality is qualitative and entails a deeper structural change of geography.

A number of social researchers across a range of academic disciplines have discerned this reconfiguration of space, albeit without invoking the term 'supraterritoriality' to describe the shift. Already half a century ago, for example, the philosopher Martin Heidegger proclaimed the advent of 'distancelessness' and an 'abolition of every possibility of remoteness' (1950, pp. 165–6). Forty years later the geographer David Harvey discussed 'processes that so revolutionize the objective qualities of space and time that we are forced to alter, sometimes in quite radical ways, how we represent the world to ourselves' (1989, p. 240). The sociologist Manuel Castells has distinguished a 'network society', in which a new 'space of flows' exists alongside the old 'space of places' (1989, p. 348). The anthropologist Marc Augè has described an instantaneity that puts 'any person into relation with the entire world' (1994, p. 95). In the field of International Relations, John Ruggie has written of a 'nonterritorial region' in the contemporary world (1993, p. 172).

Might such a geographical transformation in the longer term prove to be as epochal as the shift to territorialism was at an earlier historical juncture? After all, social relations have not always and everywhere operated with a macro spatial framework that is overridingly territorial. For instance, cultures with a metaphysical cosmology have assigned only secondary, if any, importance to territorial referents. In fact, a territorial grid to locate points on a map was not introduced anywhere until the second century AD, by Zhang Heng in China (Douglas, 1996, p. 22). Medieval people in Europe did not have a notion of territory defined by three-dimensional geometry applied to the earth's surface (Zumthor, 1993; and Hanawat and Kobialka, 2000). Images of the world showing the continents in anything like the territorial shapes that are commonly recognised today were not drawn before the late fifteenth century. It took a further 200 years before the first maps depicting country units appeared (Campbell, 1987; and Whitfield, 1994). Not until the high tide of colonialism at the end of the nineteenth century did a territorial logic dominate the construction of macro social spaces across the earth.

From then until the third quarter of the twentieth century, social spaces of a macro kind (that is, as opposed to directly perceived micro social spaces like built environments) nearly always took a territorial form. Indeed, one could say that a structure of territorial*ism* governed social geography. In a territorialist situation, people identify their location in the world primarily in relation to territorial position. (In most cases the territorial reference points are fixed, though for nomadic groups the spots may shift.) Moreover, in territorialist social relations the length of territorial distances between places and the presence or absence of territorial (especially state) borders between places heavily influences the frequency and significance of contacts that people at different territorial sites have with each other.

However, like any social structure, territorialism as the prevailing mode of geography was specific to a particular historical and cultural context. True, many people today still use the terms 'geography' and 'territory' interchangeably, as if to exclude the possibility that social space could have other than territorial forms. Yet world geography today is in an important respect not like that of the period to the mid-twentieth century. Following several decades of proliferating and expanding supraterritorial connections, territoriality has lost its monopoly hold. Territorial domains remain very important, but they no longer define the entire macro spatial framework.

Most of the rise of supraterritoriality is recent. As with any development, longer-term antecedents can of course be found. However, supraterritorial connectivity has reached by far its greatest extents during the past half-century. Earlier periods did not know jet travel, intercontinental missiles, transworld migrants with trans-border remittances, satellite communications, facsimiles, the Internet, instant transplanetary television broadcasts, intercontinental production chains, transworld retailers, global credit cards, a continuous diet of global sports tournaments, or large-scale transplanetary anthropogenic ecological changes. Contemporary history is supraterritorial to degrees well beyond anything previously known.

True, enthusiasm at discovering something new – a significant reconfiguration of social geography – must not prompt overstatements of its extent. Globalisation in the more specific sense of the spread of supraterritoriality has been less extensive than globalisation in the more general sense of the growth of transplanetary connections. The supraterritorial aspects of contemporary globalisation have far-reaching transformative potentials, but they constitute only part of the larger trend, and assessments of currently unfolding social change need to be correspondingly tempered.

c. Global, World, International and Transnational

Further clarification of the idea of globality that is suggested here may be obtained by comparing the term with cognate concepts such as 'world', 'international' and 'transnational' links. All of these words put the spotlight on social relations beyond society conceived on nation/state/country lines. However, the four notions imply different emphases and should not be conflated.

At first glance, 'world' might seem synonymous with 'global', since in contemporary modern society 'the world' is generally conceived as planet earth. Indeed, the present analysis invokes 'transworld' as a synonym for 'transplanetary'. However, people in other eras and cultures have identified their 'world' in non-global ways. For example, the ancient Chinese mapped their 'world' in terms of a Middle Kingdom surrounded by peripheries of barbarians. Other ancient civilisations unfolded in a Mediterranean 'world'. Medieval Europeans conceived of the 'world' in terms of relations between humanity, nature and God. Hence 'world' refers to the spatial totality that prevails in a given context. Globality (in the sense of connectivity across the planetary realm) has featured in some social 'worlds' throughout history, but far from all.

Moreover, the contemporary world has multiple spatial dimensions in addition to the global. World social relations today have regional, country, local, household and other geographical aspects alongside the transplanetary facets. Thus 'world' is the social-geographical whole, while 'global' is only one of its spatial qualities.

The distinction between 'global' and 'international' has been stressed already, but it bears reiteration. 'International' exhanges occur between country units, while 'global' transactions occur within a planetary unit. Whereas international relations are *inter*-territorial relations, global relations are *trans*- and sometimes *supra*-territorial relations. Thus global economics is different from international economics, global politics is different from international politics, and so on.

Finally, a number of researchers have since the 1970s adopted a discourse of 'transnational' relations to analyse social interchange beyond the state and national society (Merle, 1974; and Keohane and Nye, 1977). This conception has the merit of highlighting non-governmental relations between countries and non-national forms of social bonds (e.g. transnational religious and class solidarities). However, ideas of transnationalism offer less when it comes to elaborating a more specific conception of the character of these non-statist and non-nationalist circumstances. In contrast, notions of global relations positively identify the transplanetary and supraterritorial qualities of various social relations.

Another objection to the vocabulary of trans*nationality* is that it still takes the nation-state-country as its reference point and to that extent retains traces of methodological nationalism and statism. Indeed, transnational relations are usually conceived as transactions across state borders. On the other hand, ideas of globality avoid domestic/foreign, internal/external dichotomies and thereby foster a clear and important methodological reorientation.

d. *Methodological Implications*

If contemporary social geography is no longer territorialist in character, then traditional habits of social research need to be adjusted. Methodological territorialism has exercised a pervasive and deep hold on the conventions of social enquiry. The spread of supraterritoriality requires a major shift of approach.

Methodological territorialism refers to the practice of understanding and investigating social relations through the lens of territorial geography. Territorialist method means formulating concepts, asking questions, constructing hypotheses, gathering and interpreting evidence, and drawing conclusions in a spatial framework that is wholly territorial. These intellectual habits are so engrained that most social researchers reproduce them more or less unconsciously.

Methodological territorialism lies at the heart of currently prevailing commonsense notions of geography, economy, governance, history, literature, culture and society. Thus the vast majority of social and political geographers have conceived of the world in terms of bordered territorial (especially country) units. Likewise, macroeconomists have normally studied production, exchange and consumption in relation to national (read territorial) and international (read inter-territorial) realms. Students of politics have conventionally regarded governance as a territorial question, that is, as a matter of local and country government, with the latter sometimes meeting in 'international' (again, code for inter-territorial) organisations. Similarly, mainstream historians have examined continuity and change over time in respect of territorial contexts such as localities and countries. Literature has generally been classed in terms of national-territorial genres: English literature, Indonesian literature, etc. For their part, anthropologists have almost invariably conceived of culture and community with reference to territorial units, in the sense of local and national peoples. Meanwhile territorialist premises have led sociologists usually to assume that society by definition takes a territorial (usually national) form: hence Albanian society, Bolivian society, Chinese society, etc.

Like any analytical device, methodological territorialism involves simplification. Actual social practice has always been more complicated. Nevertheless, this assumption offered a broadly viable intellectual shortcut for earlier generations of scholars. Methodological territorialism reflected the social conditions of a particular epoch when bordered territorial units, separated by territorial distance, formed far and away the overriding framework for macro social geography.

However, territorialist analysis is not a timeless or universally applicable method. The emergence of the states-system, the growth of mercantile and industrial capitalism, and the rise of national identities all understandably encouraged researchers of earlier times to adopt methodologically territorialist perspectives. Yet today large-scale globalisation – including the substantial spread of supraterritoriality – should stimulate a reconstruction of methodology on alternative, non-territorialist premises.

This call for different intellectual foundations no doubt provokes resistance in some quarters. It is difficult and even painful to change taken-for-granted knowledge, to reassess a cornerstone of understanding of social relations, to endure the disruption and confusion that comes in the transition between abandoning one set of first principles and consolidating another. Moreover, a post-territorialist methodology has political implications that vested interests could oppose. For example, post-territorialist social knowledge would logically undercut the primacy of both state-centric research and state-centric governance.

Yet it can arguably be quite dangerous to give methodological territorialism further lease on life in the contemporary more global world. For example, territorialist assumptions are obviously unsuitable to understand – and address – transplanetary ecological issues. Likewise, if significant parts of capitalism now operate with relative autonomy from territorial space, then old intellectual frameworks cannot adequately address the issues of distributive justice that invariably accompany processes of surplus accumulation. Similarly, a political theory that offers today's world only territorial constructions of community, citizenship and democracy is obsolete. Hence the stakes in the call for post-territorialist enquiry are much more than academic alone.

e. Manifestations of Globality

The character and scale of globalisation as the spread of transplanetary connections – including many (mainly recent) links that have a supraterritorial quality – may be further clarified with a survey of transworld activities. Such a review indicates that globality can touch pretty well all aspects of social life. That said, as the final section of this chapter emphasises, it does not follow that global relations have become anything close to the only feature of social geography, either today or in the foreseeable future.

A great deal of globality is manifested through communications, that is, exchanges of ideas, information, images, signals, sounds and text. Transworld communication can be effected by means of the book trade, postal services, telegraph, telephone, facsimile, telex, text messaging, videoconference, computer networks, newspaper, magazine, radio, television, video and film. Supraterritoriality comes into global communications when, for example, certain publications (like Harry Potter books) and recordings (like Eminem CDs) are released simultaneously across the planet. In addition, satellite broadcasts and transoceanic cables enable communication to be effected instantaneously between any points on earth, irrespective of the territorial distances and territorial borders that lie between them. Toll-free telephone numbers can link up to a call centre on any continent.

The Internet is supraterritorial communication *par excellence*, instantly relaying a full range of visual and auditory signals anywhere on the planet that terminals exist to send and receive them. Much of today's globality is an 'e-world' of e-commerce, e-friendship, e-government and e-mail. Indeed, in September 2001 the Internet allowed doctors in New York, USA, to perform transoceanic robot-assisted telesurgery on a patient in Strasbourg, France (Pogue, 2001). The notion that the Internet involves new kinds of social geography is conveyed by the term 'cyberspace'.

Other globality occurs in the transplanetary movement of people. Global travel is undertaken by many migrant labourers, professionals, pilgrims, refugees, tourists, adventurers, adopted children and more. Relevant modes of transworld transport include caravans, ships, trains, motor vehicles and aeroplanes. Jet aircraft in particular have introduced something approaching a supraterritorial quality into contemporary global travel, as passengers can be flown between any two locations on the earth within a day. Transworld travel enables the occurrence of large global convocations like the *haj*, professional congresses, tourist resorts, trade fairs and United Nations (UN) summits. Transplanetary movements of domestics and sex workers have brought globalisation into many a household and brothel (Ehrenreich and Hochschild, 2002). Some business travellers have the globe as their office, working from hotels and airport lounges as much as a fixed home base. Conflicts in Afghanistan, Bosnia and Somalia have generated global waves of refugees and asylum seekers. Although state border controls restrict global travel in many cases, millions upon millions of people each year move about the planet as a single place.

Even when people are not travelling, they may be globally connected through organisations, that is, associations that coordinate the activities of individuals spread across the planet. Many of these organisations pursue mainly commercial purposes as global companies (often imprecisely named 'multinational corporations'). Examples include Inter Press Service, Mitsubishi, Nokia, Novartis, Standard Chartered, and Royal Dutch/Shell. In addition, many businesses have developed various types of transworld coalitions, often termed 'strategic alliances' (for instance, joint ventures, subcontracting arrangements, franchises, and so on). Other trans-world organisations have mainly regulatory functions and can suitably be called global governance institutions. For instance, activities of the International Monetary Fund (IMF), the United Nations Educational, Scientific and Cultural Organisation (UNESCO) and the World Trade Organisation (WTO) extend across the planet. Some regionally, nationally and locally based governance bodies like the European Union (EU), the United States government and the Hong Kong municipal authorities also have significant global reach. Along with commercial and governance agencies, many civil society associations also have a global organisation. They include faith-based groups like the World Fellowship of Buddhists, labour movements like the International Confederation of Free Trade Unions (ICFTU), NGOs like Amnesty International, peasant coalitions like Vía Campesina, and philanthropic bodies like the Ford Foundation. In addition, many localised civil society associations organise globally through coalitions and other networks. For example, the global Oxfam network encompassed nearly 3,000 local associations in some 80 countries in 2000 (Hajnal, 2002, pp. 57, 60). Still other global organisations involve clandestine operations like transworld criminal networks (Berdal and Serrano, 2002).

Some global companies also undertake transworld production. In so-called 'global factories' (Fuentes and Ehrenreich, 1983) or 'global commodity chains' (Gereffi and Korzeniewicz, 1994), different stages of the production of a commodity are sited at several (perhaps very widely scattered) locations on the planet. Thus, in principle, the research centre, design unit, procurement office, fabrication plant, finishing point, assembly line, quality control operation, data processing office, advertising bureau and after-sales service could each be situated in different provinces, countries and regions across the planet. Global production involves intra-firm trade within a transworld company as well as, if not more than, international trade between countries. Through so-called 'global sourcing', a producer draws the required inputs from a transplanetary field, rather than being restricted to a particular country or region. Differences in local costs of labour, raw materials, regulation and taxation often figure more importantly in these business calculations than the costs of transport across distance and borders between the various sites in the global production chain. This type of manufacture has developed especially in respect of textiles, clothing, motor vehicles, leather goods, sports articles, toys, optical products, consumer electronics, semiconductors, aircraft and construction equipment. A global production process has supraterritorial qualities inasmuch as it occurs simultaneously and with tight coordination across a transworld space.

Globality can be manifested in consumption as well as production. Many commodities are distributed and sold through global markets, sometimes through a tightly coordinated supraterritorial business strategy. In this way consumers dispersed across the planet purchase the same good or service, often under a single brand name like Nike, Pepsi-Cola or Toyota. Already in the 1980s, Howard Perlmutter of the Wharton Business School identified 136 industries where a global marketing strategy had supposedly become vital to commercial success (Main, 1989, p. 55). The vast range of global products has come to include many raw materials, packaged foods, bottled beverages, cigarettes, designer clothes, household articles and appliances, pharmaceuticals, music recordings, audio-visual productions, printed publications, online information services, financial instruments, office equipment, armaments, transport vehicles, travel services and more. Citicorp has proclaimed itself to be 'your global bank', and Peter Stuyvesant has marketed itself as 'the global cigarette'. Transworld products have come to figure in the everyday lives of much of humanity, whether through actual purchases or through unfulfilled desires evoked by global advertising.

Global communications, global travel, global production and global markets have all promoted, and been facilitated by, global money. That is, some units of account, means of payment, stores of value and mediums of exchange have transplanetary circulation. For example, the 'US' dollar, the 'Japanese' yen, the 'British' pound and other major denominations are much more than national currencies. As supraterritorial monies, they are used anywhere on earth at the same time and move (electronically and via air transport) anywhere on earth in effectively no time. In addition, the Special Drawing Right (SDR) and the euro have emerged through the IMF and the EU, respectively, as suprastate monies with transworld circulation. Many bankcards can extract cash in local currency from the 900,000 automated teller machines (ATMs) in over 120 countries that are today connected to supraterritorial networks like Maestro and Cirrus (MasterCard, 2003). Several credit cards like Visa, MasterCard and American Express can be used for payments at countless establishments in almost every country across the planet. Although not yet in wide usage, digital money can be stored on certain smart cards (so-called electronic purses) in multiple currencies at once, creating something of a global wallet.

Globality also appears in many areas of finance. For instance, most foreign exchange transactions today take place through a round-the-globe, round-the-clock market that connects the dealing rooms of New York, Sydney, Tokyo, Singapore, Hong Kong, Zürich, Frankfurt and London. In global banking, depositors place their savings in a global currency and/or at a global bank and/or at a global branch location such as a so-called 'offshore' financial centre. These practices contrast with territorial banking, in which clients deposit their savings in their national currency at a local or national bank within their country of residence. With transworld payments, migrant workers use global banking networks to remit some of their earnings to relations at another corner of the planet. Meanwhile global bank loans occur when a lender (or syndicate of lenders, perhaps spread across several countries) provides credit in a global currency. Thus, for example, a group of banks based in Austria, the Netherlands and the UK might issue a loan in US dollars to a borrower in the Dominican Republic. The level of interest on such a credit is generally not the prevailing national percentage, but a function of a supraterritorial benchmark like the London InterBank Offered Rate (LIBOR). At the same time, micro-credit schemes in local communities can be linked to global programmes. Similarly, global bonds (often called 'eurobonds') involve a transworld currency as well as borrowers, investors, a syndicate of managers and securities exchanges that are spread across multiple countries.

Global financial transactions also occur on similar lines in respect of medium-term notes and short-term credit instruments like treasury bills and commercial paper. In equity markets, meanwhile, global shares are company stocks that are: (a) listed on several securities exchanges across the earth; and/or (b) held by investors spread across the planet. For their part derivatives have a global character when, for example, the same futures contract is traded simultaneously on the Chicago, Singapore and London markets, as well as through electronic links between them. Insurance policies, too, can have global coverage in a global currency and/or are handled by global companies in global financial centres. In addition, many private and institutional investors maintain global portfolios. That is, they spread their funds across banks, stocks, bonds, money-market tools, derivatives contracts and insurance policies from around the globe. Indeed, with supraterritorial dealing, a broker can buy and sell financial instruments anywhere on the planet instantaneously with a telephone call or the click of a mouse. Several major financial markets like the National Association of Securities Dealers Automated Quotation system (Nasdaq) have no fixed territorial meeting place at all. In sum, then, much of today's foreign exchange, banking, securities, derivatives and insurance business occurs with considerable delinkage from territorial space.

Globality is further manifested in some military activities. Contemporary arsenals include a number of global weapons that can range across pretty well any distance over the earth. Examples include spy satellites, long-range bomber and surveillance aircraft, and unpiloted intercontinental missiles. Global warfare occurs when a campaign of armed combat is pursued from widely spread points across the planet. For instance, although the battlefields lay in Iraq, the 2003 war against Saddam Hussein's Ba'ath regime involved command headquarters in the USA and Qatar, air bases in Europe and Kuwait, troops and arms from several continents, and satellites in outer space. Likewise, the British military had a global presence with troops in over 80 countries as of 2002 (*Financial Times*, 12 July, 2002). So-called 'rapid reaction forces' can be deployed anywhere on the planet within hours. UN peacekeeping operations involve multinational armies deployed anywhere on earth. Certain paramilitary groups like al'Qaeda and the Irish Republican Army (IRA) have also operated as transworld networks. The attacks of 11 September, 2001, brought home as never before the potential impact of informal global armies using global communications and global finance.

Ecologically, a planetary life-support system has of course operated from the moment that the first organisms appeared on earth. However, some matters of social ecology can also have global qualities. Several major anthropogenic (i.e. human-induced) environmental changes have had a pronounced transworld dimension. For example, the anthropogenic greenhouse effect is allegedly pro-ducing planetary climate change, popularly known as 'global warming'. Neither the causes nor the effects of this trend can be territorially specified and restricted. Similarly, stratospheric ozone depletion (and its reversal) is effectively a dis-tanceless and borderless process. With respect to the biosphere, the contemporary global world is experiencing major reductions in the diversity of ecosystems, in the number of species of life, and in the variety of genes that circulate within individual species. In contemporary genetic engineering, recombinant DNA tech-niques allow a gene to be taken from one organism anywhere on earth and put in a second at any other location. Another headline global ecological issue asks how many people the planet can support at one time. Further environmental conditions with global aspects include radioactive fallout, flows of sulphur dioxide and nitrogen oxide (so-called 'acid rain'), the depletion of tropical moist forests, desertification, changes in sea level, marine pollution, management of ocean fish stocks, big dams, possible future shortages of fresh water and arable soil, and waste disposal in outer space. Although the severity of these various ecological problems can be debated, it is clear that none of them is confined to a particular country or region.

Sometimes closely related with ecological concerns, a number of health matters, too, have global dimensions (WHO, 2001; and Pirages, 2006). Since prehistory natural forces of waters and winds have transported microorganisms across the planet. In addition, people have for many centuries carried a number of communicable diseases across and between continents, including plague, smallpox, anthrax, cholera, syphilis, measles, tuberculosis and influenza. Contemporary times have raised the speed and magnitude of global spreads of various human, animal and plant diseases. Examples include HIV/AIDS, SARS, BSE, foot and mouth disease, and gemini viruses. For viruses and bacteria, the planet is one microbial pool in which pathogens do not carry passports. Other questions of human health with clear transplanetary aspects include those related to diet, drug use, occupational conditions and tobacco consumption. Needless to say, successful strategies to address these issues also require a partly global approach.

Much globality is also found in the area of law. Countless formal rules and regulations have acquired a transworld character. The widely diverse examples include various arms control schemes, criminal laws, environmental agreements, human rights conventions, technical standards and trade rules. In addition, some law firms have developed transworld networks of offices, while police forces have pursued transplanetary cooperation through the International Criminal Police Organisation (Interpol). Global suprastate courts include the International Court of Justice (ICJ), ad hoc war crimes tribunals, and the recently established International Criminal Court (ICC). In addition, some national courts hear cases that relate to transworld issues, such as various global intellectual property claims that are brought before US tribunals.

Finally, globality is evident in social relations through global consciousness. In other words, people often think globally. In addition to holding microcosmic conceptions of the social realm as a district or a country, people can also hold macrocosmic notions, where the planet is regarded as a 'global village'. Globally minded people regard the planet as a principal source of their food supplies, their entertainments, their threats and their friends. Some workers like Ghanaian traders and Filipina domestics see the whole earth (as opposed to a particular locality or country) as their potential workplace. Transworld consciousness also takes form in certain languages (e.g. English, Esperanto and Spanish), certain icons (e.g. Coca-Cola labels and world heritage sites), certain narratives (e.g. soap operas), certain fashions (e.g. blue jeans), certain rituals (e.g. sending postcards) and other symbols. Awareness of the planet as a single social place is furthermore evident in events like global sports competitions (including global supporters clubs), global exhibitions, global film festivals, global tours by music superstars, global conferences and global panics. In addition, global consciousness arises when people conceive of their social affiliations in transplanetary, supraterritorial terms, for instance, with transworld solidarities based on class, gender, generation, profession, race, religion, sexuality and indeed humanity as such. Stories of aliens from outer space seem telling in this regard: the foreign other is conceived not as another nationality from another territory, but as another being from another planet, thereby defining humanity and the earth as one.

The preceding survey of the many instances of globality demonstrates the widespread incidence of transplanetary – including more particularly supraterritorial – circumstances across contemporary social life. Cumulatively, all of this global communication, global travel, global organisation, global production, global consumption, global money, global finance, global military, global ecology, global health, global law and global consciousness indicates that contemporary social relations cannot be described without extensive reference to transworld spaces.

5. QUALIFICATIONS

The preceding discussion has made a strong case for what globalisation *is*, in terms of a change in social space that is both quantitatively and qualitatively significant. However, it is equally important to emphasise what the growth in transplanetary connections and the spread of supraterritoriality do *not* entail. In particular it is crucial to reject the following six *non sequiturs*: globalism, reification, global/local binaries, cultural homogenisation, universality and political neutrality.

a. Globalism

First, then, the rise of supraterritoriality in no way means that territorial space has ceased to matter. We should not replace territorialism with a globalist methodology that looks *only* at transplanetary relations and ignores the importance of territorial spaces. We do not live in a 'borderless world' where territory is 'obsolescent' (Ohmae, 1990; and Rosecrance, 1995). Although contemporary history has witnessed the end of territorial*ism* (where social space is effectively reducible to territorial grids), we have certainly not seen the end of territoriali*ty*. To say that social geography can no longer be understood in terms of territoriality alone is of course not to say that territoriality has become irrelevant.

On the contrary, territorial production, territorial governance mechanisms, territorial ecology and territorial identities remain highly significant at the start of the twenty-first century, even if they do not monopolise the situation as before. For example, many communications links like airports, roads, railways and shipping lanes remain territorially fixed. Several recent economic studies have suggested that territorial distance remains a strong influence on trade in manufactures as well as – perhaps more surprisingly – financial assets (Portes and Rey, 1999; and Aviat and Coeurdacier, 2004). In other words, people are still more likely to do foreign business with countries that are territorially closer. In addition, territorial borders continue to exert strong influences on movements of material goods and people (Helliwell, 1998). It can take months to complete the dozens of official documents required to export legally from India. Meanwhile, countless localised products remain bound to particular territorial markets. Largely territorially bound commodities derived from agriculture and mining have persisted at the same time that largely supraterritorial commodities like information and communications have risen to prominence. While US dollars and Visa card payments cross the planet instantly, many other forms of money continue to have restricted circulation within a given territorial domain, and national currencies show no sign of disappearing altogether (Gilbert and Helleiner, 1999). Most people today still hold their bank accounts at a local branch or do no banking at all. Much ecological degradation is linked to specific territorial locations, for instance, of overgrazing, salination or dumping of toxic wastes. In terms of social affiliations, some observers have suggested that territorially bound identities could even have become more rather than less significant in a world of diminishing territorial barriers (Mlinar, 1992; and Harvey, 1993).

So the end of territorialism has not marked the start of globalism. The addition of supraterritorial qualities of geography has not eliminated the territorial aspects (Brenner, 1998 and 1999). Indeed, contemporary globalisation has been closely connected with certain forms of *re*territorialisation like the rise of micro-nationalist politics, urbanisation and the growth of globally connected cities, and the proliferation of offshore arrangements.

Perhaps the most striking reterritorialisation to accompany recent globalisation has been regionalisation. Some of this regionalisation has occurred within states, in cases like Flanders in Belgium or Siberia in Russia. Other regionalisation has had a trans-state character, such as the Basque area across France and Spain or the Kurdish movement across Iran, Iraq, Syria and Turkey. Still other regionalisation has happened between states, in projects like the East African Community and Asia-Pacific Economic Cooperation. And considerable regionalisation has had an unofficial character, as in citizen action initiatives like the European Social Forum.

Clearly, social space in today's world is *both* territorial *and* supraterritorial. Indeed, in social practice the two qualities always intersect. Supraterritoriality is only relatively deterritorialised, and contemporary territoriality is only partly supraterritorialised. Territorial relations are no longer purely territorial, and supraterritorial relations are not wholly non-territorial.

Thus, for example, every Internet user accesses cyberspace from a territorial location. Global products, global finance and global communications always 'touch down' in territorial localities. Supraterritorial military technologies like spy satellites are generally directed at territorial targets. So-called 'global cities' such as London and Tokyo still have a longitude, latitude and altitude. Global ecological changes have territorially specific impacts: for example, rising sea level has different consequences for coastal zones as against uplands.

In short, contemporary society knows no 'pure' globality that exists independently of territorial spaces. The recent accelerated growth of supraterritoriality has brought a relative retreat rather than a complete removal of territoriality. In this sense the term 'deterritorialisation' can have misleading connotations and is therefore avoided here. Global relations today substantially rather than wholly transcend territorial space. Although territoriality does not place insurmountable constraints on supraterritoriality, the new flows still have to engage with territorial locations. The present world is globalising, not totally globalised.

By the same token, however, little if any territoriality today exists independently of supraterritoriality. Most contemporary regional, national, provincial and local conditions co-exist with – and are influenced by – global circumstances. Indeed, territoriality is changed by its encounters with supraterritoriality. For example, territorial states act differently in a globalising world than in a territorialist one. Similarly, territorial identities obtain different dynamics when they are associated with global diasporas (e.g. of Armenians and Sikhs). Territorial environmental issues like local water shortages acquire different significance when they form part of a transworld problem.

In sum, current globalisation is not replacing one compact formula (territorialism) with another (globalism). Rather, the rise of supraterritoriality is bringing greater complexity to geography – and by extension to culture, ecology, economics, history, politics and social psychology as well. The relative simplicity of a territorialist-statist-nationalist world is fading.

b. Reification

The preceding point regarding the interrelation of supraterritorial and territorial spaces points to a second caution, namely, regarding reification. While globality is a discrete concept, it is not a discrete concrete condition. It is helpful, analytically, to distinguish different spheres of social space; however, concretely, the global is not a domain unto itself, separate from the regional, the national, the provincial, the local and the household. There is no purely global circumstance, divorced from other spaces, just as no household, local, provincial, national or regional domain is sealed off from other geographical arenas.

So social space should not be understood as an assemblage of discrete realms, but as an interrelation of spheres within a whole. Events and developments are not global *or* national *or* local *or* some other scale, but an intersection of global *and* other spatial qualities. The global is a dimension of social geography rather than a space in its own right. It is heuristically helpful to distinguish a global quality of contemporary social space, but we must not turn the global into a 'thing' that is separate from regional, national, local and household 'things'.

For example, a government may be sited at a country 'level', but it is a place where supranational, national and subnational spaces converge. Thus states are involved in transworld law and regional arrangements as well as national regulation and relations with provincial and local authorities. Likewise, firms and other actors in today's globalising circumstances are meeting points for co-constituting transworld, regional, national, local and household aspects of geography. Hence the vocabulary of interconnected 'scales' is preferable to that of separated 'levels'.

Avoidance of reification is especially important in these early days of global studies. Several centuries of international studies have suffered dearly from a reified distinction between the national and the international, where the 'internal' and 'domestic' was ontologically separated from the 'external' and 'foreign'. In practice, of course, the 'inside' and the 'outside' of countries are deeply intertwined. These old errors of reifying the international must not be carried over into new research of the global.

c. *Global/Local Binaries*

The interrelatedness of dimensions of social space (as opposed to the existence of separate domains) suggests that it is mistaken – as many have done – to set up oppositions between the global and the local. Such a binary resurrects in new form the misguided domestic/international dichotomy of old. Typically, local/global polarisations have depicted the local as 'here', immediate and intimate, and the global as 'there', distant and isolating. The local is concrete, grounded, authentic and meaningful, whereas the global is abstract, unconnected, artificial and meaningless. The local purportedly provides security and community, while the global houses danger and violence. The local is innocent, the global manipulative. The local is the arena for autonomy and empowerment, the global the realm of dependence and domination. On such assumptions, some critics have rejected globalisation with calls for localisation (Hewison, 1999; and Hines, 2000).

Yet these binaries do not bear up to closer scrutiny. After all, people can have very immediate and intimate relationships with each other via jet travel, telephone and Internet. In contrast, many next-door neighbours in contemporary cities do not even know each other's names. Supraterritorial communities of people (for example, sharing the same class position, ethnicity, religious faith or sexual orientation) can have far-reaching solidarity, whereas localities can experience deep fear, hatred and intolerance. Indigenous peoples have used transworld networks and laws to promote their self-determination, while many a local elite has exercised arbitrary authoritarian power. Global flows frequently involve ordinary people leading everyday lives (listening to radio and munching brand-name fast food), while various exhibits of local culture are contrived. In short, there is nothing inherently alienating about the global and nothing intrinsically liberating about the local.

Instead, both the local and the global have enabling and disabling potentials. Indeed, as already stressed, the two qualities are inseparable in social practice; so terming one circumstance 'local' and another 'global' is actually arbitrary and confusing. For example, globally mobile companies may follow locally tailored marketing strategies, while locally grounded peasants may be globalised through their televisions and religions. A social condition is not positive or negative according to whether it is local as against global, since the situation is generally both local and global at the same time. It is the particular blend of local and global (and other spatial spheres) that matters, not locality versus globality.

d. Cultural Homogenisation

The complexity of multidimensional social space likewise suggests that it is mistaken – as many observers have done – to link globalisation with homogenisation. The growth of transplanetary and supraterritorial connectivity does not *ipso facto* reduce cultural diversity. After all, the global, the regional, the national, the provincial, the local and the household aspects of social space can intertwine in innumerable different combinations. Indeed, by injecting a further dimension into the geographical spectrum – thereby adding to its complexity – globalisation could just as well increase cultural pluralism.

True, the contemporary world has experienced considerable cultural destruction. For example, languages have been disappearing at rates as worrying as those for species extinction (Wurm, 1996). Indigenous peoples' heritages have been undercut or erased across the planet. A high tide of consumerism has seemingly imposed cultural levelling across the world, including via a multitude of global agents such as Carrefour, Michael Jackson, Microsoft and Madison Avenue advertisers.

On the other hand, perceptions of cultural homogenisation in the context of globalisation can be exaggerated. What appears on the surface to be the same transplanetary language can in fact harbour widely varying vocabularies and understandings across different social contexts. So the English of Nairobi markets is not the English of the Scottish Highlands, and the Spanish of East Los Angeles barrios is not the Spanish of Santiago office blocks (Rhedding-Jones, 2002). Likewise, as reception research has shown, different parts of a transworld audience can read hugely different meanings into a Hollywood blockbuster. In this regard it can be questioned how far the diverse viewers actually 'see' the same global film (Tomlinson, 1991). Similarly, global marketers often have to adjust the design and advertisement of transworld products in ways that appeal to diverse cultural contexts. Even an icon of global Americanisation like McDonald's varies its menu considerably across the planet in relation to local sensibilities. Globalisation is also glocalisation (Robertson, 1992, pp. 173–4; and Salcedo, 2003).

In any case, decreasing cultural diversity is not intrinsic to globalisation as such. On the contrary, transplanetary and supraterritorial relations can host great cultural heterogeneity (cf. Breidenbach and Zukrigl, 1998). Multiple world religions occupy sites on the Internet, and all manner of peoples from ethnic diasporas to sexual minorities have formed transworld associations. Indeed, globalisation has offered opportunities to defend cultural diversity, as when indigenous peoples have used UN mechanisms and electronic mass media to promote their particularity (Dowmunt, 1993; and Wilmer, 1993). Globality can also foster cultural innovation. To take one specific example, youth in Frankfurt-am-Main have combined aspects of African-American rap music and hip-hop culture with elements of their North African and Turkish heritages to create novel modes of expression for their hybrid identities in Germany (Bennett, 1999). Some observers take such developments as evidence that contemporary globality is increasingly less westo-centric (Appiah and Gates, 1997, p. ix; and Leclerc, 2000).

In any case, it is clear that globalisation can have heterogenising as well as homogenising effects. There can be, and are, many globalisations (Berger and Huntington, 2002). The overall balance between cultural divergence and convergence lies not in globality as such, but in contextual circumstances. The social power relations that shape transplanetary connections are particularly important in this regard. Thus, to the extent that cultural imperialism afflicts contemporary history, it is largely a problem of the voracity of western modernity rather than an outcome of globalisation *per se*.

e. Universality

A further qualification to notions of globalisation as increased transworld and supraterritorial connectivity must note that the trend has not touched all of humanity to the same extent. Globality links people *anywhere* on the planet, but it does not follow that it connects people *everywhere*, or to the same degree. To repeat the earlier disclaimer, under the definition suggested here globalisation is not universalisation. On the contrary, the incidence of contemporary transplanetary connectivity has varied considerably in relation to territorial and social location. Indeed, some people continue to live lives that are relatively untouched by globality.

In terms of territorial position, global networks have generally involved populations of North America, Western Europe and East Asia more than people in other world regions. Variations in the intensity of globality have also occurred among regions within countries. For example, coastal provinces of China have undergone greater globalisation than the interior of the country. In the USA, residents of Silicon Valley have been more enveloped in global communications than inhabitants of the Dakotas. Across the world, patterns of contemporary globalisation have broadly followed urban-rural lines, with cities and towns generally experiencing more transplanetary connectivity than countrysides.

With regard to social position, wealthy people have on the whole accessed transworld relations more than the poor. While those with the means rush from their global bank to the airport lounge, hundreds of millions of low-income people alive today have never made a telephone call. With respect to gender, men have generally linked up to the Internet much more than women (HDR, 1999, p. 62). Other patterns of uneven entry to, and benefit from, global flows can be discerned in respect of civilisation and race.

To be sure, contemporary globality has not been an exclusively Northern, urban, elite, male, western, white preserve. At the territorial margins, for example, transworld links have extended to remote villages in Africa (Piot, 1999; and Mendonsa, 2001). At the social margins, the homeless of Rio de Janeiro often request a television even before they demand running water (Mariana, 2002). Yet, although globality may have become pervasive, prevailing cultural frameworks, resource distributions and power relationships have produced a highly uneven spread of transplanetary and supraterritorial relations in today's world.

f. Political Neutrality

The foregoing remarks concerning unequal opportunities to use and shape transworld connections highlight the thoroughly political character of globalisation. Human geography is no more politically neutral than any other aspect of social relations like culture or economics. Space always involves politics: processes of acquiring, distributing and exercising social power. A social field is never a level field. Thus transplanetary and supraterritorial connections invariably house power relations and associated power struggles, whether latent or overt. Global links are venues of conflict and cooperation, hierarchy and equality, opportunity and its denial.

Indeed, nothing in globalisation is apolitical. Even seemingly tame questions of transplanetary technical harmonisation have provoked power struggles. For example, in the nineteenth century the British and French governments competed to have the prime meridian (for the measure of longitudes and universal standard time) pass through their respective capitals, with Greenwich eventually winning out. More recently, different computer operating systems have offered users different degrees of initiative and control (Raymond, 1999). It is illusory to think that anything in globality can be divorced from issues of power – and thus also social justice.

Any analysis of globalisation must therefore examine the political aspects involved. On the one hand, these politics involve actors: that is, power relations among individuals, households, associations, firms and governance organisations. In addition, the politics of globalisation involve social structures: that is, power relations between age groups, between civilisations, between classes, between genders, between races, between people holding different sexual orientations, and so on. Like any significant historical trend, the growth of transplanetary and supraterritorial connections empowers some people and disempowers others.

So, as a political process, globalisation is about contests between different interests and competing values. The spread of globality is – and cannot but be – normatively laden and politically charged. It is important to determine whose power rises and whose suffers under currently prevailing practices of globalisation and to consider whether alternative policies could have better political implications.

Indeed, much of the politics of globalisation is about choices. True, powerful forces connected with dominant actors, deep social structures and long-term historical processes have promoted the recent large-scale expansion of transplanetary and supraterritorial connectivity. However, all social actors have opportunities (admittedly unequal) to respond to and mould this trend.

Multiple globalisations are possible. There is nothing inevitable about the scope, speed, direction and consequences of the trend. In particular, as stressed earlier, globalisation as a geographical process and neoliberalism as a political project are not the same thing. Alternative paths of globalisation might be more desirable than the directions that have prevailed over the past quarter-century. Personal and collective decisions (both active and passive) can make a substantial difference.

These ethical choices and political moves include the way that one defines globalisation. As ever, theory and practice are inseparable. Who gets to define globalisation, and who benefits (and loses) from the resultant definition? To deal with the challenges of contemporary globality people need a conception that not only provides intellectual clarification, but also helps to make relevant, wise, responsible and empowering decisions about how to engage with globalisation. Notions of globality as transplanetary and supraterritorial connectivity can well serve the promotion of human security, social justice and democracy in contemporary history.

6. CONCLUSION

This chapter argues that, when defined in a particular geographical fashion, notions of 'globality' and 'globalisation' can be valuable additions to the conceptual toolkit for understanding social relations. Yes, much globe-talk of recent years has revealed nothing new. And yes, loose thinking and careless politics has devalued many ideas of 'globalisation'. However, these shortcomings do not discredit the concept in every form. After all, widespread sloppy usage of other key ideas – 'class', 'democracy', 'rationality' and 'soul', to name but a few – has not been reason to discard these notions altogether.

On the contrary, a definition of globalisation as a respatialisation of social life opens up new knowledge and engages key policy challenges of current history in a constructively critical manner. Notions of 'globality' and 'globalisation' can capture, as no other vocabulary, the present ongoing large-scale growth of trans-planetary – and often also supraterritorial – connectivity. Such an insight offers a highly promising entry point for research and action on contemporary history.

To reiterate, this conception of globalisation has a distinctive focus. It is different from ideas of internationalisation, liberalisation, universalisation and westernisation. The trans-territorial connections of globality are different from the inter-territorial connections of internationality. The transborder transactions of globality are different from the open-border transactions of liberality. The transplanetary simultaneity and instantaneity of supraterritoriality is different from the worldwideness of universality. The geographical focus of globality is different from the cultural focus of western modernity. Although globalisation as defined here has some overlap with, and connections to, internationalisation, liberalisation, universalisation and westernisation, it is not equivalent to any of these older concepts and trends.

Of course, the conception of globalisation elaborated in this chapter is in no way intended to be the last word about what the term might mean. No definition is definitive. The aim is not to issue a final pronouncement, but to offer ever-provisional ideas that provoke further reflection and debate.

REFERENCES

Appiah, K. A. and H. L. Gates (eds.) (1997), *The Dictionary of Global Culture* (New York: Knopf).
Augè, M. (1994), *An Anthropology for Contemporaneous Worlds* (Stanford, CA: Stanford University Press, 1999).
Aviat, A. and N. Coeurdacier (2004), 'The Geography of Trade in Goods and Assets', Paper for the CESifo Venice Summer Institute Workshop on Dissecting Globalization (21–22 July).
Bennett, A. (1999), 'Hip Hop am Main: The Localization of Rap Music and Hip Hop Culture', *Media, Culture and Society*, **21**, 1, 77–91.
Bentham, J. (1789), *An Introduction to the Principles of Morals and Legislation* (London: Hafner, 1948).
Berdal, M. and M. Serrano (eds.) (2002), *Transnational Organized Crime and International Security: Business as Usual?* (Boulder, CO: Rienner).
Berger, P. L. and S. P. Huntington (eds.) (2002), *Many Globalizations: Cultural Diversity in the Contemporary World* (Oxford: Oxford University Press).
Bradford, S. and R. Z. Lawrence (2004), *Has Globalization Gone Far Enough? The Costs of Fragmented Markets* (Washington, DC: Institute for International Economics).
Breidenbach, J. and I. Zukrigl (1998), *Tanz der Kulturen. Kulturelle Identität in einer globalisierten Welt* ['The Dance of Cultures: Cultural Identity in a Globalizing World'] (Munich: Kunstmann).
Brenner, N. (1998), 'Global Cities, Glocal States: Global City Formation and State Territorial Restructuring in Contemporary Europe', *Review of International Political Economy*, **5**, 1, 1–37.

Brenner, N. (1999), 'Beyond State-centrism? Space, Territoriality, and Geographical Scale in Globalization Studies', *Theory and Society*, **28**, 1, 39–78.

Brenner, N., B. Jessop, M. Jones and G. MacLeod (eds.) (2003), *State/Space: A Reader* (Oxford: Blackwell).

Campbell, T. (1987), *The Earliest Printed Maps 1472–1500* (London: British Library).

Castells, M. (1989), *The Informational City: Information Technology, Economic Restructuring, and the Urban-Regional Process* (Oxford: Blackwell).

CSGR (2005), CSGR Globalisation Index, available on the website of the Centre for the Study of Globalisation and Regionalisation (www.csgr.org, accessed on 16 February).

Douglas, I. (1996), 'The Myth of Globali[z]ation: A Poststructural Reading of Speed and Reflexivity in the Governance of Late Modernity', Paper presented at the 38th Annual Convention of the International Studies Association (San Diego, April).

Dowmunt, T. (ed.) (1993), *Channels of Resistance: Global Television and Local Empowerment* (London: BFI/Channel 4).

Ehrenreich, B. and A. R. Hochschild (eds.) (2002), *Global Woman: Nannies, Maids, and Sex Workers in the New Economy* (New York: Metropolitan Books).

Fuentes, A. and B. Ehrenreich (1983), *Women in the Global Factory* (Boston, MA: South End).

Gamble, C. (1994), *Timewalkers: The Prehistory of Global Civilization* (Cambridge, MA: Harvard University Press).

Gereffi, G. and M. Korzeniewicz (eds.) (1994), *Commodity Chains and Global Capitalism* (Westport, CT: Praeger).

Giddens, A. (1990), *The Consequences of Modernity* (Cambridge: Polity).

Giddens, A. (1996), 'On Globalization', excerpts from a keynote address at the UNRISD Conference on Globalization and Citizenship (1 December – at www.unrisd.org) (under 'viewpoints').

Gilbert, E. and E. Helleiner (eds.) (1999), *Nation-states and Money: The Past, Present and Future of National Currencies* (London: Routledge).

Hajnal, P. I. (2002), 'Oxfam International', in P. I. Hajnal (ed.), *Civil Society in the Information Age* (Aldershot: Ashgate), 57–66.

Hanawat, B. A. and M. Kobialka (eds.) (2000), *Medieval Practices of Space* (Minneapolis, MN: University of Minnesota Press).

Harvey, D. (1989), *The Condition of Postmodernity: An Enquiry into the Conditions of Cultural Change* (Oxford: Blackwell).

Harvey, D. (1993), 'From Space to Place and Back Again: Reflections on the Condition of Post-modernity', in J. Bird, B. Curtis, T. Putnam, G. Robertson and L. Tickner (eds.), *Mapping the Futures: Local Cultures, Global Change* (London: Routledge), 3–29.

HDR (1999), *Human Development Report 1999* (New York: Oxford University Press).

Heidegger, M. (1950), 'The Thing', in *Poetry, Language, Thought* (New York: Harper & Row, 1971), 165–82.

Held, D. and A. McGrew (2003), *The Global Transformations Reader: An Introduction to the Globalization Debate* (Cambridge: Polity).

Helliwell, J. F. (1998), *How Much Do National Borders Matter?* (Washington, DC: Brookings Institution Press).

Hewison, K. (1999), *Localism in Thailand: A Study of Globalisation and Its Discontents* (Coventry: ESRC/University of Warwick Centre for the Study of Globalisation and Regionalisation, Working Paper No. 39/99).

Higgott, R. A. and A. Payne (eds.) (2000), *The New Political Economy of Globalization* (Cheltenham: Edward Elgar).

Hines, C. (2000), *Localization: A Global Manifesto* (London: Earthscan).

Hirst, P. and G. Thompson (1999), *Globalization in Question: The International Economy and the Possibilities of Governance* (Cambridge: Polity, 2nd ed.).

Kearney, A. T. (2001), 'Measuring Globalization: Who's Up, Who's Down?', *Foreign Policy*, **122** (January–February), 56–65.

Keohane, R. O. and J. S. Nye (1977), *Power and Interdependence: World Politics in Transition* (Boston, MA: Little, Brown).

Lechner, F. J. and J. Boli (eds.) (2000), *The Globalization Reader* (Oxford: Blackwell).

Leclerc, G. (2000), *La mondialisation culturelle. Les civilisations à l'épreuve* ['Cultural Globalisation: Civilisations to the Test'] (Paris: Presses Universitaires de France).

Lefebvre, H. (1974), *The Production of Space* (Oxford: Blackwell, 1991).

Levitt, T. (1983), 'The Globalization of Markets', *Harvard Business Review*, **61**, 3, 92–102.

LoC (2005), Website of the Library of Congress (http://catalog.loc.gov/, accessed on 7 February).

Main, J. (1989), 'How To Go Global – and Why', *Fortune*, **120**, 5 (28 August), 54–8.

Mariana (2002), Activist with the Homeless Workers Movement (MTST), interviewed by the author in Rio de Janeiro on 28 January.

Marrison, A. (ed.) (1998), *Free Trade and Its Reception 1815–1960* (London: Routledge).

MasterCard (2003), Website of MasterCard (www.mastercard.com, accessed on 18 July and 23 August).

Mendonsa, E. (2001), *Continuity and Change in a West African Society: Globalization's Impact on the Sisala of Ghana* (Durham, NC: Carolina Academic Press).

Merle, M. (1974), *Sociologie des relations internationales* (Paris: Dalloz).

Mittelman, J. H. (2002), 'Globalization: An Ascendant Paradigm?', *International Studies Perspectives*, **3**, 1, 1–14.

Mlinar, Z. (ed.) (1992), *Globalization and Territorial Identities* (Aldershot: Avebury).

MWD (2003), *Merriam-Webster Dictionary* (www.m-w.com/cgi-bin/dictionary, accessed on 16 September).

Nescafé (2003), Website of Nescafé (www.nescafe.com/main_nest.asp, accessed on 14 July).

O'Rourke, K. H. and J. G. Williamson (1999), *Globalization and History: The Evolution of a Nineteenth-century Atlantic Economy* (Cambridge, MA: MIT Press).

OED (1989), *The Oxford English Dictionary* (Oxford: Clarendon, 2nd ed.).

Ohmae, K. (1990), *The Borderless World: Power and Strategy in the Interlinked Economy* (New York: HarperCollins).

Petras, J. and H. Veltmeyer (2001), *Globalization Unmasked: Imperialism in the 21st Century* (London: Zed Books).

Piot, C. (1999), *Remotely Global: Village Modernity in West Africa* (Chicago: University of Chicago Press).

Pirages, D. (2006), 'Disease', in R. Robertson and J. A. Scholte (eds.), *Encyclopedia of Globalization* (London: Routledge).

Pogue, Z. (2001), 'A Look at the First Transatlantic Telesurgery' (accessed at www.stanford.edu/~zpogue/telemedicine/first.htm).

Portes, R. and H. Rey (1999), 'The Determinants of Cross-border Equity Flows', NBER Working Paper 7336.

PTT (1951), *Verslag van het Staatsbedrijf de Posterijen, Telegrafie en Telefonie over het jaar 1950* ['Annual Report for the Year 1950 of the State Post, Telegraph and Telephone Company'] (The Hague: Staatsdrukkerij).

Raymond, E. S. (1999), *The Cathedral and the Bazaar: Musings on Linux and Open Source by an Accidental Revolutionary* (Cambridge, MA: O'Reilly).

Reiser, O. L. and B. Davies (1944), *Planetary Democracy: An Introduction to Scientific Humanism* (New York: Creative Age Press).

Rhedding-Jones, J. (2002), 'English Elsewhere: Glocalization, Assessment and Ethics', *Journal of Curriculum Studies*, **34**, 4, 383–404.

Robertson, R. (1983), 'Interpreting Globality', in *World Realities and International Studies Today* (Glenside, PA: Pennsylvania Council on International Education), 7–20.

Robertson, R. (1992), *Globalization: Social Theory and Global Culture* (London: Sage).

Robertson, R. (2001), 'Globality', in N. J. Smelser and P. B. Baltes (eds.), *International Encyclopedia of the Social and Behavioral Sciences* (Oxford: Elsevier/Pergamon), 6254–8.

Robertson, R. and J. A. Scholte (eds.) (2006), *Encyclopedia of Globalization* (London: Routledge).

Rodrik, D. (2001), *The Global Governance of Trade as if Development Really Mattered* (New York: United Nations Development Programme).

Rosecrance, R. (1995), 'The Obsolescence of Territory', *New Perspectives Quarterly*, **12**, 1, 44–50.

Rosenau, J. N. (1980), *The Study of Global Interdependence: Essays on the Transnationalization of World Affairs* (London: Pinter).

Rosenberg, J. (2001), *The Follies of Globalization Theory: Polemical Essays* (London: Verso).

Ruggie, J. G. (1993), 'Territoriality and Beyond: Problematizing Modernity in International Relations', *International Organization*, **47**, 1, 139–74.

Salcedo, R. (2003), 'When the Global Meets the Local at the Mall', *American Behavioral Scientist*, **46**, 8, 1084–103.

Scholte, J. A. (2005), *Globalization: A Critical Introduction* (Basingstoke: Palgrave Macmillan, 2nd ed.).

Schreiter, R. J. (1997), *The New Catholicity: Theology between the Global and the Local* (Maryknoll, NY: Orbis Books).

Shaw, M. (ed.) (1999), *Politics and Globalisation: Knowledge, Ethics and Agency* (London: Routledge).

Suganami, H. (1978), 'A Note on the Origin of the Word "International"', *British Journal of International Studies*, **4**, 3, 226–32.

Tomlinson, J. (1991), *Cultural Imperialism: A Critical Introduction* (London: Pinter).

Waters, M. (1995), *Globalization* (London: Routledge).

Webster (1961), *Webster's Third New International Dictionary of the English Language Unabridged* (Springfield, MA: Merriam).

Whitfield, P. (1994), *The Image of the World: 20 Centuries of World Maps* (London: British Library).

WHO (2001), 'Special Theme: Globalization', *Bulletin of the World Health Organization*, **79**, 9, 802–4, 827–93.

Wilmer, F. (1993), *The Indigenous Voice in World Politics: Since Time Immemorial* (London: Sage).

Wurm, S. A. (ed.) (1996), *Atlas of the World's Languages in Danger of Disappearing* (Paris: United Nations Educational, Scientific and Cultural Organisation).

Zumthor, P. (1993), *La mesure du monde. Représentation de l'espace au Moyen Age* ['The Scale of the World: Representation of Space in the Middle Ages'] (Paris: Seuil).

9

Globalisation and Values

John Whalley

1. INTRODUCTION

*T*HIS chapter discusses how globalisation processes can affect social values and vice versa. It takes as its notion of values communally shared beliefs (such as rankings of considerations in defining social arrangements such as responsibility and freedom, order and liberty, religious beliefs, attitudes towards materialism, attitudes towards the natural environment, communal identification). Accepting that values differ between both societies and economies, I treat social values as providing a broad framework within which economies operate as a part of a linked social system. I consider values as a system of jointly accepted constraints on individual behaviour in the tradition of Parsons (1949), and as the central defining entity of what we understand by the term society. I then examine how globalisation viewed in its economic dimensions as ever deeper market-based integration can influence values and how values can influence the impacts of globalisation.

I suggest that the main focus of literature on social values in disciplines outside of economics (sociology, political science) has been to describe, classify and rationalise alternative conceptualisations of both society and communally accepted value systems. The discussion is of the historical evolution of societies; whether social structures can be adequately represented by equilibrium processes (or whether conflict and discrete change is the norm); whether collectively held values are consistent with individual rationality; and what descriptions of value systems best represent different social entities (communities, nations, families, civilisations). These discussions occur along with various speculations and arguments as to how value systems may evolve in the future given historical patterns from the past.

Earlier versions of this chapter were presented at a CESifo area group meeting held in Munich, 29/30 January, 2004, and at CSGR (Warwick), prior to the CESifo conference 'Dissecting Globalisation', held in Venice, 23/24 July, 2005. The author is grateful to Robin Cohen, Sian Sullivan, Marc Muendler, Syed Ahsan, Ray Riesman, Hans Werner Sinn and James Brassett, and seminar and conference participants for comments. Referees on the earlier draft also provided helpful remarks. It draws on discussions with Jan Aart Scholte, Richard Higgott, Andrew Cooper and Bob Young. The author is grateful to Edgar Cudmore, Manish Pandey and Josh Svatek for research support.

In broader globalisation debate how a more globalised world both changes and interacts with nationally based value systems in a central issue. My objective here is narrower, namely to discuss possible interactions between social values and globalisation shocks from viewpoints that seem natural to economists who work with analytical structures that can be used for comparative static analyses. Accepting that different value systems occur in different societies, I ask how they can jointly interact, change and adapt when societies are subjected to various shocks associated with globalisation, such as deeper market integration, increased speed of transactions across societies, more rapid technical progress, economic marginalisation within and between societies and other globally driven forces for changes. Can the values of one society come to dominate or subsume those of another if, say, market-based integration occurs across two or more economies?

And if economies are only part of wider social systems, what form of inter-connection/interpenetration of values inevitably occurs if market-driven globalisation occurs? Can value systems blend one with another under the influence of market-based globalisation, assimilating features of each? Can values of weaker societies effectively become dysfunctional and collapse, and what are the consequences if this happens? What might happen if the values of one society are myopically (or naively) transplanted into another society; and what can be the impact on economic (and wider) social performance? Are the impacts on economic performance of value erosion or strengthening likely to be large or small compared to existing estimates of more conventional economic impacts of market liberalisation and integration? How should effects on values be traded off against more conventional economic impacts of policy reform, such as the gains from trade when trade liberalisation occurs.

My aim is to transplant the thinking of economists into other disciplines in ways which other disciplines may find helpful, while at the same time posing issues raised by other disciplines for economists in language closer to theirs. In the process the idea ultimately is to blend analytical techniques from economics into the discussion and language of other disciplines when analysing the effects of globalisation. I suggest that considerable portions of analytical economics literature, such as that on tax competition, policy coordination, currency competition (bimetallism), the design of international institutions and other matters can be drawn on and results from these might suggest how value systems could interact in various circumstances. I discuss what some of the elements of value system interaction could be in global trade policy disputes/clashes, and discuss the relationship of these to Huntington's (1996) characterisation of globalisation as a clash of civilisations. In some (but not all) cases I also suggest that the indirect channels of globalisation's impacts first on social values and as a consequence on economic performance, may be as, if not more, important for evaluating what impacts globalisation on economic performance are than the direct effects discussed in more conventional economics literature (such as impacts on consumption, production and welfare).

The (perhaps unsurprising to some) conclusion is that social values can interact under globalisation in complex ways and likely there is no general statement as to what outcomes will be observed since there are many scenarios as to how things might unfold. But if gains (or losses) from globalisation go beyond conventional economic impacts such as the gains from trade, and if globalisation pressures which modify societal values both for better and for worse are (as I believe) central to the globalisation process, then this may be an area also worthy of other economists' attention. These conclusions may not seem insightful for analytical economists seeking clean general statements from formalised analytical models allowing deductive logic to be carefully applied, but value system interaction is frequently raised as a potentially important area of impact for globalisation-driven change, and the relative lack of discussion by economists of these issues motivates the discussions here.

2. SOCIAL VALUES AND SOCIAL CAPITAL

For the purposes of the current discussion, I use the term social values in the sense of Parsons (1949) as relating to shared beliefs within a group of individuals living in a society which have the effect of constraining and partially determining individual behaviour. These may be religious beliefs, attitudes to materialism and property in general, attitudes towards the natural environment, agreements on collective governance, or jointly shared positions on the relative importance of objectives in defining social arrangements. The latter may reflect the relative importance of responsibility and freedom (an Asian/European-North American difference), of between order and good government and individual liberty (a difference between the US Constitution and the British North America Act which shaped Canadian identity).[1]

Typically social values are not shared in the same way by all members of a society and opinions will differ and conflict will occur over what should be the jointly accepted commitments underlying the value system reflected in constitutional

---

[1] The distinctiveness of national character, and hence social value systems is repeatedly stressed in nationalistic literature. For instance, Lin (1935) in his famous discussion of the Chinese character (p. 57) remarks '. . . the Chinese are a hard-boiled lot. There is no nonsense about them; they do not live in order to die, as the Christians pretend to do, nor do they seek for a Utopia on earth, as many seers of the West do. They just want to order this life on earth, which they know to be full of pain and sorrow, so that they may work peaceably, endure nobily, and live happily. Of the noble virtues of the West, of nobility, ambition, zeal for reform, public spirit, sense for adventure and heroic courage, the Chinese are devoid. They cannot be interested in climbing Mont Blanc or in exploring the North Pole. But they are tremendously interested in this commonplace world, and they have an indomitable patience, an indefatigable industry, a sense of duty, a level-headed commonsense, cheerfulness, humour, tolerance, pacificism, and that unequalled genius for finding happiness in hard environments which we call contentment – qualities that make this commonplace life enjoyable to them. And chief of these are pacificism and tolerance, which are the mark of a mellow culture, and which seem to be lacking in modern Europe'.

and legal arrangements. For now, I will assume that some system of beliefs can be represented as the jointly agreed values of the collective itself (the nation, if you will).

As such, social values is a considerably broader term than social capital, as emphasised in recent literature in economics and sociology (Loury, 1977; Coleman, 1988; Portes, 1998; and Manski, 2000). Social capital relates to collective commitment in the form of trust, honesty and other elements of social arrangements necessary for the execution of individual optimisation plans, and is something whose level can be raised by investment of time and resources. Social values define the constraints on behaviour that mutually accepted beliefs imply and can be thought of as reflecting shared beliefs as to how individuals relate to one another in many aspects of their daily lives. Values differ from social capital in providing the framework for communally acceptable individual behaviour within which both societies and economies function. If accepted as determinants of individuals' behaviour they qualify (or add to) the view that individual self-interest alone motivates individual behaviour.

In the humanities societal values are taken as embodied in the literature, music, art, architecture and other forms of expression created by a smaller number of members of society as a distinctive representation and manifestation of the collective identity of society itself. Cunningham and Reich (1994) document the emergence of Western societies from prehistory to the present day in these terms, equating the evolution of Western values with the development of Western civilisation. Embree (1972) describes a similar process for the emergence of Vedic culture and values in South Asia and neighbouring areas.

Since Parsons, social values have been taken to be important for the many social structures in which individuals simultaneously participate, many of which cross national boundaries (families, religious or ethnic groups, local or regional communities, work, related groups, gender groups, and many more). Whether acceptance of social value-based arrangements is in the individual self-interest is an issue discussed in sociological literature on values, as is how and why value systems embodying such implicit agreements come about. Economists in their workings tend to focus more on the ways in which societal values (norms) can influence individual behaviour, and less on how they arise. Akerlof (1984) and Leibenstein (1950) are examples. The classical economist most centrally credited with discussion of how societal norms and individual behaviour interact is Veblen (1899), who used the term conspicuous consumption to indicate consumption activity undertaken largely for its effects on an individual's reputation with others.

For the purposes of the discussion here, I will adopt a narrow concept of social values which I adopt specifically for my discussion of links between values and globalisation seen in terms of market-based integration. I follow Granovetter (1985) and stress that market-based economies function in ways that reflect their embedment in wider social structures. Arrangements for private property will differ, mechanisms to protect natural habitat in the presence of market-based activities will vary, religious beliefs may limit both the type and form of market transactions, and social conventions will come into play as it is not possible to rely on legal contracts alone to detail what exchange or production activity will actually take place since there are always elements of ambiguity in the execution of all contractual arrangements. Thus, what economists typically characterise as an economy, i.e. a set of individuals (or households) with endowments and preferences in an Arrow-Debreu (1954) pure exchange or with production framework, should in reality be placed in a wider social context in which social values play potentially a major role in both facilitating and constraining the market-based transactions at the heart of an Arrow-Debreu world. In turn, social values are themselves affected as different market-based transactions occur.

Earlier discussions of the embeddedness of market transactions in social systems can be found in Arrow (1970) and the literature on social capital (Loury, 1977; Coleman, 1988; Matthews, 1986; North, 1997; Collier, 1998; Portes, 1998; Manski, 2000; and Durlauf and Falchamps, 2004), where social capital is taken to refer to communal arrangements that affect individual behaviour (such as the trustworthiness and honesty of others). Social capital, in turn, is something that can be invested in through joint commitment of time and resources. Social capital is thus something which can be added to through investment in joint commitment, and in a *de novo* world no social capital would exist.

Values in contrast denote the environment into which individuals are born as social animals and live their lives. They reflect shared religious beliefs, attitudes to property, accepted codes of moral conduct and other elements of social arrangements which both constrain individual behaviour and act as shared or collective identity. Their sharing and acceptance is a key part of the socialisation process stressed by Parsons, and a *de novo* world without values is hard to imagine. Children are raised by parents in ways which reflect how, as children, they were similarly treated. As mature adults they expect to both care for their parents and their own children since this is what they learn from their own parents. Within communities (villages, for instance) members accept that they will help each other in times of stress (bad harvests and weather) since they jointly implicitly agree to coinsurance and experience such arrangements from birth. The commitments reflected in value systems do not involve investment of time and resources, as with social capital (such as the accumulation of trust when implementing transactions as stressed in social capital literature). They exist as part of the social endowment, and they change and evolve over time with changed beliefs, perspectives and circumstances, some of which can reflect globalisation-induced change.

One example how market-based arrangements and social values interact reflects the inability in practice of individuals to fully synchronise the timing of all transactions and to fully monitor the quality and reliability of goods transacted upon delivery. Thus, if buyers and sellers of commodities in markets do not accept each other as having shared values, they may suspect that their market partner may not faithfully execute what is agreed between them. If values differ between the transactors, market transactions may be more difficult to execute and overall economic efficiency may suffer.

One might claim on these grounds that market-oriented reforms were implemented in Russia after 1991 in part as property-right-enhancing reforms in the hope they might make reversion to the previous regime of collectivist central planning more difficult and that the outcome in the absence of needed modifications to shared social values to allow for efficient market transactions was economic implosion on a major scale. This precipitated a large fall in income per capita over seven years in both Russia and most other former Soviet republics (by perhaps 35–50 per cent), with reversion to inefficient barter trade, extensive tax evasion and asset stripping in enterprises. Underlying this economic collapse was the delayed value system changes needed to fully support the newly established market arrangements. Growth in Russia since the financial crisis of 1998 could then be taken to represent the eventual evolution of supportive value system change for the market-oriented reforms of 1991. This explanation also raises the issue of whether slower and more successful policy change in China reflected realism as to the initial smaller value system modification.

The contention I make for the purposes of this chapter is that for their efficient functioning market-based economies in reality need a supportive system of reasonably widely shared social values which provide a fair degree of certainty to market transactors of the behaviour they will encounter from others. If value systems become less supportive of markets or new market arrangements need changes in value-based arrangements for their successful implementation, economic transactions can take more time with more resources devoted to verify completion of agreed contracts. Individuals find *ex post* mechanisms to resolve disputes (returning goods, receiving refunds, etc.) less satisfactory, and weakened social values impair market-based economic performance.

At the same time, the social values that perform this role can themselves be affected by changed market activity and in ways which affect both collective identity and how individuals see their own participation in the wider social structure. This may be in ways which are either beneficial or retrograde. Growth, for instance, may lead to more dynamism and confidence in the future which might strengthen supportive value system arrangements. But if economic growth reinforces a sense of collective identity which is seen as excessively materially oriented and neglectful of people in their own right over property and possessions, such changes in values might alternatively be viewed as retrograde.[2]

---

[2] See recent literature in economic psychology (Kasser and Kasser, 2001; and Kasser and Kanner, 2004) which reports on research showing that when people rate the relative importance of materialistic values highly compared to other values such as self-acceptance, community belonging and interpersonal relationships, a lower quality of life is also reported. For instance, in clinical studies mature adolescents with stronger materialistic motivation report lower vitality, as well as more depression and anxiety.

3. SOCIAL THOUGHT AND SOCIAL VALUES

The literature on social thought does not discuss social value in quite the same ways as I do above, but it does build centrally on the notion that there is a distinct entity which one can term society, and that (at least in older thought) this can both be studied objectively and its jointly shared values both constrain and partly determine individual actions. Sociologists over the years have devoted much energy to discussing society and its associated value systems in these terms, and I perhaps do this literature poor justice in the ways I bring it into my discussion here.

Sociological theories of society are often traced to the Enlightenment and to Auguste Comte whose ideas were formed during the French Revolution, and the political and social instability which followed involving republican governments, monarchy and the Napoleonic empire. Comte's objective was to develop a vision for France of a better society which he hoped would take France out of its instability and provide social progress for all. He saw society as an organism progressively evolving from simple to more complex forms, and he tried to uncover rules that governed both the structure and evolution of social inter-actions. In so doing, he studied the implicit rules and institutions which organise society as a whole, separate from the direct interests of the individuals who live in the social structure. He tried to explain how social structures come about and analyse how individual self-interest can best be restrained by social conventions so that social stability ensues. He emphasised the role of family, government and religion in the emergence and operation of social value systems.

Subsequent nineteenth-century writers further developed the same notion that society is an entity shaping and constraining individual behaviour that exists beyond the individual interests of its participants. This included thinkers that modern-day economists think of as analysing largely only individualistic behaviour, such as Marshall and Pareto (both of whose views on these matters are discussed at length along with Durkheim and Weber as founders of modern sociology by Parsons, 1949). Thus Marx (see Avineri, 1978) developed a class-based framework for looking at society, with individuals (or households) seen as members of classes and history as largely reflecting the outcome of class struggles. Later, Durkheim (1933) analysed modern society as evolving from segmented traditional structures to more formally organised entities with laws and supporting institutions. His study of society (in Siedman's, 2004, words) was of 'shared institutions, cultural beliefs, and social conventions that are irreducible to individual psychology'. Weber (1951 and 1958) studied the social value systems of Western Europe and China, seeking in part to explain why religious value systems in Europe had generated the Industrial Revolution, and why this same outcome had not occurred in Imperial China.

Twentieth-century writers developed more complex conceptualisations of both society and its associated value systems. Parsons (1949) saw the actions of individuals within any social structure as determined both by individually based choice and jointly accepted constraints on these choices, with these constraints determined simultaneously along with the precise form of the social structure itself. Parsons explicitly rejected notions of individual self-interest is reflecting Darwinian natural selection and survival (genetic determinism) and accounting for the evolution of social structure as appears in contemporary socio-biology literature (see Dawkins, 1976; and Wilson, 1980). Instead, social order arose from a process of social coordination and cultural consensus. In this, the needs and motivations of the individual and the role requirements of the social entity fitted each other. Social disorder arose from allocative conflict; divisions over who gets what. Disruption of social order was inevitable as societies were subject to external shocks. If social order broke down all together, the coercive force of the state (police, military, law) might be resorted to so as to restore social order.

In Parsons' approach to society, individuals are seen as having both identification with and a sense of joint ownership in society as a whole. Individuals are attached to class, ethnic, racial and other groupings, and in modern states also to national communities; communities of national citizens. Parsons did not discuss global identity, and how a process of globalisation might eventually fuse separate national identities into a combined and multifaceted global identity. Nor is there any discussion of how societies and social values may cross national borders in ways which no longer overlap with nation states. The Parsonian view of the world centred on societies as nation states.

Later sociological literature contains many elaborations on this theme as well as challenges to its central notions. Berger and Luckmann (1967), for instance, further developed Parsons' ideas by asserting an objective reality for society which they saw (again in Siedman's, 2004, words) as

> part of a more encompassing supra-human order of nature or the divine. Social institutions are granted authority not by mere human but by divine decree, natural law, or historical destiny. Religion, philosophy, myth, and science have been the chief symbolic strategies of social legitimation. They re-establish everyday perceptions of the social world as an objective order that can ground our subjective experience as orderly, coherent, and purposeful.

Subsequent writers, such as Blau (1975) and Collins (1986) advanced what they portrayed as a scientific theory of social structure. Collins saw all human beings as 'sociably conflict-prone animals'. Blau explained how social order prevailed using a theory of social structure reflecting distributions of individuals across a range of social metrics (gender, age, race, income), some of which were discrete (race) and others continuous (income).

Other literature fundamentally challenges the Parsonian view of society. Conflict theory, as advanced by Dahrendorf (1959), suggests that role structures within society inevitably generate conflict and hence societies continually change and evolve; ideas taken further in a widely cited reformulation and extension of

Parsons' ideas by Giddens (1973) captured in the term structuralism. Related notions of symbolic interactionism were developed by Blumer (1969) and Roch (1979) as a new societal construct, as were phenomenological sociology and ethnomethodology by Garfinkel (1967) and Cicourel (1973).

In recent literature on globalisation, Beck (1999) focuses on the need to understand what he calls a 'world risk society', looking at ecological and technological risk, and their social and political implications. This forms the basis for Beck's call for a 'Cosmopolitan Manifesto' to address the joint evolution of global and local communities responding to issues which national politics cannot adequately address.

Wallerstein (2001) emphasises the need to re- (or, un)think the paradigms of nineteenth-century social thought that limit discussion of the ways in which contemporary processes such as globalisation can be dealt with at a societal level. Wallerstein's world-systems analysis is less a theory of the social structures of the modern world than a critique of how he sees scientific social inquiry being undertaken. Castells (2004), in an influential three-volume piece, tries to account for the complex intertwinings of progressive and reactionary forces underpinning globalisation and its related forces, which he sees as changing our current world. The objectives of anti-globalisation movements are analysed in this work, along with associated economic and political implications.

For the purposes of my discussion here, I simply take all of this literature as supporting the claim that individuals do indeed have collective identity and this is part of the system of social values. Both this collective identity and other elements of the system of social values both constrain and influence individual behaviour in ways which go beyond narrowly conceived individual self-interest.

If this is accepted, then concern both over how values affect behaviour, and changed market behaviour can change values become part of discussion of the effects of globalisation, including analyses undertaken by economists. Understanding how collective identity enters individual decision making may be necessary to make realistic assessments of the impacts of globalisation on economic performance; and market-based globalisation itself may have important implications for values and collective identity. As globalisation in the form of market-based integration moves forward, the conjecture is that an evolving multifaceted global social value system will evolve. If supportive it will more easily facilitate market-based transactions, and if less supportive may retard economic progress. How global value systems change for better or for worse under a globalisation (integration) process involving individual nation states is also an issue.

This line of inquiry points in several directions. One is how we evaluate both the positive and negative influences of value system change and adaptation when discussing particular global policy initiatives as elements of globalisation, such as trade liberalisation. Another is to how the process of value system change under globalisation shocks can be analysed; does it necessarily lead to improved societal performance or can value system displacement be harmful? Yet another (and even more difficult) task is to quantify such effects. These and other questions are taken up in the next sections which discuss how economic literature might be brought to bear in thinking through ways in which globalisation shocks and socially-based value systems might jointly evolve.

4. THE GLOBALISATION PROCESS AS EXTERNAL SHOCKS AFFECTING VALUE SYSTEMS

Globalisation debate often seems to revolve around a set of repeatedly asked but ill-defined questions; is globalisation good or bad; does it hurt the poor; has it gone too far; should it be stopped, banned, or even imprisoned? Anti-globalisation literature (Greider, 1997; Klein, 1999; and others) in turn covers many sub-areas, including corporatism, branding, outsourcing, financial mania, the impacts on power of multinational companies, and other elements.[3]

The reality as Higgott (2002) points out is that globalisation is a contested concept; something we all talk about, have opinions over, are not quite sure what it is. But whatever globalisation is, there is little doubt that people are talking about it, and globally. Alan Greenspan, for instance, suggested in a recent speech that WTO trade liberalisation should be accelerated to protect globalisation, without fully specifying the interest of the Federal Reserve in this matter, what globalisation and WTO trade liberalisation really were, and why, anyway, globalisation was in need of protection.

A central difficulty when discussing globalisation is that the term means different things to different disciplines, and even to individual researchers within disciplines. Discussing the effects of globalisation on social value systems can thus involve many different discussions with disjoint terminology which can be hard to simultaneously join.

To economists globalisation is typically growing trade, ever more foreign investment, increased speed of transactions in financial markets, international diffusion of technology, internationally more mobile labour, and other facets of ever deeper economic integration across national borders. The central element is market-based integration as a process in which national barriers to flows of goods, capital and labour come down and the global economy moves ever closer towards a single globally integrated market economy and away from nationally segmented markets. Along with this goes globally integrated production units, global companies, global branding and issues of power of corporate entities.

---

[3] Economists have responded to anti-globalisation arguments in a series of pieces (see Deardorff, 2003; and Segerstrom, 2003) which broadly argue that conventional neoclassical economics gives little support to anti-globalisation positions.

With the focus on globalisation also come analyses of such issues as the costs of remaining barriers to flows of goods and factors between national economies (especially labour flows; see Hamilton and Whalley, 1984), the effects of more rapid transmission of information and execution of contracts, global product mandates, tax competition, cooperative treaty-based arrangements in the face of strategic non-cooperative national incentives, macro policy coordination, out-sourcing, labour immobility, and other related matters.

To political scientists, globalisation suggests global political processes in which there are challenges to national authority structures as mobility across nations accelerates and transfer of nation state functions to supra-national authorities occurs. It leads to evaluation of transnational political processes, assessments of constraints on the autonomy of national authorities, and even the emergence of partial identification of national citizenry within a new emerging global identity. Analyses of these issues inevitably imply different approaches from those used by economists in their globalisation work.

To modern sociologists (following Beck, 1999) globalisation is a process of global social interaction, seen as elevating global risk and providing implications for social structures at all levels of interaction (global, national, local). Stress occasioned on local communities by market-based integration, and the impact of large adjustments in globally more interdependent labour markets in which larger production units (multinationals) dominate provide a major focus, with related concerns over marginalisation of smaller, poorer societies and groups within societies. Whether global values can emerge as a fusion of separate national values (if that is possible) is a question which arises, as is what happens to local values as global integration occurs. Yet again, different directions of research are suggested compared to that of other disciplines.

To those with roots in the anti-globalisation movement (such as Klein, 1999) the key issue is the role played by globalisation in elevating corporate concentration and in intensifying global corporate power via outsourcing, branding and integrated global markets in which goods sell. Anti-globalisation protesters also raise issues of the manic behaviour of modern capitalism (Greider, 1997; and Strange, 1995); the negative elements of global standardisation (McDonaldisation, as discussed in Ritzer, 2000), the influence of media misrepresentation and portrayal as Glassner (1999) documents, and other issues.

While the globalisation debate, in reality, encompasses all of the above and more, my point of departure is to ask how should we approach this process from an analytical viewpoint? Can we envisage what processes of value systems adaptation may unfold in certain circumstances, and can we evaluate what elements of the process may be desirable or undesirable? Does globalisation (whatever it is) represent a move towards global collective identity with preserved distinctiveness in a global fusion of national values which simultaneously implies global synthesis and conflict among nationally-based social systems? Or is the process where value systems of large entities displace those of the small, and are such processes stable or unstable?

Clearly, some form of abstraction (and simplification) is needed in such a discussion, and inevitably in the process some of the issues raised in the disciplinary portrayals above cannot be adequately addressed. The dilemma for analytically-based researchers is that fully capturing all the links between globalisation and social values in a framework which also spans all of the concerns reflected in the current disciplinary foci seems to be beyond reach.

Accepting that market-based integrative economic policy components of globalisation (such as trade liberalisation) need be considered in their wider social context, one can try to analyse some of the consequences using a verbal analytical approach. For this, I take this as my position, that the central Arrow-Debreu model of general equilibrium that economists use to represent market-based economic behaviour (for either an exchange or production economy) should ideally be embedded within wider models of social interaction where social values influence individual behaviour, and also affect the functioning of market-based allocative arrangements.[4] Equally, the effects of market-based outcomes on social values need to be captured. A wholism is seemingly needed for models of economic behaviour if they are to have full credibility for those from other disciplines and used to shed light on the impacts of globalisation.

A simple example of such an approach (and in the spirit of the new institutional economics) would be that if as a result of globalisation shocks trust is less firmly shared between market participants, the time taken to execute transactions may become longer. In this case, the monitoring applied to product quality may be lengthier, and other negative (or positive) effects on economic behaviour from changed value systems attributable to globalisation could follow. This would suggest that socially embedded models of market interactions could yield different perceptions of the impacts of market-driven global integration than models that have no social embedment.

The particular choice of joint economy-wide construct and representation of social value systems affects the perceived outcomes of any given policy or other change taken to reflect the process of globalisation, but the impacts could be substantial. For example, in a somewhat trivial formalisation of a socially embedded model of market behaviour, one could conceive of an economy as having two groups of workers, urban and rural. Labour market transactions involving urban workers selling their labour to urban employers might involve small transactions costs, since these groups already know and trust each other, and similarly

---

[4] There seem to be relatively few models developed by economists which explicitly consider how formalisations of social interactions can be constructed. One which does so is an early piece by Simon (1952) presenting a formal theory of interactions in social groups based on Homans' (1950) earlier work. See Granovetter (1985) for a more recent discussion.

for rural workers transacting with rural employers. However, rural workers moving to urban areas might face significantly higher transactions costs (especially in the short run) if trust is not already established between migrating rural workers and urban employers.

Thus, if the desirability of trade liberalisation were considered in a traditional small open-economy Arrow-Debreu model it would (in the absence of complicating factors such as other distortions, rent shifting, market structure, infant industry considerations) be welfare improving, but if considered in a simple socially embedded structure of this form it could be welfare worsening. Chia and Whalley (1997) report on a numerical model of welfare-worsening service trade liberalisation using a structure incorporating differential intermediation transactions costs in two countries. Usually the presumption for small open economies is that trade liberalisation is a good thing, but Chia and Whalley show that this need not be so in the case for intermediation services and transactions costs, and similar results might apply for a socially embedded model as sketched. Another example might be a model with disjoint urban and rural networks with consumption externalities in which average and marginal network values differ. Where differences in average values of networks affect migration between urban and rural areas rather than marginal values, inefficient migration can occur. In this case, much as in Lewis (1954) models of development with traditional practices in the agricultural sector, market-based integration (trade liberalisation) could be welfare worsening.

Such socially embedded models in either simple or more refined form seem to be little considered by economists since general analytical results are difficult to obtain, and there is a tradition of separation of discussion of economic policy impacts from the social impacts usually verbally discussed in sociological literature. But using numerical simulation methods models incorporating social embedment might produce some of the results sketched out here for certain model parametrisations, which would then be opposite to prevailing economic opinion. An implication would seem to be that the concerns of globalisation protesters over market-based integration and trade liberalisation over negative impacts on social structure, values and culture could be seen by economists as having more analytic credibility than currently. Using a numerical simulation approach, one might also ask how globalisation shocks could impact value systems in some simple socially embedded models, and how the interaction/interpenetration of value systems could in turn provide feedback effects that could also influence the impacts of globalisation assessed in more conventional economic terms.

As part of this process one needs to discuss how globalisation shocks and their effects might be represented in any such modelling exercises. The idea would be to view globalisation as a process of interaction and integration across societies which involves changes in both market-based arrangements and social value systems. In this process both become enmeshed independently of the type of change occurring. Under this view of the world, economic integration inevitably generates changes in social value systems which then themselves also impact social and economic performance.

Many details would be needed to implement such modelling approaches in concrete instances of interaction, including what are the entities whose value systems are seen as entwined in this way. Is it nation states, sub-national communities or civilisations, as Huntington (1996) suggests? Whichever is chosen (and maybe all need to be considered), analytic models of interaction would need to be accordingly developed. If globalisation is viewed in narrower economic terms as movement towards deeper market-based integration, one place to begin in analysing its effects may be to accept that the differing social systems surrounding market activities in national economies also inevitably come into contact as the globalisation process moves forwards. A move from, say, autarky to free trade can change the social systems of the countries involved in various ways.

This may involve, say, Chinese trading with Americans relying on social values that characterise the other country's market transactions. In such cases it may be that transactions across social systems are inherently more difficult to execute than those which occur inside socially more homogeneous borders. Maybe these difficulties recede with the passage of time. Maybe the social systems of each entity themselves change in the process and are in some way enriched. Maybe mutual distrust intensifies with unsatisfactory market transactions across social structures. Maybe all of the above occur to some degree. But the hypothesis would be that change of some form (for better or worse) results in social systems from market-based globalisation which involves moves towards deeper economic integration. Similar outcomes could be claimed for other forms of economic globalisation, such as increased cross-border investment, labour flows, globalisation-speeded financial market activity, heightened transfer of technology and other processes. Formalising and eventually quantifying both the social value system consequences of these changes and feedback effects as value systems change and further modify outcomes is the challenge.

In addition, social value system differences clearly influence and may even constrain how economic globalisation unfolds as a process. For instance, the limited trade between most African economies and OECD countries is variously ascribed to infrastructural problems in Africa (including civil war), transportation problems, macroeconomic instability and other factors. But if value systems are so different across social structures that market-based transactions between OECD and African economies are inherently more difficult to execute, then evaluating what the key differences in value systems are may offer an approach to speeding market integration and offer a new way of thinking on how to promote more trade. Value system differences might also limit technological diffusion, provide barriers to labour mobility, and have other (to economists) unanticipated effects.

Simply put, then, the conjecture I offer is that the process of globalisation (whatever it is) influences social value systems (whatever they are), and changes in them (again whatever they are) can influence how globalisation plays out as a process in terms of its impacts on economic and social performance indicators. The size and importance of these interactions is for now inevitably only the subject of conjecture since there are sharply competing views of how social structures organise themselves and evolve. Many types of economic models could be built to analyse them, and many elements of globalisation could be considered in such models. But the effects stemming from interactions between value systems and globalisation could be substantial.

5. VALUE SYSTEM COMPETITION, COLLAPSE, ASSIMILATION, FUSION AND CONFLICT

Analysing the links between social values and globalisation requires analytic frameworks to help understand how and why value system changes occur and how globalisation shocks to national societies and economies impact societal performance. One approach which could be used is the comparative statics which typifies much postwar economic theorising, as originally set out in Samuelson (1947), Hicks (1939) and in subsequent literature. This approach analyses what if counterfactuals for hypothetical *ex ante* change, and goes beyond the tradition of aiming largely to characterise societal structures and the constraints which value systems place on individual behaviour, and assess historical patterns in the evolution of social structures to unearth tendencies for future patterns. To economists it often seems that other disciplines hold back from such analyses perhaps because they are inevitably dependent on assumptions and model structures which themselves are inevitably hypothetical; but without some formal comparative static framework to analyse globalisation and value linkage judgements on what is likely or unlikely to occur, or even what are good or bad developments, are difficult to arrive at.

To implement such an approach, one first needs to formalise a joint model of economic behaviour and societal interaction characterised by a joint equilibrium structure. One can then attempt to assess how behaviour in the model chosen would change if various globalisation-driven shocks to the system occurred, such as policy-driven global economic integration or changes in global social arrangements (such as, for instance, new communications technologies).

One might, for instance, use comparative statics to ask how social value systems would compete under globalisation shocks? Could it be they could partially or wholly assimilate each other, fusing and taking features from each as economic integration occurred? Could there be an outcome in which value systems of smaller social entities were subsumed? Is cooperation between value systems possible in such a structure, such that cooperative outcomes from interactions between value systems with strategic elements could be generated by globalisation shocks? And what if the values from one society were to be naively (or myopically) implanted to another, could perverse or unfair outcomes result?

In the process of developing such comparative statics one might ask what types of change in social value systems represent an improvement and which regress, and according to which criteria? And quantitatively, one might assess whether any effects attributed to value system change are likely to be large or small compared to traditional effects of market-based integration usually studied by economists, such as the gains from trade.

The model used to capture both social value systems and globalisation shocks would be central to such an undertaking. Differential adjustment costs of the type sketched out above might be one simple formulation. Another could be an explicit economic network structure in which preferences of individuals were defined not only over their own consumption, but over the consumption of others. Such a formalisation has been recently used by Bhattarai and Whalley (2006) to analyse the effects of global liberalisation in network structures in service areas such as telecoms. Applied to social value systems these could be models of disjoint or overlapping networks covering subsets of societies, with a value to each network going beyond the immediate direct benefits of consumption of goods to individuals. These are at best sketches of simple, and even rudimentary, formalisations of social value system interactions with economic behaviour but they could provide a starting point for such investigations.

Comparative static exercises using such formalisations could also draw on several strands of recent economic literature depending on the types of globalisation shocks considered. These might be models of how jurisdictional policies interact under assimilation, how coordination between national policies might or might not improve things, or how international institutions are best designed given the incentives involved.

The tax competition literature (Wilson, 1999) analyses possibilities of races to the top or bottom in inter-jurisdictional tax rates as mobile factors move between jurisdictions and tax bases expand and contract. International macro policy coordination literature (Obstfeld and Rogoff, 1996) discusses among other things the benefits to joint intervention in multi-country macroeconomic policies and the gains to coordination more generally. Myatt et al. (2002) and Currie and Levine (1993) provide a more focused discussion of games of coordination in this setting. Recent discussion of international institution arrangements (Stiglitz, 2002; and Bagwell and Staiger, 1999, 2001 and 2003) focuses on the considerations involved in framing international rules and organising institutional processes to restrain individual country incentives to depart from globally beneficial arrangements.

How might value systems interact and compete with one another? Suppose two societies, one with a high level and one with a low level of trust, were to integrate. Would shared or common levels of trust emerge somewhere between the two, or could there be a race to the top (both high levels of trust) or the bottom (both low levels of trust) as transactions moved between the two types of value systems. Likely, as in tax competition literature, either outcome may occur but exploring the conditions for one outcome or the other could be informative. Another conjecture might be that much like the role of national currency in the global economy, the persistence of multiple value systems in the long run might not characterise an efficient globality. If values must be shared for common and joint use, then if I connect (or transact) with you my values become yours and yours mine. Just as bimetallism is not viable in the long run as a global specie mechanism, so multiple value systems might not prevail in a long-run homogenised globality. Literature on tax competition from Kanbur and Keen (1993) and Zodrow and Mieszkowski (1986) could be relevant here; and how value systems (like jurisdictions) interact in either non-cooperative Nash form (Wildasin, 1988) or cooperative form (Burbidge et al., 1997) might also be analysed.

This discussion also presumes that all individuals are to be fully globally connected with all others under globalisation, and for all purposes. If subsets of interconnections (transactions) can remain disjoint from each other (either spatially or functionally, or both) then distinct value subsystems might survive. Questions of how common value systems also evolve mirror those surrounding the emergence of common standards for shared technologies. If homogenisation is the trend, which one prevails is an issue; just as with cellphones and VCRs, how a common value standard is determined is key.

Another set of issues is whether in some sense the most efficient value system will prevail under globalisation, or whether bad values can drive out good? For example, once corruption is established in an economy can it spread and drive out pro-social honest behaviour. Good values (in some sense) may not be able to withstand individual incentives to adopt socially undesirable behaviour (such as corruption) experienced elsewhere. Will social value systems of large entities overpower those of smaller entities? This may well be the tendency based on the number of transactions conducted by one or more agents using the larger society's value system, but the ability of values to change and modify under globalisation shocks may differ from society to society.

Can assimilation across value systems occur? Clearly this seems to be both likely and even probably happening to some degree at present. Chinese traders selling in US markets learn US practices and vice versa, and from these experiences they also change their own practices. A global value system might therefore be conceived of as possibly taking the best, in some sense, from all nationally-based values to yield a mutated but globally more efficient set of global norms.

Can local collapse in values occur? Where distinctive value systems operate in relatively small and distinct societies, a move to a globalised or socially more widely used value system may result in the submergence and near destruction of local value systems. Traditional societies world-wide seemingly bear testimony to these possibilities. Morrisseau (1998), for instance, both documents and discusses the near disintegration of local community-based value systems among North American Indian bands in the last two centuries, and the social and individual consequences which result.

What of naive transplantation of values from one society to another? Here clearly undesirable outcomes can occur. Suppose society X collectively sees itself as embodying a value system upheld by the rule of law and protection of individual rights and liberties, and as a large society seeks (even if well intentioned) to transplant its own value system abroad as a form of global social advancement. Suppose that the legal structure in the receiving society is corrupted with bribable judges, police officers and other elements of a less than legally bound society. Corruption can intensify under such transplantation by an elevation in the role of legal structure in the recipient society.

In traditional societies with complex informal rights to use, transit or otherwise employ land, formal systems of land title and registration have been introduced with the purpose of firming-up property rights and allowing market trade in land with improved economic efficiency as the objective. The result has been in some cases that informal rights remain as the respected right serving to confuse new legal title, but with new legal title used for the purposes of mortgage access with resulting financial complexity in financial instruments and confusion in title for productive use.

And what of the quantitative consequences of value system interaction of the type speculated on above as occurring along with market-driven globalisation? Seemingly, where collective identity is a prime and perhaps the key social value, the consequences of social value system changes stemming from globalisation can be profound. Morrisseau (1998) also documents gas sniffing, drug abuse, teenage pregnancy and other personally retrograde behaviour in North American Indian bands attributed to the shared loss from the weakening and near disappearance of collective identity. Morrisseau documents how in such cases collective healing is the route to re-establishment of both collective identity and individual self-worth. Seemingly in such cases, while hard to quantify, these elements of value system interaction, if occurring under globalisation, could well outweigh conventional Ricardian gains from trade.

It is perhaps worth concluding this section with the comment that similar integrative processes involving the assimilation and mixing of social arrangements now analysed under globalisation, while previously not occurring simultaneously in most countries around the world, characterise large parts of the human historical record. Embree (1972), for instance, discusses how Hindu transitions reflect a long period of assimilation of different cultures and traditions during the Vedic age (1500BC–600BC) which fused scattered populations who spoke Dravidian languages (the modern representatives of Tamil and Telugu), embraced a wide range of different deities, and practised a wide range of sacrificial and warrior-based practices. The fusion produced the golden Vedic age. Many other instances of social clash, assimilation and inevitable forward movement could be cited.

In this sense value system change under globalisation is hardly a new phenomenon or even a new concern. But both the large and central role played by the economic component in modern globalisation discussions and the simultaneous reach of globalisation into most societies and cultures seems to mark a departure from earlier experiences. If so, this may be a further reason to explore how the theorising of economists enables a better understanding of current episodes of globally-driven social change.

6. CONCLUDING REMARKS

This chapter discusses how the many processes of globalisation might interact with social value systems and collective identity, and through these interactions how overall societal and economic performance may be impacted. Its thrust is to suggest that economists may be able to contribute to this part of the wider debate on globalisation by formalising simple notions of social value systems (collective identity) and using comparative statics to assess how societal performance might be impacted by globalisation shocks. Writings from other disciplines largely document and identify these concerns without using a comparative statics approach.

While at times much maligned by some from other social disciplines (see Wallerstein's (2001, p. 258) call 'Away with economists' remark), my belief is that working jointly with those from other disciplines, economists can nonetheless make a contribution to debates on how globalisation affects social process and how induced societal change affects economic performance by bringing their analytical skills to bear in an interdisciplinary communicatory manner. To think in terms of processes of interaction, competition, cooperation and assimilation between value systems and to more formally develop new analytics and comparative statics of collective rationality beyond the initial ideas set out in this cursory piece is the direction I suggest. Debate on globalisation is now centre stage in our emerging global polity, and economists can offer their analytical skills to other disciplines and make important contributions to debate on wider and potentially larger issues than impacts on trade and factor flows.

REFERENCES

Akerlof, G. (1984), *An Economic Theorist's Book of Tales* (Cambridge: Cambridge University Press).

Arrow, K. J. (1970), 'The Organization of Economic Activity: Issues Pertinent to the Choice of Market verses Non-market Allocation', in R. H. Haveman and J. Margolis (eds.), *Public Expenditure and Policy Analysis* (Chicago: Markham).

Arrow, K. J. and G. Debreu (1954), 'Existence of an Equilibrium for a Competitive Economy', *Econometrica*, **22**, 3, 265–90.

Avineri, S. (1978), *The Social and Political Thought of Karl Marx* (Cambridge: Cambridge University Press).

Bagwell, K. and R. W. Staiger (1999), 'An Economic Theory of GATT', *American Economic Review*, **89**, 1, 215–48.

Bagwell, K. and R. W. Staiger (2001), 'Domestic Politics, National Sovereignty, and Economic Institutions', *Quarterly Journal of Economics*, **116**, 2, 519–62.

Bagwell, K. and R. W. Staiger (2003), *An Economic Theory of GATT* (Cambridge, MA: MIT Press).

Beck, U. (1999), *World Risk Society* (Cambridge: Polity Press; Malden, MA: Blackwell).

Berger, P. and T. Luckmann (1967), *The Social Construction of Reality: A Treatise in the Sociology of Knowledge* (New York: Anchor).

Bhattarai, K. and J. Whalley (2006), 'The Division and Size of Gains from Liberalization in Service Networks', *Review of International Economics*, **14**, 3, 348–61.

Blau, D. (1975), *Inequality and Heterogeneity: A Primitive Theory of Social Structure* (New York: Free Press).

Blumer, H. (1969), *Symbolic Interaction: Perspectives and Method* (Englewood Cliffs, NJ: Prentice Hall).

Burbidge, J. B., J. A. DePater, G. M. Myers and A. Sengupta (1997), 'A Coalition-formation Approach to Equilibrium Federations and Trading Blocs', *American Economic Review*, **87**, 5, 940–56.

Castells, M. (2004), *The Information Age: Economy, Society, and Culture* (3 Volumes, Malden, MA: Blackwell).

Chia, N. C. and J. Whalley (1997), 'A Numerical Example Showing Globally Welfare-Worsening Liberalization of International Trade in Banking Services', *Journal of Policy Modeling*, **19**, 2, 119–27.

Cicourel, A. V. (1973), *Cognitive Sociology* (Harmondsworth: Penguin).

Coleman, J. (1988), 'Social Capital in the Creation of Human Capital', *American Journal of Sociology*, **94** (Supplement), S95–121.

Collier, P. (1998), 'Social Capital and Poverty', Social Capital Initiative, Working Paper No. 4 (World Bank).

Collins, R. (1986), *Weberian Sociological Theory* (Cambridge: Cambridge University Press).

Cunningham, L. and J. Reich (1994), *Culture and Values* (San Francisco: Harcourt Brace, 3rd ed.).

Currie, D. and P. Levine (1993), *Rules, Reputation, and Macroeconomic Policy Coordination* (Cambridge: Cambridge University Press).

Dahrendorf, R. (1959), *Class and Class Conflict in an Industrial Society* (London: Routledge & Kegan Paul).

Dawkins, R. (1976), *The Selfish Gene* (Oxford: Oxford University Press).

Deardorff, A. (2003), 'What Might Globalization's Critics Believe?', *The World Economy*, **26**, 5, 639–58.

Durkheim, E. (1933), *The Division of Labor in Society* (New York: Free Press).

Durlauf, S. and M. Falchamps (2004), 'Empirical Studies of Social Capital: A Critical Survey' (Mimeo).

Embree, A. T. (1972), *The Hindu Tradition: Readings in Oriental Thought* (London: Vintage Books).

Garfinkel, H. (1967), *Studies in Ethnomethodology* (Englewood Cliffs, NJ: Prentice Hall).

Giddens, A. (1973), *The Class Structure of Advanced Societies* (London: Hutchinson).

Glassner, D. (1999), *The Culture of Fear* (New York: Basic Books).

Granovetter, M. (1985), 'Economic Action and Social Structure: The Problem of Embeddedness', *American Journal of Sociology*, **91**, 3, 481–510.

Greider, W. (1997), *One World, Ready or Not: The Manic Logic of Global Capitalism* (New York: Simon & Schuster).

Hamilton, B. and J. Whalley (1984), 'Efficiency and Distributional Implications of Global Restrictions on Labour Mobility: Calculations and Policy Implications', *Journal of Development Economics*, **14**, 1–2, 61–75.

Hicks, J. R. (1939), *Value and Capital* (Oxford: Oxford University Press).

Higgott, R. (2002), CSGR Working Paper on Globalization as a Contested Concept (Warwick, UK).

Homans, C. (1950), *The Human Group* (New York: Harpers).

Huntington, S. P. (1996), *The Clash of Civilizations and Remaking of World Order* (New York: Simon & Schuster).

Kanbur, R. and M. Keen (1993), 'Jeux Sans Frontières: Tax Competition and Tax Coordination when Countries Differ in Size', *American Economic Review*, **83**, 4, 877–92.

Kasser, T. and A. D. Kanner (ed.) (2004), *Psychology and Consumer Culture* (Washington, DC: American Psychological Association).

Kasser, T. and V. G. Kasser (2001), 'The Dreams of People High and Low in Materialism', *Journal of Economic Psychology*, **22**, 6, 693–719.

Klein, N. (1999), *No Space, No Choice, No Jobs, No Logo: Taking Aim at the Brand Bullies* (New York: Picador USA).

Leibenstein, H. (1950), 'Bandwagon, Snob, and Veblen Effects in the Theory of Consumer Demand', *Quarterly Journal of Economics*, **64**, 2, 183–207.

Lewis, W. A. (1954), 'Economic Development with Unlimited Supplies of Labour', *Manchester School of Economic and Social Studies*, **22**, 2, 139–91.

Lin, Y. (1935), *My Country and My People* (Beijing: Foreign Language Teaching and Research Press).

Loury, G. (1977), 'A Dynamic Theory of Racial Income Differences', in P. Wallace and A. LaMond (eds.), *Women, Minorities, and Employment Discrimination* (Lexington, MA: Lexington Books).

Manski, C. F. (2000), 'Economic Analysis of Social Interactions', *Journal of Economic Perspectives*, **14**, 3, 115–36.

Matthews, R. C. O. (1986), 'The Economics of Institutions and Sources of Growth', *Economic Journal*, **96**, 384, 903–18.

Morrisseau, C. (1998), *Into the Daylight: A Wholistic Approach to Healing* (Toronto: University of Toronto Press).

Myatt, D. P., H. S. Shin and C. Wallace (2002), 'The Assessment: Games and Coordination', *Oxford Review of Economic Policy*, **18**, 4, 397–417.

North, D. C. (1997), 'The Contributions of the New Institutional Economics to an Understanding of the Transition Problem', UNU/Wider 1997 Annual Lecture (Helsinki).

Obstfeld, M. and K. Rogoff (1996), *Foundations of International Macroeconomics* (Cambridge, MA: MIT Press).

Parsons, T. (1949), *The Structure of Social Action: A Study in Social Theory with Special Reference to a Group of Recent European Writers* (Glencoe, IL: Free Press, 2nd ed.).

Portes, A. (1998), 'Social Capital: Its Origins and Applications in Modern Sociology', *Annual Review of Sociology*, **24**, 1–14.

Ritzer, G. (2000), *The McDonaldization of Society* (Thousand Oaks, CA: Pine Forge Press).

Roch, P. (1979), *The Meaning of Symbolic Interaction* (Basingstoke: Macmillan).

Samuelson, P. A. (1947), *Foundations of Economic Analysis* (Cambridge, MA: Harvard University Press).

Segerstrom, P. (2003), 'Naomi Klein and the Anti-globalisation Movement', in M. Lundahl (ed.), *Globalization and its Enemies* (Stockholm: EFI, Economic Research Institute, Stockholm School of Economics).

Siedman, S. (2004), *Contested Knowledge: Social Theory Today* (Oxford: Blackwell, 3rd ed.).

Simon, H. A. (1952), 'A Formal Theory of Interaction in Social Groups', *American Sociological Review*, **17**, 2, 202–11.

Stiglitz, J. (2002), *Globalization and its Discontents* (New York: W. W. Norton).

Strange, S. (1995), *Mad Money* (Manchester: Manchester University Press).

Veblen, T. (1899), *The Theory of Leisure Class: An Economic Study in the Evolution of Institutions* (New York: The Macmillan Company; London: Macmillan & Co., Ltd.).

Wallerstein, I. (2001), *Unthinking Social Science: The Limits of Nineteenth Century Paradigms* (Philadelphia, PA: Temple University Press).

Weber, M. (1951), *The Religion of China: Confucianism and Taoism* (New York: Free Press).

Weber, M. (1958), *The Protestant Ethic and the Spirit of Capitalism* (New York: Free Press).

Wildasin, D. E. (1988), 'Nash Equilibria in Models of Fiscal Competition', *Journal of Public Economics*, **35**, 2, 229–40.

Wilson, E. (1980), *Sociobiology* (Cambridge, MA: Belknap Press of Harvard University Press).

Wilson, J. D. (1999), 'Theories of Tax Competition', *National Tax Journal*, **52**, 2, 269–304.

Zodrow, G. R. and P. Mieszkowski (1986), 'Pigou, Tiebout, Property Taxation, and the Under-provision of Local Public Goods', *Journal of Urban Economics*, **19**, 356–70.

Index

A. T. Kearney 94
Abu Dhabi International Petroleum Investment
    Corporation 64
Abu Dhabi Investment Authority 64
administered prices, Indonesia 20
Afghanistan 106
Africa and OECD countries, trade between 136
Africa, Caribbean and Pacific (ACP) countries
    28–9, 45, 47
African Growth and Opportunity Act (AGOA,
    USA) 42, 45
Agreement on Agriculture, WTO 58
Agreement on Government Procurement (GPA)
    56
agricultural sector
    East African Community 40, 45
    EU 57
    GATT 81, 82
    Indonesia 19, 21, 22
    Israel 57–8, 60
    Japan 3–6, 7–8, 9
    USA 57, 81
Akerlof, G. 126
al'Qaeda 109
Albania 54
American Express 108
anti-dumping measures
    Israel 57
    Indonesia 20
anti-globalisation movement 95, 131, 132, 133,
    135
    Indonesia 22
Anti-monopoly Act (AMA, Japan), 2006
    amendment 3
Argentina 59
Army, Israeli 55
Arrow, K. J. 127, 134, 135
Asian Economic Community 18
Asian economic crisis 11, 12, 22, 23
Asia-Pacific Economic Cooperation (APEC)
    87, 112
Association of Southeast Asian Nations
    (ASEAN) 18

Free Trade Area 18–19, 23
    Indonesia 18
    Japan's FTA negotiations with 6, 7
asylum seekers 106
Augè, Marc 101
Australia 7, 8, 64

bacteria, global dimensions 110
Bahrain 54, 69
balance of payments, Indonesia 15
Bangladesh 54
Bank of International Settlements (BIS)
    87
bankcards 108
banking sector, UAE 64, 65
Basic Plan for Food, Agriculture and Rural
    Areas, Japan 5
Basque area 112
Batam special export zone 21
Beck, U. 131, 133
Belgium 112
Bentham, Jeremy 92
Berger, P. 130
Bhattarai, K. 138
bilateral investment treaties (BITs) 65
    Kenyan 43
    Tanzanian 43
    UAE 65–8, 70, 71
    Ugandan 43–4
biosphere 109
Blau, D. 130
Blumer, H. 131
border protection, Japan 5
Bosnia 106
Brazil 85
Brunei 6, 7, 54
Bulog 23
bureaucracy
    East African Community 44
    mission creep 77
Burundi 27, 28, 29
business environment improvements, East
    African Community 43

Business Studies 92
buying networks, East Asia 24

Cambodia 54
Cameroon 28
Canada 52, 61, 85
Cancún Ministerial Meeting 75, 86
capacity building 84
capital/financial account balance, Indonesia 14, 15
capital formation, Indonesia 13
carbon dioxide emissions, Indonesia 16
Caribbean countries 47
Carribean Community and Common Market (CARICOM) 28
Castells, Manuel 101, 131
Central Africa 30, 31, 47
Centre for the Study of Globalisation and Regionalisation 94
cereals, Kenya 36–7
Chad 54
Chia, N. C. 135
Chile 6, 7, 56
China
    competition with Indonesia 24
    export performance 17
    FTA negotiations with the UAE 64
    globalisation 116
    Imperial 129
    investment in Kenya 43
    Japanese trade with 8
    trade liberalisation 23
    value systems 128, 129, 139
Cicourel, A. V. 131
Cirrus 108
Citicorp 107
citizen action initiatives, regionalisation 112
civil society associations 106–7
climate change 16, 109
club of clubs, and WTO effectiveness 86–8, 89
Collins, R. 130
colonialism 97, 101
Committee on Government Procurement, Israel 56
Common External Tariff (CET) 27, 35, 38–40, 49
Common Market for Eastern and Southern Africa (COMESA) 44
communications 105–6
comparative statics 137–8

competition policy
    East African Community 45
    Indonesia 20
    Japan 3
    UAE 62, 63, 64, 65, 70
    WTO controversies 84
Comte, Auguste 129
conflict theory 130
conspicuous consumption 126
consumer nominal assistance coefficient (NAC), Japan 4
consumer protection, UAE 65
consumer support estimates (CSE), Japan 3–4
consumerism 115
consumption
    conspicuous 126
    Indonesia 13
contract enforcement, East African Community 44
corruption
    Indonesia 15, 21
    value systems 139, 140
Cotonou Agreement 28–9
Council on Economic and Fiscal Policy, Japan 5–6
credit, Indonesia 13
credit cards 108
Cuba 54
cultural homogenisation 115–16
cultural innovation 116
Cunningham, L. 126
currency, supraterritorial 100, 107–8
current account, Indonesia 14, 15, 16
customs
    East African Community 43, 44, 47
    East Asian production and buying networks 24
    Indonesia 22, 24
    Japan 2, 9
Customs Envelope Agreement 52–3

Dahrendorf, R. 130
Debreu, G. 127, 134, 135
debt service ratio, Indonesia 14, 15
decentralisation, Indonesia 22
deforestation, Indonesia 16
democracy
    Indonesia 15, 22
    international organisations 80
    legitimacy 80

Democratic Party (DP), Japan 6
deterritorialisation 113
developed countries
    criticisms of the WTO 75, 85
    fragmentation among 86
developing countries
    criticisms of the WTO 75, 84, 85
    electronics exports 24
    GATT 82
    Israel's invoking of developing country
        status 56
    Israel's trade with 53, 55
    and Japan 8–9
development issues, Japan 8–9
digital money 108
dispute settlement
    bilateral investment treaties 65
    COMESA 44
    East African Community 44
    GATT 81, 82
    WTO 83, 84, 85, 89
Dispute Settlement Body (DSB) 83, 85, 89
distribution networks
    East African Community 46
    Japan 2, 6
    UAE 62
distributive justice 105
Doha Development Agenda (DDA)
    Israel 60
    Japan 9
    UAE 64
Dubai Holding 64
Dubai Ports Authority 64
Durkheim, E. 129
duty drawback schemes, East African
        Community 41
duty exemptions, Tanzania 43

ease of doing business see trade facilitation
East Africa
    intra-regional trade 40
    regional trade cooperation 28
    tariffs 30
    trade changes 31
    trade liberalisation 29
    trade policy reform 29–30
East Africa Cooperation 27
East African Community (EAC) 27–9, 49
    Competition Committee 43
    Economic Partnership Agreements 45, 47–9

and the EU, changing relations between 27
exports 41–2, 45–7, 49
intra-regional trade 40–1, 47, 48, 49
investment measures 42–4, 49
prospective issues for trade policy 45–9
regionalisation 112
tariffs 32–8, 45
trade policy 38–44
trade policy reform 29–38
East Asia
    Japanese trade with 2, 8
    production and buying networks 24
    trade cost reduction 9
Eastern and Southern Africa (ESA) group 29,
        47
economic growth
    Indonesia 12
    and social values 128
    UAE 63
Economic Partnership Agreements
    Cotonou Agreement 28–9
    East African Community 45, 47–9
    Japan 6, 7
Ecuador 85
education, UAE 65
Egypt 51, 59
electronics sector, Indonesia 24
Embree, A. T. 126, 140
emiratisation policy, UAE 62, 65, 68
Enlightenment 129
environmental issues
    globality 109–10
    and methodological territorialism 105
    supraterritoriality 100
    territoriality 112, 113
    WTO controversies 84
Estonia 56
ethnomethodology 131
eurobonds 108
European Free Trade Area (EFTA) 52, 53
European Social Forum 112
European Union (EU) 87
    agricultural sector 57
    and the East African Community 27, 29, 45,
        47–9
    Cotonou Agreement 28–9
    euro 108
    and the Gulf Cooperation Council, FTA with
        64
    imports from sub-Saharan African countries 45

Israel's agricultural trade with 60
Israel's FTAs with 52
Lomé conventions 45, 47
protectionism 57
retaliation authorisation by the WTO 85
Tanzanian BIT with 43
and the UAE, trade between 61
Ugandan BIT with 44
US disputes with 82
exchange rate policy
   Gulf Cooperation Council currency union 62
   Indonesia 13, 15, 16, 17, 23
   Kuwait 64
   UAE 64
export processing zones (EPZs), East African
      Community 41, 42
export promotion bodies, East African
      Community 41
Export Promotion Council, Kenya 42
exports
   from China 17
   from developing countries 24
   from the East African Community 41–2, 45–
      7
   from the EU 47, 48–9
   from India 112
   from Indonesia 12, 13, 14, 15, 16, 21, 23–6
   from Israel 57, 59
   from Japan 1
   from Kenya 40, 41–2, 45, 46, 48
   from Malaysia 24
   from the Philippines 24
   special export zones, Indonesia 21
   from sub-Saharan African countries 30–2,
      40, 45
   from Tanzania 40, 41, 42, 46–7
   from Thailand 24
   from the UAE 61, 63
   from Uganda 40, 41, 42, 45, 46–7
expropriation, limiting the threat of 44

facilitation of trade see trade facilitation
FDI see foreign direct investment
Federal Reserve 132
federalism, global 80
financial instruments, global 100, 109
financial sector
   globality 108–9
   Japan 2
fiscal deficit, Japan 1

fiscal policy
   Indonesia 13, 15
   UAE 64
Flanders 112
food prices, global rise in 16
foreign direct investment
   Bahrain 69
   bilateral investment treaties 65
   East African Community 43–4
   Indonesia 24
   Japan 3
   Kenya 43, 44
   Tanzania 43
   UAE 62, 63, 64, 65, 68–70, 71
   Uganda 43–4
   WTO 83, 84
foreign exchange reserves
   Indonesia 14, 15
   Israel 54
foreign exchange transactions, globality 108
Foreign Policy magazine 94
France 112, 129
free-riding behaviour, international
      organisations 78, 79
free trade agreements/areas (FTAs)
   ASEAN (AFTA) 18–19, 23
   Greater Arab Free Trade Area 64
   Gulf Cooperation Council currency union 62
   between Israel and the EU 52
   Japan 6–7, 8, 9
   UAE 62, 63, 68, 70, 71
fuel prices
   global rise in 16
   Indonesia 16, 20

Gabon 28
Gambia 28
Gamble, Clive 96
game theory 76
Garfinkel, H. 131
GDP see gross domestic product
General Agreement on Tariffs and Trade
      (GATT)
   mission 81
   transition to the WTO 81–4
General Agreement on Trade in Services
      (GATS) 83
generalised system of preference (GSP)
      scheme, Japan 8
genetic engineering 109

geographical concentration of production,
    Japan 5
Germany 43
Giddens, Anthony 93, 131
global banking 108
global bonds 108
global cities 113
global commodity chains 107
global companies 106–7
global consciousness 110–11
global derivatives 108–9
global economy
    and East Asia 2
    and Indonesia 16
global factories 107
global federalism 80
global financial transactions 108
global identity 130, 133
global insurance policies 109
global/local binaries 114–15
global markets 107
global organisations 106–7
global portfolios 109
global production 107
global products 107, 115–16
global relations 99
global shares 108
global sourcing 107
Global Studies Associations 93
global village 110
global warfare 109
global warming 16, 109
global weapons 109
globalisation
    cultural homogenisation 115–16
    defining 91–3, 118–19, 132–3
    as external shocks affecting value systems
        132–8, 141
    global identity 130
    global/local binaries 114–15
    global, world, international and transnational
        terms, comparison of 102–3
    as internationalisation 93–5, 119
    as liberalisation 95–6, 119
    methodological implications 104–5
    politics 117–18
    qualifications 111–18
    redundant concepts 93–8
    reification 113–14
    rise of term 92–3

space 98–9
transplanetary relations and
    supraterritoriality 98, 99–102
uneven spread 116–17
as universalisation 96, 119
and universality 116–17
values see values and globalisation
way forward 98–111
as westernisation 96–7, 119
Globalisation Studies Network 93
globalism 111–13
globality 99–103, 118–19
    manifestations 105–11
globally connected cities 112
glocalisation 116
governance
    indicators, UAE 67–8
    WTO 83, 84
government procurement
    Indonesia 20
    Israel 55–6
    Japan 3
    WTO Agreement on Government
        Procurement 20
    WTO controversies 84, 85
Granovetter M. 126
Greater Arab Free Trade Area 64
greenhouse effect 109
Greenspan, Alan 132
gross domestic product (GDP)
    Indonesia 13
    Japan 1
Gulf Cooperation Council (GCC) 61
    currency union 62, 64
    foreign direct investment 69, 70
    FTA with the EU 64
    Japan's FTA/EPA negotiations with 7

Habibie, B. J. 23
Harvey, David 101
health matters, global dimensions 110
Heidegger, Martin 101
Hicks, J. R. 137
Higgott, R. 132
Hindu transitions 140–1
Hirst, Paul 94
homogenisation 115–16
    globalisation as universalisation 96
human rights campaigns, supraterritoriality 100
Huntington, S. P. 136

identity 130, 131, 133, 140, 141
immigration to Israel 53
imports
    to the East African Community 29,
        39–40, 47, 48–9
    from the EU 29
    to Indonesia 13, 14, 15, 16, 21, 23
    to Israel 52–4, 57, 58
    to Japan 1, 4
    to Kenya 36–7, 40, 41, 48
    to sub-Saharan Africa 30–2
    to Tanzania 37–8, 40, 41, 48
    to the UAE 61, 62, 63, 68
    to Uganda 37–8, 40, 41, 48
India 7, 23, 112
indigenous peoples 114–15
Indonesia 11–12, 22–6
    exports to Israel 54
    Japan's FTA/EPA with 6, 7, 18
    principles and practice of trade policy 18–22
    recent economic developments 12–17
industrial cooperation, Israel 56
Industrial Revolution 129
industry policy, Indonesia 23
inflation
    Indonesia 12–15, 17
    UAE 62
infrastructure
    East African Community 43, 46
    Indonesia 15, 24
    UAE 64
Intellectual Property Rights
    Indonesia 20
    Israel 56
    TRIPs see Trade-Related Intellectual
        Property
interactionism, symbolic 131
interest groups, Japan 5
intermediation services 135
International Country Risk Guide (ICRG),
    political risk index 65–7
International Court of Justice (ICJ) 110
International Criminal Court (ICC) 110
International Criminal Police Organisation 110
international institutional arrangements 138
International Labour Organisation (ILO) 87
international macro policy coordination
    literature 138
International Monetary Fund (IMF)
    inadequate means 78

Indonesia 22, 23
Special Drawing Right 108
international organisations 75–6, 88–9
    club of clubs, and WTO effectiveness 86–8,
        89
    dilemma 76–86
    GATT to WTO 81–4
    inadequate means 78–9
    legitimacy 79–86
    mission creep 76–7
    WTO under fire 84–6
international relations 92, 99
international standards 55
'international' term 102–3
internationalisation, globalisation as 93–5,
    119
Internet 105–6, 113
Interpol 110
investment
    East African Community 42–4, 47
    foreign direct see foreign direct investment
    Indonesia 12, 14, 15–16, 17
    sub-Saharan Africa 42
Investment Law (Indonesia, 2007) 15
Iran 112
Iraq 64, 112
Iraq war 109
Irish Republican Army (IRA) 109
Israel 60
    inter-sectoral differences 57–60
    non-tariff barriers 51, 53–5
    standards and procurement 55–7
    tariff barriers 51–3
Israeli Standard 55

Japan 9
    agricultural protection 3–6
    development, consideration for 8–9
    effective checklist in the Trade Policy
        Review exercise 1
    improvements and remaining issues 1–3
    Indonesia's FTA/EPA with 6, 7, 18
    regionalism 5, 6–8
    and the UAE, trade between 61
Jordan
    bilateral trade agreement with the UAE 64
    Israel's partial preferential agreement with
        52
    textile sector 51, 59
justice, distributive 105

Kanbur, R. 139
Keen, M. 139
Kenya
    Common External Tariff 39–40, 49
    EPAs 29, 47–8
    FDI 43, 44
    imports 36–7
    manufacturing sector 40
    protectionism 29, 37, 38
    tariffs 30, 32–3, 35–7, 38
    trade changes 31
    trade liberalisation 35
    transport costs 46
    see also East African Community
Korea 7, 8
kosher certificate requirement, Israel 53, 56
KPPU, Indonesia 20
Kurdish movement 112
Kuwait 54, 64

labour markets
    Indonesia 12, 16, 22
    UAE 62
    WTO controversies 75, 84
laissez-faire economics 95
languages, disappearing 115
law, globality 110
least developed countries (LDCs)
    and Japan 8–9
    Tanzania and Uganda's access to the EU 47
leather and leather products, Japan 3
Lebanon 54, 55, 64
legal system, East African Community 44
legitimacy, international organisations
    79–86
    GATT 81, 82, 83
    WTO 85, 86, 88
Leibenstein, H. 126
Levitt, Theodore 92
Lewis, W. A. 135
Liberal Democratic Party (LDP), Japan 6
liberalism, Indonesia 22
licences, Israel 51, 53, 54
lobbying, Israel 59, 60
local/global binaries 114–15
logistics
    East Asian production and buying networks
        24
    Japan 2
Lomé conventions 45, 47

London InterBank Offered Rate (LIBOR) 108
Luckmann, T. 130

macroeconomic management, Indonesia 12–15
Maestro 108
Malaysia
    electronics exports 24
    exports to Israel 54
    and Indonesian smuggling 21
    and Indonesian sub-national governments in
        close proximity to 22
    Japan's FTA with 6, 7
Mandatory Tenders Regulation (Preference for
    Israeli Products and Mandatory Business
    Cooperation) (1995) 56
manufacturing sector
    Indonesia 18, 22, 24
    Israel 52
    Japan 3, 7–8
    Kenya 37, 40
    UAE 64
maps 101
market transactions, and social values 127–8
Marrakech Agreement
    Israel 57
    labour standards 75
    Trade Policy Reviews 1
Marshall, A. 129
Marx, Karl 129
mass media, supraterritoriality 100
MasterCard 108
McDonald's 116
media, supraterritoriality 100
Mercosur 52
methodological territorialism 104–5
Mexico 6, 7, 52
MFN see most favoured nation (MFN)
    treatment
micro-credit schemes 108
microeconomic policy, Indonesia 15–16
micro-nationalist politics 112
Mieszkowski, P. 139
military activities, global 109
minimum wages, Indonesia 12
Ministry for Trade and Industry, Indonesia 21, 23
Ministry of Agriculture, Forestry and Fishery
    (MAFF), Japan 4, 5, 6
Ministry of Agriculture, Indonesia 21
Ministry of Agriculture, Israel 58, 60
Ministry of Defence, Israel 55, 56

Ministry of Finance, Indonesia 21, 23
Ministry of Industry, Trade and Labour, Israel
    54, 55, 58, 60
Ministry of Rural Development, Israel 58
mission creep, international organisations 76–7
    GATT 82, 83
    WTO 83
modernisation 97
monetary policy, UAE 64
money supply, Indonesia 13
monopolies, Israel 60
Morocco 54, 64
Morrisseau, C. 140
most favoured nation (MFN) treatment
    East African Community 43
    GATT 81
    Israel 51, 52, 53, 54–5, 57–8, 59
MUB 41, 42

nation state, and global federalism 80
National Association of Securities Dealers
    Automated Quotation system (Nasdaq)
    109
nationalisation, Indonesia 11
neoliberalism 95, 118
Netherlands 43
nominal assistance coefficient (NAC), Japan 4
non-governmental actors, and the WTO 85
non-tariff barriers (NTBs)
    GATT 82
    Indonesia 18, 19, 20, 21, 23
    Israel 51, 53–5
    Japan 3

Official Israeli Standard 55
offshore arrangements 112
oil consumption, Indonesia 16
oil production, Indonesia 16
oligopolies, Israel 59–60
Olson, Mancur 78–9
one country, one vote system 79
openness
    Indonesia 11, 12, 20, 22–3
    Israel 51
    Japan 1, 2
    UAE 61, 63
    WTO 85
Organisation for Economic Co-operation and
    Development (OECD)
    accession to 56

and African countries, trade between 136
    as a club of clubs 87
    Israel 56
    Multilateral Agreement on Investment 75
Organisation of Eastern Caribbean States
    (OECS) 28
Oxfam 107
ozone depletion 109

Pacific countries 47
Pakistan 54
Palestinian Authority (PA) 52–3, 54, 55
parallel imports, lacking in Israel 54
Pareto, V. 129
Parsons, T. 125, 126, 127, 129–31
pensions, Japan 1
Perlmutter, Howard 107
Peter Principle 77
Peter Stuyvesant 107
petroleum prices, Indonesia 16, 20
phenonemological sociology 131
Philippines, the 6, 7, 24
police forces, transplanetary cooperation 110
political party funding, Indonesia 22
political risk index, UAE 65–7, 68
political science 133
politics, and globalisation 117–18
Polo, Marco 100–1
port clearance procedures, East African
    Community 44, 47
portfolio investment, UAE 64
power relations in globalisation 117–18
preferential trade agreements (PTAs)
    Indonesia 18
    Israel 55, 58
    Southeast Asia 18
    see also Economic Partnership Agreements;
        free trade agreements/areas
pressure groups, Japan 5
price stabilisation, Japan 5
private sector, UAE 63, 65
privatisation
    Japan 2–3
    Tanzania 43
producer nominal assistance coefficient (NAC),
    Japan 4
producer support estimates (PSE), Japan 3
production networks
    East Asia 24
    Japan 2, 6

professional services sector, Japan 2–3
property rights
East African Community 44
UAE 63, 65–8, 70, 71
value systems 140
protectionism
East Africa 29
East African Community 49
Indonesia 11, 21, 22, 23
Israel 52, 55–6, 57–8, 60
Japan 1, 3–6, 9
Kenya 37, 38
reduction *see* trade liberalisation
Southeast Asia 18
sub-Saharan African countries 46
Tanzania 38
Uganda 38
see also tariffs
public debt, Indonesia 13, 15
public expenditure, Israel 51, 55

quality controls, Israel 53, 55
quarantine, Indonesia 22
quotas
GATT 82
Israel 51, 53, 58
Japan 8
UAE 62, 65, 68

rapid reaction forces 109
refugees 106
regional integration, East African Community 47
regionalisation 112
regionalism 9
Japan 5, 6–8
regulatory quality, UAE 67
Reich, J. 126
reification of globalisation 113–14
religion 96, 116, 129
retaliation, WTO 85, 89
reterritorialisation 112
rice
Indonesia 23
Japan 5, 6
Robertson, Roland 92
Roch, P. 131
Rodrik, Dani 94
Romania 59
Rosenau, J. N. 92

Rosenberg, J. 93
Ruggie, John 101
Rules of Origin requirements, EU 45, 47, 48
Russia
emigration to Israel 53
market-oriented reforms and social values 128
OECD 56
regionalisation 112
Rwanda 27, 28, 29

safeguard levy, Israel 52
Samuelson, P. A. 137
Sanitary and Phytosanitary Measures (SPS) 83
Indonesia 20
Japan 3, 5
savings, Indonesia 14
Seattle meeting, labour standards 75
self-interest, individual 130
September 11, 2001 terrorist attacks 109
service link costs, Japan 2
services sector, Japan 2–3
severance pay, Indonesia 12
Siberia 112
Simai, M. 79
Singapore
and Batam special export zone 21
and Indonesian smuggling 21
and Indonesian sub-national governments in close proximity to 22
intra-ASEAN trade 18
Japan's FTA with 6, 7
Singapore Issues 75
Slovakia 56
smuggling, Indonesia 21, 23
social capital 126–8
social life, geographical dimension of 99
social space 113–15
social thought 129–32
social values *see* values and globalisation
socially embedded models of market behaviour 134–5
sociology 92, 129–30, 133
Soeharto regime 11, 15, 23
Somalia 106
South Africa 30, 43
Southeast Asia 18
Southern Africa 29, 47
tariffs 30
trade changes 31

Spain 112
spatiality, and globalisation 98–9
special and differential treatment, GATT 82
Special Drawing Right (SDR) 108
special export zones, Indonesia 21
standards
    Indonesia 20
    international 55
    Israel 53
Standards Institution of Israel 55
Standards Law (Israel, 1998) 55
state enterprises, Indonesia 20
state trading, Japan 3, 5
strategic alliances 106
structuralism 131
sub-Saharan African (SSA) countries
    bilateral investment treaties with Tanzania
        43
    exports 45, 46
    integration 28
    intra-regional trade 40
    investment 42
    protectionism 46
    trade changes 30–1
    trade liberalisation 29
    trade policy reform 29–31
    Trade Policy Reviews 28
subsidies
    Indonesia 16
    Japan 3, 5, 6
    WTO controversies 85
Subsidies and Countervailing Measures (SCM)
    83
supraterritoriality 98, 99–102, 111, 119
    cultural heterogeneity 116
    global communications 105–6
    global production 107
    methodological territorialism 104
    politics 117, 118
    and territoriality 111, 112, 113
    uneven spread 117
Switzerland 7, 43
symbolic interactionism 131
Syria
    bilateral trade agreement with the UAE
        64
    normalisation of trade relations with Israel
        55
    prohibition on exports to Israel 54, 55
    regionalisation 112

Tanzania
    Common External Tariff 39–40, 49
    Eastern and Southern Africa group 29
    Economic Partnership Agreements 47–8
    FDI 43
    imports 37–8
    privatisation 43
    protectionism 29, 38
    Southern Africa group 29
    tariffs 30, 31, 34–5, 36, 37–8
    trade changes 31
    transport costs 46
    see also East African Community
tariffication, Israel 57
tariffs
    Common External Tariff 27, 35, 38–40,
        49
    East Africa 30
    East African Community 27, 29, 32–8, 45,
        47–8, 49
    GATT 81, 82
    Greater Arab Free Trade Area 64
    Indonesia 19–20, 21, 23
    Israel 51–3, 57–8, 59
    Japan 3, 4, 5, 7–8, 9
    Kenya 32–3, 35–7, 38
    sub-Saharan Africa 30, 31
    Tanzania 31, 34–5, 36, 37–8
    Uganda 32, 33–4, 35, 37–8
tax competition literature 138, 139
tax holidays, Kenya 43
tax revenue, Indonesia 13
taxation, Indonesia 19
Technical Barriers to Trade (TBT) 83
technocracy 80
telecommunications
    Japan 2–3
    supraterritoriality 100
    UAE 64
Telecommunications Regulatory Authority,
    UAE 64
terms of trade, Indonesia 14, 16
territorial banking 108
territorialism 101, 102, 111
    methodological 104–5
territoriality 111–13
textile sector, Israel 51, 59
Thailand 6, 7, 24
Thompson, Grahame 94
time deposit, Indonesia 13

tit-for-tat strategies, in international
    organisations 78
Tokyo Round 82
tourism, UAE 64
trade costs
    East African Community 47
    Japan 2, 9
trade deficit, sub-Saharan Africa 31
trade facilitation
    East African Community 43, 44, 47
    Indonesia 15
    Japan 2, 9
trade liberalisation
    China 23
    controversies 85
    developing countries 85
    East African Community 27, 29, 40, 45, 46,
        48–9
    global 23
    globalisation as 95–6, 119
    Greenspan, Alan 132
    India 23
    Indonesia 18, 21, 23
    Israel 51, 55, 60
    Japan 7–8, 9
    Kenya 35
    social values 131, 134–5
    sub-Saharan African countries 29
    UAE 64, 65
    Uganda 32
    see also free trade agreements/areas
Trade Policy Reviews 61–2
Trade-Related Intellectual Property (TRIPs) 75, 83
    controversies 84
    Israel 56
Trade-Related Investment Measures (TRIMs)
    75, 83
training, UAE 65
transactions costs
    East African Community 44
    trade liberalisation 135
transcontinental spread of humans 96
'transnational' term 103
transoceanic trade 96
transparency see openness
transplanetary movement of people 106
transplanetary relations 98, 99–102, 111, 119
    cultural heterogeneity 116
    politics 117, 118
    uneven spread 117

transport
    costs 46, 54, 107
    East African Community 46
    and global sourcing 107
    globality 106
    Israel 54
    supraterritoriality 100–1
    UAE 64
transworld instantaneity 100, 101, 105
transworld organisations 106–7
transworld simultaneity 100, 101, 105
TRIMs 75, 83
TRIPs see Trade-Related Intellectual Property
trust, and globalisation 134–5, 138–9
Tunisia 54
Turkey 52, 112

Uganda
    Common External Tariff 38–40, 49
    EPAs 29, 47–8
    FDI 43–4
    imports 37–8
    protectionism 29, 38
    tariffs 30, 32, 33–4, 35, 37–8
    trade changes 31
    trade facilitation 44
    trade liberalisation 32
    transport costs 46
    see also East African Community
unemployment, Indonesia 12, 13
unilateral trade reform, Indonesia 18
United Arab Emirates (UAE) 61–3,
    70–1
    economic developments and challenges
        63–5
    exports to Israel 54
    FDI performance 68–70
    free trade zones 68
    property rights protection and bilateral
        investment treaties 65–8, 70
United Kingdom 43
United Nations
    as a club of clubs 87
    free-riding behaviour 79
    inadequate means 78
    peacekeeping operations 109
United States of America
    agricultural sector 57, 81
    Australia's FTA with 8
    EU disputes with 82

Federal Reserve 132
GATT 81
globalisation 116–17
imports from sub-Saharan African countries
    42, 45
and Israel, trade between 52, 53, 56, 58
Korea's FTA with 8
labour standards and the WTO 75
protectionism 57
retaliation authorisation by the WTO 85
sub-prime market 16
Trade Representative 56
and the UAE, trade between 61, 64
value systems 139
United States Trade Representative 56
universalisation, globalisation as 96, 119
urbanisation 112
Uruguay Round 83, 84
founding of the WTO 75
Israel's invoking of developing country
    status 56
Japan 9

value-added tax (VAT)
East African Community, zero-rated exports
    41
Indonesia 19
Tanzania 43
Uganda 44
values and globalisation 123–5, 141
globalisation as external shocks affecting
    value systems 132–8, 141
social thought and social values 129–32
social values and social capital 125–8
value system competition, collapse,
    assimilation, fusion and conflict 137–41
variable import levy, Israel 58

Veblen, T. 126
Vedic age 140–1
vehicles sector, Israel 54
veto rights, international organisations 79
Vietnam 7
viruses, global dimensions 110
Visa 108
voluntary export restraints 82
vote buying, Indonesia 22

Wallerstein, I. 131, 141
war crimes tribunals 110
Weber, M. 129
West Africa 47
regional integration 28
tariffs 30
trade changes 31
westernisation, globalisation as 96–7, 119
Whalley, J. 135, 138
Working Group on Economic Partnership
    Agreements and Agriculture, Japan 5
world religions 96, 116
world risk society 131
world-systems analysis 131
'world' term 102–3
World Trade Organisation (WTO)
as a club of clubs 86–8, 89
controversies 75–6, 84–6
founding 75, 84
legitimacy 85, 86, 88
means 85, 88
mission 87–8
transition from GATT to 81–4

Zanzibar 42
Zhang Heng 101
Zodrow, G. R. 139